George Washington and the Origins of the American Presidency

EDITED BY
Mark J. Rozell,
William D. Pederson,
AND Frank J. Williams

Westport, Connecticut
London

JK
511
.G48
2000

Library of Congress Cataloging-in-Publication Data

George Washington and the origins of the American presidency / edited by Mark J.
    Rozell, William D. Pederson, and Frank J. Williams.
        p.   cm.
    Includes bibliographical references and index.
    ISBN 0–275–96867–7 (alk. paper)
    1. Presidents—United States—History.   2. Washington, George, 1732–1799.
    3. United States. President (1789–1797 : Washington)   4. United States—Politics and
    government—1789–1797.   I. Rozell, Mark J.   II. Pederson, William D., 1946–
    III. Williams, Frank J.
    JK511.G48   2000
    973.4'1'092—dc21   99–054740

British Library Cataloguing in Publication Data is available.

Library of Congress Catalog Card Number: 99–054740
ISBN: 0–275–96867–7

First published in 2000

Praeger Publishers, 88 Post Road West, Westport, CT 06881
An imprint of Greenwood Publishing Group, Inc.
www.praeger.com

Printed in the United States of America

∞™

The paper used in this book complies with the
Permanent Paper Standard issued by the National
Information Standards Organization (Z39.48–1984).

10 9 8 7 6 5 4 3 2 1

Contents

Introduction

George Washington and the Origins of the American Presidency

MARK J. ROZELL

The Constitutional Convention of 1787 formally created the American presidency. George Washington put the office into effect. Indeed, Washington was very cognizant of the fact that his actions as president would establish the office and have consequences for his successors. The first president's own words evidenced how conscious he was of the crucial role he played in determining the makeup of the office of the presidency. He had written to James Madison, "As the first of everything, *in our situation will serve to establish a precedent*, it is devoutly wished on my part that these precedents be fixed on true principles."[1] In May 1789 Washington wrote, "Many things which appear of little importance in themselves and at the beginning, may have great and durable consequences from their having been established at the commencement of a new general government."[2]

All presidents experience the burdens of the office. Washington's burdens were unique in that only he had the responsibility to establish the office in practice. The costs of misjudgments to the future of the presidency were great. The parameters of the president's powers remained vague when Washington took office. The executive article of the Constitution (Article II) lacked the specificity of the legislative article (Article I), leaving the first occupant of the presidency imperfect guidance on the scope and limits of his authority. Indeed, it may very well have been because Washington was the obvious choice of first occupant of the office that the Constitutional Convention officers left many of the powers of the presidency vague. Willard Sterne Randall writes, "No doubt no other president would have been trusted with such latitude."[3] Acutely aware of his burdens, Washington set out to exercise his powers prudently yet firmly when necessary.

Perhaps Washington's greatest legacy to the presidency was his substantial success in establishing the office for the future. He was a model for the office at a time when that was most needed. Indeed, as the historian Forrest McDonald has written, "[T]he office of president of the United States could scarcely have been created had George Washington not been available to become its first occupant."[4]

Washington was a reluctant first occupant of the office of the presidency. He loved private life and wished to fulfill his days tending to the business of agriculture at Mount Vernon. But duty had called on the nation's most famous and admired citizen in the past, and he had answered the calls. He had sworn off attending the Constitutional Convention, but when others had placed his name as a participant and implored him to go, he did so. Although he had misgivings about certain provisions of the Constitution, he lent his support to the document, understanding that his say carried enormous clout and that the furtherance of the nation depended on a strong government. He expressed his wish that some other qualified person come forward to assume the presidency, but there was no other who had the nearly universal esteem of his people, and he knew it. Washington left the private life he desired to answer the call of duty. He determined that the well-being of the young nation had to override his personal preference for the comforts of private life.

Although Washington was careful to distinguish his own political interests from those of the nation, he recognized that for many Americans he personally embodied the office of the presidency. He traveled throughout much of the young nation so that the people could see their president, and this action fostered the notion of democratic governance. He resisted calls for elaborate titles and ill-founded advice that he close himself off to the people and remain aloof except to a select few. He opened the doors to the White House during selected hours to meet with regular citizens, and although he found the exercise at times exasperating, he continued it. On the one hand, Washington wanted to be a people's president. On the other hand, he understood the need to imbue the office of the presidency with dignity.

Throughout his two terms Washington took care to exercise his powers properly. He deferred to Congress where appropriate, but he was not at all reluctant to protect the powers of his office. He took some of his constitutionally based powers quite literally, as when he went to the Senate in person to seek the "advice and consent" of its members on a proposed treaty. He learned from this experience that perhaps the Constitution need not be interpreted so precisely, as he found the meeting with the senators a counterproductive one at which he became visibly angry and reportedly left the room, saying that he would be "damned" if he ever returned. Washington never repeated the experience of personally visiting the Senate to seek advice or consent prior to making such a decision. No president since has gone to the Senate chamber to seek either advice or consent on a treaty or an appointment. In this action, Washington helped establish the independent power of the president to act in foreign affairs *before* seeking the legislative input.

On a host of matters Washington, in a sense, "filled in the blanks" of Article II. He established the presidential power to remove executive branch officials, a position that some attacked as an intrusion on the legislative authority. If the president has to seek advice and consent to appoint, some reasoned, then he should not have the unilateral power to remove officials. During a lengthy House debate on the issue in May 1789 some members argued that the necessary and proper clause of Article I of the Constitution empowered the legislative to carry into execution all departments and officers. Yet both houses of the Congress ultimately sided with Washington's interpretation of exclusive presidential power to fire top-level executive branch officers.[5] Washington's action also helped to establish in practice the principle of an independent executive branch of the government.

Similarly, Washington established in practice the independent power of the president to act in foreign policy when he issued the controversial Neutrality Proclamation. Congress had been in the midst of a debate over the proper U.S. position in the war between France and Great Britain. By acting alone and issuing the proclamation, the president had settled the issue. Although many in Congress protested, the legislative lacked the authority to challenge Washington's action. Many presidents since have claimed that the executive holds the upper hand in the making of foreign policy, and the courts generally have sided with presidents in such disputes (i.e., in those cases where the courts have decided rather than declared such disputes political questions).

Washington established a British-style system of cabinet government with appointed secretaries (with Senate approval) leading the departments of State, War, and Treasury. The Senate gave wide deference to the president to have the cabinet secretaries of his own choosing, which established another long-standing precedent. The practice of "senatorial courtesy" also originated with Washington when he appointed an officer to command a Georgian naval port, and the state's two senators protested. Washington deferred to the senators and withdrew the appointment. Hence, he established the precedent that for federal appointments within a state the president must consult the state's senators (in the modern era of party competition that practice is modified to include the senior senator of the president's own party within the state).

Not every precedent that Washington established succeeded or stood the test of time. He believed that Congress properly was the chief lawmaking branch of the government and that the executive did not share the legislative power. Consequently, he would veto legislation only on Constitutional grounds, a practice that presidents mostly followed until the Jackson era. Today, of course, the veto is a policy instrument allowing the executive to share in a part of the legislative power.

In appointing officials to government posts, Washington generally applied merit-based criteria. Constitutional scholar Henry Abraham praises the first president for using merit as the primary criterion for nominations to the Supreme Court and the strict avoidance of the pernicious modern practice of various litmus tests.[6] Although admirable, that precedent did not last long.

Washington similarly appointed cabinet secretaries and key presidential advisers based on their qualifications. He perhaps created the only truly bipartisan and merit-based cabinet. And in choosing Hamilton, Jefferson, and Madison as his three leading aides, he brought together three prodigious and independent minds destined to do battle with one another over policy. Scholars Sidney M. Milkis and Michael Nelson praise the lineup as generally successful despite the acrimony, but the experiment in merit selection did not appeal to Washington's successors.[7] Washington of course had warned against the establishment of party competition in the United States, and the nation did not long heed that call. The political scientist Woodrow Wilson would later characterize the dual roles of the president as head of the nation and head of a political party as not altogether compatible. Although modern presidents occasionally invite a member of the other party into their cabinet (President Bill Clinton's choice of William Cohen as defense secretary is the most recent example), the established practice is far from Washington's precedent.

Perhaps Washington's best-known precedent was the two-term limit—an informal practice broken only once in our history but then later foolishly amended into the Constitution. Washington surely could have served a third term. The Constitutional Convention delegates had ultimately favored indefinite re-eligibility for the president, in part because of the widespread expectation that Washington would hold the office. In this case the well-being of the young Republic and Washington's personal wishes converged. It is not clear that Washington actually acted in this case out of concern for establishing a good precedent. Edward S. Corwin wrote that Washington made this decision "purely on grounds of personal preference." But as Corwin correctly added, the effect was the same: Jefferson followed in Washington's footsteps, and in so doing he emphasized Washington's precedent.[8]

Although not all of Washington's precedents lasted, many important ones did, and the success of the office is due in large part to the prudent actions of the first occupant of the office. It is unfortunate that Washington does not receive the respect and attention of contemporary presidential scholars and students who are wedded to a model of the office derived from idealized interpretations of the first "modern" president, Franklin Roosevelt. This state of affairs led Milkis and Nelson to lament that the academic community in presidency studies treats 1933 "as the year 1 A.D. of presidential history."[9] The largest-selling and most influential presidency text in the history of the profession begins with the FDR years and makes only a single passing reference to George Washington.[10]

Yet there is evidence of the beginning of a resurgence of interest in the Washington presidency. Political scientist David K. Nichols inaugurated a healthy scholarly debate when he suggested that many of the origins of the modern presidency generally associated with FDR reside instead with the Washington administration.[11] Journalist Richard Brookhiser's more recent volume on George Washington attracted wide reviewing interest in journals of opinion, scholarly recognition, and substantially stronger sales than most works of political history.[12] In 1998 and 1999 two academic conferences on the Washington presidency together attracted well over 100 scholarly papers.[13]

The chapters in this volume represent a portion of the growing academic inquiry into the importance of Washington to our understanding of the presidency. This volume is largely the outcome of the September 17–19, 1998, conference on the Washington Legacy sponsored by the American Studies Program at the Louisiana State University in Shreveport. Eight of the following 10 chapters originally were presented at that conference. The other two chapters were specially commissioned for this volume. A major grant from the Louisiana Endowment for the Humanities funded the conference and made this volume possible.

The volume is divided into three parts, beginning with "Washington's Leadership and Legacy." Political scientist Byron W. Daynes opens with the central question of this entire endeavor: in essence, whether the study of George Washington is germane to the study of the modern presidency. Like Nichols and others before him, Daynes demonstrates the enormous impact that Washington's actions had on the development of the presidency. Daynes builds his summary of Washington's accomplishments and impact around the themes of the president as chief executive, chief diplomat, Commander in Chief, and opinion/party leader. He ultimately differs with those who have argued that Washington's impact largely was an accident of timing—that is, anyone who first served as president would have been ultimately judged as the premier precedent-setter. Daynes finds that Washington's character and competence properly established the presidency and that the nation indeed benefited from the actions of its first occupant of the highest office. Daynes concludes that "yes, political scientists would do well to study carefully the Washington presidency."

Political theorist Thomas Engeman and political scientist Raymond Tatalovich directly challenge the Nichols thesis that George Washington was the first "modern" president.[11] Their chapter offers first a description of the Nichols thesis and the evidence for his argument. They counter with their own theory "that the 'modern' understanding of the presidency originates not with the Constitutional Founding but from the Second American Constitution beginning with the Progressive critique and culminating in the mid-twentieth century." The authors conclude with the presentation of their own empirical support for that theory. Engeman and Tatalovich concede that Nichols is correct about Washington's impact on the president's diplomatic role. But ultimately, it is inaccurate, they maintain, to characterize the Constitutional Framers or Washington as the originators of most of the elements of the modern presidency.

Political psychologist Elizabeth W. Marvick sees Washington as one of the few truly transforming leaders in the history of the West. Washington had dreamed of a newly independent nation characterized by liberty and order, and he "strove to transform that dream into reality." One could identify fewer than a handful of other leaders of the modern Western world who fit that description: perhaps de Gaulle of France, Kumal of Turkey, or Mandela of South Africa. "But," as Marvick adds, "among American leaders Washington stands alone." Yet for historians there has long been a greater fascination with the character of Abraham Lincoln than of Washington. Whereas the former is known to us for his earlier failures, insecurities, triumphs, and then martyrdom, the latter is treated as an icon. Marvick delves into the family background and learning experiences that framed Washington's character. She presents a more complex picture of the man than offered by some of the reverential studies of the first president.

Part II of the volume examines "Presidential Powers and the Washington Administration." It begins with political scientist Malcolm L. Cross' analysis of one of Washington's major precedents: the president as chief of state and the government's active chief executive. For the former, the president is a symbol and the ceremonial leader of the country. For the latter, the president staffs and supervises the executive branch. Washington set out "to make the American presidency both efficient and dignified," writes Cross. We assume these two roles for the presidency today. Yet the Constitution did not mandate these roles. It was Washington who perceived the dual role of the presidency, and his closest adviser, Alexander Hamilton, urged the first president to adopt such a vision for the office. Washington and Hamilton are in large part responsible for the creation of the dignified-efficient presidency.

Historian John W. Kuehl examines the debate over the controversial Jay Treaty, focusing on the contending arguments advanced by Washington and James Madison. Washington initially was conflicted about the treaty, but he ultimately believed its ratification was necessary to avoid war with Great Britain. Once Washington took a stand, he defended it as proper, despite public disapproval and the opposition efforts led by Madison. In refusing congressional requests for all papers related to the treaty negotiations, Washington created the important precedent of the president's independent role in establishing treaties. Kuehl evaluates the impact that Washington's actions had on establishing this precedent and the development of the executive's predominant role in foreign policy.

Constitutional scholars Henry J. Abraham and Barbara A. Perry characterize Washington, not President Franklin D. Roosevelt, as truly the nation's first "court-packer." The four-times-elected FDR appointed nine members of the Supreme Court. His ill-conceived attempt to pack the Court failed and became a blot on his legacy. Washington nominated 14 individuals to the Court during his two terms, and 11 of those persons actually served. More importantly, Washington established criteria for selection to the Court, some of which exist today, including "support and advocacy of the Constitution," prior judicial experience, and geographic suitability, among others. More than any other president he was "directly involved in identifying and choosing his nominees." Washington never resorted to the kinds of "litmus tests" on issues that have generated so much controversy in the modern era. Washington was concerned first and foremost with creating a strong, independent judicial branch staffed by qualified individuals who revered the Constitution and had a deep commitment to public service.

Part II closes with an analysis of one of Washington's lesser-known, yet important, precedents: the creation of what is today called "executive privilege." Although that phrase was an invention of the Eisenhower era, all presidents since Washington have exercised some form of what we call executive privilege: the right of the president and high-level White House officers to withhold information from Congress, the courts, and ultimately the public. Washington did not exercise this authority lightly. Indeed, his actions set the ultimate standards for the future—that presidents withhold information only when it is absolutely necessary to do so to protect the national security or the public interest. Washington showed by example that he did not equate his own political interests with those of the nation, a lesson that has been truly lost on some of his successors in the modern era.

Part III examines "Washington and the Press." Historian Carol Sue Humphrey shows that Washington was not immune to the fickle nature of press coverage of presidents, often thought to be a modern phenomenon. His coverage ranged from hero worship to outright hostility and contemptuousness. Washington understood the utility of newspapers to his various causes. As general, Washington encouraged favorable reporting of the Revolutionary War, and he wrote angrily about negative reports that he felt potentially compromised the American cause. As president he encouraged a free and informative press, although he disapproved of much of his own coverage. He particularly detested the development of the partisan press as unfavorable to the nation's stature and a poor means of informing the governed about the issues. Humphrey notes that although Washington was ultimately disappointed in the press' performance, his own reputation survived despite some harsh treatment by editorialists.

Historian Frank E. Dunkle examines the earlier roots of the Washington legend by examining coverage of him in the Boston newspapers in the mid-to-late 1750s. As a young man, Washington had achieved fame in the

Boston newspapers because of his role in a conflict between France and Britain for control of the Ohio River valley that led to the French and Indian War. As a young officer, Washington's actions received wide and favorable coverage in the New England newspapers, despite the fact that he had suffered more defeats than he had achieved victories. In part, the newspapers were promoting support for the war and therefore exaggerating the achievements of the British American soldiers. Washington "was cast in the role of a hero." The chapter's analysis of the content of the early newspaper coverage shows how Washington achieved early recognition that would later play an important role in his selection to lead the fight for independence.

Political scientist Graham G. Dodds examines Washington's precedents in establishing relations between presidents and the press. Among those was the first presidential "honeymoon" with the press, followed by growing contentiousness over time. Dodds reviews the important role that the partisan press of the time played in the deteriorating relationship between Washington and the newspapers. During Washington's administration domestic coverage of events for the first time played an important role in influencing foreign policy. Washington was also the first president to have to deal with government leaks to the press. Furthermore, like modern presidents, Washington was acutely aware of the importance of press coverage and a presidential image to achieving his goals. He was not reluctant to use the press to promote himself and his goals, as he did when he leaked his Farewell Address to a friendly printer. Yet Washington, unlike some of the modern presidents, did not engage in open battle with the press when he received unfavorable coverage. Dodds reports that Washington generally did not engage the press in feuds, except when he responded through his aides—a practice very common in the modern era. Despite his reservations about the quality of press coverage at times, Washington respected the need for a free press and did not advocate suppressing information.

The sum total of these chapters is a portrait of the nation's first president as a man who was very conscious of his potential place in history and who sought to fulfill his role in a manner that would best serve future generations. Yet Washington himself was not certain that the new Republic would long survive. His legacy in large part is that he established the presidency in practice, and that institution has survived to this day, as Rossiter once wrote, as "one of the few truly successful institutions created by men in their endless quest for the blessings of free government."[14]

NOTES

1. George Washington, letter to James Madison, May 5, 1789, quoted in John C. Fitzpatrick, ed., *The Writings of George Washington*, 39 vols. (Washington, DC: U.S. Government Printing Office, 1931–1944), 30:311.

2. "Queries on a Line of Conduct," May 10, 1789, quoted in Fitzpatrick, *The Writings of George Washington*, 30:321.

3. Willard Sterne Randall, *George Washington: A Life* (New York: Henry Holt, 1997), p. 435.

4. Forrest McDonald, "Presidential Character: The Example of George Washington," in Philip G. Henderson, ed., *The Presidency: Then and Now* (Lanham, MD: Rowman & Littlefield, 2000), p. 1.

5. See Charles E. Morganston, *The Appointment and Removal Power of the President of the United States* (Washington, DC: U.S. Government Printing Office, 1929).

6. See Henry J. Abraham, *Justices and Presidents: A Political History of Appointments to the Supreme Court*, 3rd ed. (New York: Oxford University Press, 1992); Henry J. Abraham, *Justices, Presidents, and Senators* (Lanham, MD: Rowman & Litlefield, 1999).

7. Sidney M. Milkis and Michael Nelson, *The American Presidency: Origins and Development* (Washington, DC: Congressional Quarterly Press, 1990), p. 75.

8. Edward S. Corwin, *The President, Office and Powers: 1787–1957* (New York: New York University Press, 1957).

9. Milkis and Nelson, *The American Presidency*, p. xii.

10. The original "classic" version is Richard Neustadt, *Presidential Power* (New York: John Wiley and Sons, 1960). This book has now sold over 1 million copies and remains a standard in presidency courses. An editor consulted me several years ago about the value of putting Pofessor Clinton Rossiter's classic presidency text back into print. I enthusiastically endorsed the idea. My editor has since told me that the book barely sells about 400 copies a year.

11. David K. Nichols, *The Myth of the Modern Presidency* (University Park: Pennsylvania State University Press, 1994).

12. Richard Brookhiser, *Founding Father: Rediscovering George Washington* (New York: Free Press, 1996).

13. The American Studies Program at Louisiana State University in Shreveport sponsored the 1998 conference. The Heritage Foundation and the Intercollegiate Studies Institute cosponsored the 1999 conference.

14. Clinton Rossiter, *The American Presidency* (Baltimore: Johns Hopkins University Press, 1987), p. 1.

Part I

Washington's Leadership and Legacy

Chapter 1

George Washington: Reluctant Occupant, Uncertain Model for the Presidency

BYRON W. DAYNES

INTRODUCTION

In looking at the presidency of George Washington, the one question that needs to be asked by political scientists is, *Can we learn anything about the modern presidency by examining the presidency of George Washington, or will the net effect be negligible?*

The answer, as one might expect, is unclear. Evidence from the records of the Constitutional Convention and other early documents is imprecise. While the Framers respected Washington as an outstanding leader among them, his leadership attributes were highly unusual. For example, he appeared uncomfortable in possession of power,[1] wished to remain out of the focus of attention,[2] and did not seek position[3]; in fact, he even resisted attending the Constitutional Convention because of conflicting loyalties he felt as a leader in the Society of Cincinnati—an elite society of retired revolutionary officers—that was meeting in Philadelphia at the same time. He came to the convention only at the insistence of Edmund Randolph, Alexander Hamilton, and James Madison, who recognized Washington's importance and prominence among his political peers. Once there, he was appointed by his colleagues to preside over the convention, despite his initial hesitation. While he said very little in the debates and discussions and made a point of giving up his position whenever the convention broke into a "committee of the whole," his mere presence was extremely important, as he became the acknowledged *model* for what an exemplary president might become.[4]

Those same persons who saw Washington as an eminent presidential model, however, structured Article II of the Constitution in such a way as to accommodate the *"non-Washingtons"* who might succeed him as president, recognizing that "George Washingtons" were rare and would not be available very often. Thus, the delegates, rather than writing Article II in such a way as to attract *other* "Washingtons," followed the suggestions of Alexander Hamilton in *Federalist* No. 72. They made the presidency attractive to the most egregious among us, rewarding the occupant with *fame*, with *power*, and with a substantial *salary* in case the presidential aspirant was ambitious or avaricious.[5] One might reasonably argue, therefore, that the presidency of George Washington was unique and "uncertain" as a model for those who would follow and that an examination of his presidency might add little to our understanding of the presidency today.

Examining the evidence of political scientists regarding the worth of the Washington *model* only adds to the confusion. Some presidential scholars agree that we can learn little, if anything, about the modern presidency by looking at eighteenth- and early nineteenth-century presidents. Those taking this position would begin their examination of the modern presidency with an assessment of the presidency of Franklin Roosevelt,[6] while others would see Dwight Eisenhower as the first modern president.[7] Countering these views, David K. Nichols, in his book *The Myth of the Modern Presidency*, sees comparable leadership characteristics in George Washington and the other early presidents that he finds in modern presidents. These common attributes found in those early presidents, Nichols argues, include "legislative leadership, administrative control, the exercise of unilateral authority, and popular symbolic leadership."[8]

Such conclusions about the importance of the early presidents seem to be sustained in the presidential scholarly ratings that have been published over the years that find George Washington consistently rated among the top two or three great presidents. In the Arthur Schlesinger Sr. polls of 1948 and 1962, for example, Washington placed second only to Abraham Lincoln.[9] Washington rated second to Lincoln in the 1970 Maranell–Dodder poll as well.[10] But in the 1982 Murray–Blessing poll and the latest (1996) Arthur Schlesinger Jr. poll, Washington ranked third behind Lincoln and Franklin Roosevelt.[11] Thus, in these five surveys from 1948 through 1996, Washington has repeatedly ranked as one of the exceptional leaders of all times among scholars.[12]

Other students of the presidency, however, acknowledge Washington's great character traits but still think of him in a much less admired category, as did James David Barber, who saw Washington's character as reflecting traits of "dignity, judiciousness, . . . reserve and dedication to duty" but labeled him a *passive-negative* president, a president who failed to be innovative in his presidency.[13]

METHODS

It is unclear as to the impact Washington has had on the presidency. I therefore examine his presidency from the perspective of the following five presidential roles.

1. *Opinion/Party Leader*—a combined role suggesting a president's relationship to party and public opinion.
2. *Legislative Leader*—a role suggesting a president's relationship with the Congress.
3. *Chief Executive*—a role involving a president's relationship with the cabinet, administrative staff, and bureaucracy.
4. *Chief Diplomat*—the role that relates the president to other nations.
5. *Commander in Chief*—a role referring to a president as the nation's highest military leader.[14]

One probably will notice from the description of these five roles that they are not equally powerful. Under normal circumstances, a president acting as Commander in Chief is in a more powerful position than a president who has assumed the role of opinion/party leader. A president using his Commander in Chief role has access to more *legal authority*, can have an increased dominance in *decision making*, is increasingly protected from interfering *organized interests*, is of greater interest to *public opinion*, and has an ability to rally the nation behind him in a *crisis*. These five roles may thus be arranged on a power continuum with Commander in Chief ranked as the most powerful presidential role, followed by chief diplomat, chief executive, and legislative leader, with opinion/party leader the president's weakest role. It is this power arrangement among the roles that I assume in this study of Washington.[15]

THE ROLES

Opinion/Party Leader

This composite role suggests the direct relationship the president has with the people through the political party and public opinion. Unfortunately for any president, this role is generally the president's weakest. Its effective use by a president depends on individual skill and not on the number of resources or substantial authority available to him.[16] Thus, few presidents have dominated this role, and Washington was no exception. He was cautious about how he should interact with others as president. He even wrote to John Adams in 1789 asking for advice as to whether it would be improper for a president to make

informal visits; that is to say, in his calling upon his Acquaintances or public Characters for the purposes of sociability or civility: and what (as to the form of doing it)
might evince these visits to have been made in his private character, so as that they
may not be constructed into visits from the President of the United States.[17]

The people were very important to Washington, and he was willing to make
the effort to reach out to them, but it often would involve long, tiring days.
As he stated: "From the time I had done breakfast and thence till dinner
and afterwards till bedtime I could not get relieved from the ceremony of
one visit before I had to attend to another."[18]

Maintaining Contact with the People

Although Washington gave few formal speeches in public and held no
"press conference-like" sessions where he could use the press as an instrument to communicate with the people, he did make an effort to reach out
and make social contact with the citizens through a number of contact
points:

The Socials. If a person was "respectably dressed," Washington's rule
stated, men could join the president at one of his regularly scheduled "levees" held every Tuesday from three to four in the afternoon, while men and
women were hosted by Martha Washington at her many tea parties, held
on Friday evenings. The Washingtons also staged dinners on Thursdays at
four o'clock in the afternoon, inviting only "official characters and strangers
of distinction."[19] To avoid any allegations of favoritism, government work-
ers and officials and their families would be asked to the dinners on a regular
rotation.[20] These social hours helped to make the presidency more visible
to the people as well as allowed the president to procure needed information
from sources he might not otherwise seek out.

Travels. Washington also, on the advice of Hamilton, Adams, Madison,
Jay, and Knox, visited every section of the country. He did this to become
acquainted with his fellow citizens and to encourage support for and discourage opposition to the federal government. Washington told Alexander
Hamilton that he wanted to visit the eastern states "to acquire knowledge
of the face of the Country, the growth and agriculture thereof, and the
temper and disposition of the inhabitants towards the new government."[21]

The president made four official tours. On October 15, 1789, Washington began his monthlong visit to New England, traveling to each of the
states except Rhode Island and Vermont, which were not yet in the federal
system. He visited Long Island on April 20, 1790, and Rhode Island in
August of that same year. The next year George Washington left on April
7, 1791, for a three-month tour of the South that covered 1,816 miles,
spending most of his time in North and South Carolina and Georgia.[22] In
reaching out to each section of the nation, Washington, in effect, put a
personal face on government, making it less threatening and more under-

standable. Even the newspapers took note of his success, as the *Philadelphia Gazette* and the *Boston Gazette* both wrote that Washington's travels had given him the image of "the man who united all hearts."[23]

The Speeches. Washington's public addresses were somewhat limited, but compared to other early presidents, Washington held his own. While on his tours, Washington gave 20 official public addresses and five unofficial ones, according to Jeffrey Tulis' tabulations. While Jefferson and Monroe averaged five speeches a year, Washington, with an average of three speeches a year, placed third ahead of John Adams, John Quincy Adams (both of whom averaged but one speech a year), and James Madison (who gave no recorded speeches).[24] For Washington the general purpose of these tours was not to make formal speeches but to make a public appearance and to be seen by the citizenry. The president, of course, was not unusual in limiting his speaking engagements, according to Tulis, with the early presidents making only 7 percent of their speeches (N = 23) to the public, while directing 85 percent of them (N = 272) to the Congress. Twentieth-century presidents, by contrast, divided their speaking responsibilities, giving 41 percent of them (N = 138) to the public and 21 percent (N = 71) to the Congress.[25]

Public Opinion. Washington was sensitive to public opinion and took guidance from what the public thought. As he pointed out in a letter to Comte De Rochambeau:

In a government which depends so much in its first stages on public opinion, much circumspection is still necessary for those who are engaged in its administration. Fortunately the current of public sentiment runs with us, and all things hitherto seem to succeed according to our wishes.[26]

He was also aware of the consequences that would occur if leaders were too far ahead of the public's knowledge and concerns. Washington also felt a responsibility to teach the citizens about politics and citizenship and to help shape supportive public opinion. While he believed that Americans were headed in the right direction, there were concerns. As he wrote to Governor John Jay: "I am *sure* the Mass of Citizens in the United States *mean well*, and I firmly believe they will always *act well*, whenever they can obtain a right understanding of matters."[27] He intended to do all he could to give them that "right understanding." He knew that a public servant was not the same as someone in private life. He pointed out, for example,

Men in responsible positions cannot, like those in private life, be governed solely by the dictates of their own inclinations, or by such motives as can only affect themselves. . . . A man in public office . . . [i]s accountable for the consequences of his measures to others.[28]

Washington, of course, was not always successful in getting on with the citizenry, and the public was not always persuaded by the direction Washington was taking them. When Washington declared neutrality in the war between France and Great Britain, for example, the public opposed his stand and let him know this in no uncertain terms. Biographer Paul Leicester Ford in his book *The True George Washington* wrote that after Washington's Neutrality Proclamation, John Adams wrote, "Ten thousand people in the streets in Philadelphia, day after day, threatened to drag Washington out of his house and effect a revolution in the government, or compel it to declare in favor of the French and against England."[29] The public also reacted in similar fashion after Washington signed the Jay Treaty with Great Britain, with the public response described as producing "a popular outburst from one end of the country to the other."[30]

Washington was aware of the mixed public reaction to his actions. As he wrote to Henry Lee:

That there are in this, as well as in all other Countries, discontented characters, I well know; as also that these characters are actuated by very different views: Some good, from an opinion that the measures of the General Government are impure: some bad, and (if I might be allowed to use so harsh an expression) diabolical; inasmuch as they are not only meant to impede the measures of that Government generally, but more especially. . . . to destroy the confidence, which it is necessary for the people to place (until they have unequivocal proof of demerit) in their public servants; for in this light I consider myself, whilst I am an occupant of office; and if they were to go further and call me their slave (during this period) I would not dispute the point.[31]

The Press. The president right from the beginning has been the object and focus of the press' attention. The press is skeptical of power, which leads it to scrutinize all presidents. Certainly, Washington was no exception, but this scrutiny did not dissuade him from doing what he felt was the best thing for the nation at the time. As he wrote to his friend Colonel David Humphreys concerning what was said by certain Republican newspapers that did not support Washington's stance on the Jay Treaty:

[T]he gazettes . . . will . . . shew you in what manner I am attacked for a steady opposition to every measure which has a tendency to disturb the peace and tranquility of it. But these attacks, unjust and unpleasant as they are, will occasion no change in my conduct; nor will they work any other effect in my mind, than to increase the anxious desire which has long possessed my breast, to enjoy in the shades of retirement the consolation of having rendered my Country every service my abilities were competent to, uninfluenced by pecuniary or ambitious considerations as they respected myself. . . . no earthly power can deprive me of the consolation of knowing that I have not in the course of my administration been guilty of a *wilful* error, however numerous they may have been from other causes.[32]

In October 1792 Washington wrote a letter to Gouverneur Morris expressing his concern about the effect he saw the press was having on the image of the United States abroad. As Washington stated: "From the complexion of some of our Newspapers Foreigners would be led to believe that inveterate political dissensions existed among us, and that we are on the very verge of disunion; but the fact is otherwise."[33]

Washington proved, near the end of his eight years in office, that he had no more tolerance for an attacking press than any other president has had. The *Aurora*, a Philadelphia journal, came out reflecting on those eight years of his presidency, stating that "The name of Washington ceases from this day to give currency to political insults and to legalize corruption" and that

[I]t is a subject of the greatest astonishment that a single individual should have cankered the principles of republicanism in an enlightened people just emerged from the gulf of despotism, and should have carried his designs against the public liberty so far as to put in jeopardy its very existence.[34]

This did not sit well with the president, since he saw an injustice in these reflections. Washington's reply was:

To misrepresent my motives, to reprobate my politics, and to weaken the confidence which has been reposed in my administration, are objects which cannot be relinquished by those who will be satisfied with nothing short of a change in our political system.[35]

Washington as Party Leader

In the earliest years of Washington's presidency there were only Federalists, with only the slightest evidence in the 1790s of scattered informal "democratic" or "republican" societies organized around the country. These societies had grown in number from 11 in 1793 to 24 societies by 1794, helping to "nationalize" American politics as they became a national movement.[36]

Washington's relationship to the Federalist Party was interesting. In one way he felt himself "above" political warfare; on the other hand, Washington's policies became the mainstay of the Federalist Party, and many of his appointments were clearly Federalist. The president wrote to Jefferson in July 1796:

I was no party man myself . . . and the first wish of my heart was, if parties did exist, to reconcile them. . . . Until within the last year or two, I had no conception that parties would or even could go the length I have been witness to.[37]

He did believe in a strong presidency and strong federal government, and he did, as George Nordham argued, surround himself with persons who also believed in a strong federal government,[38] with one glaring exception, namely, Thomas Jefferson, who served as his first Secretary of State.

Washington at first could not fully understand that there would be those in government so dissatisfied with Federalist policies that they would want to leave government service to become involved in an opposition party. Yet near the end of his years of service in the presidency, Washington found himself worrying about the *consequences* of that party. He wrote Jefferson in July 1796, "My mind is so perfectly convinced that if these self-created societies [Democratic–Republican societies] cannot be discountenanced, they will destroy the government of this country."[39] He felt also that those same societies were largely responsible for the Whiskey Rebellion in Pennsylvania, where he found it necessary to call out troops to put down the rebellion. As he stated:

[S]elf-created Societies. . . . Have been laboring incessantly to sow the seeds of distrust, jealousy, and of course discontent; thereby hoping to effect some revolution in the government. . . . That they have been the fomenters of the Western disturbances, admits of no doubt. . . . I shall be more prolix in my speech to Congress.[40]

And in his Farewell Address, Washington referred to "party"—undoubtedly, the Democratic–Republicans—as a "scourge." Americans were encouraged to avoid partisan politics. In Washington's words:

This spirit [of party], unfortunately, is inseparable from our nature, having its root in the strongest passions of the human mind. It exists under different shapes in all Governments, more or less stifled, controuled (sp.), or repressed; but in those of the popular form it is seen in its greatest rankness, and is truly their worst enemy.

It [party] serves always to distract the public councils and enfeeble the public administration. It agitates the community with ill-founded jealousies and false alarms; kindles the animosity of one part against another; foments occasionally riot and insurrection.[41]

Legislative Leader

The active presidents have shaped this particular relationship between the president and Congress. Edward Corwin and Louis Koenig, years ago, suggested that "virtually all presidents who have made a major impact on American history have done so in great degree as legislative leaders."[42]

George Washington: A Semi-Involved Legislative Leader

A Feeling of Separation. Washington's legislative leadership is made up of a series of confrontations and differing interpretations between the executive and Congress. While Washington saw some success as a legislative leader (viz., obtaining funds for the debt built up from the war, as David K. Nichols maintains),[43] Washington felt strongly about preserving separation of powers and kept his distance from involvement with the Congress. When asked if he would campaign for one particular congressperson, he replied that he thought it "highly improper" for a president to do so.[44] Indeed, Washington felt so keenly about protecting this distinction between the two institutions that on receiving an unopened packet from a foreign nation addressed to both the president and the Congress, Washington first consulted with congressional leaders to determine who should open the packet.[45] Washington was no Thomas Jefferson, who, on becoming president, became fully absorbed by the Congress, mastering both the formal and informal techniques of getting one's way with the Congress. Douglas Freeman describes Washington's attitude about Congress in these words:

This same caution—so deep as almost to be instinctive—marked Washington's steps in exploring his relations with Congress. He regarded the executive branch as a "department" distinct from the Federal Legislature, but on parity with it and bound by oath and by the letter of the Constitution to show proper deference toward it. If he made any suggestion for action by Congress the occasion had to be one of importance. . . . The President's power over lawmaking, as he saw it, was confined to his veto. Washington held unswervingly to this view from the first, but he did not understand, at the outset, exactly how he should proceed with respect to subjects that called for joint action by the President and the Senate.[46]

Freeman argues that the president's relation with Congress had been established in the Constitution and required little more than "deference, the delivery of messages, and a steady compliance with the lawmakers' requests when reasonable."[47]

Contact with Congresspersons through the Socials and the Formal Speeches. While Washington could not be described as an involved legislative leader, he did meet his responsibility by giving annual addresses to the Congress, as Table 1.1 indicates, as well as the other speeches on various issues and policies. In addition, Washington made an effort to contact individual congresspersons during the regularly scheduled levees, teas, and dinner parties held at the president's residence.[48]

The Veto. A president's most effective legislative tool is the veto. Its effectiveness can be seen in that only 7 percent of all presidential vetoes (2,538 regular and pocket vetoes) have ever been overridden.[49] George Washington vetoed two pieces of legislation he considered unconstitutional. Neither was overridden. His first veto came April 5, 1792, on an apportionment act,[50] and his second one came five years afterward on February 28, 1797, on a bill reducing the size of the army. Washington felt that the latter bill interfered with the president's foreign affairs authority. Washington's two vetoes were two more than either John Adams or Thomas Jefferson cast. In fact,

Table 1.1
Annual Messages to Congress by Role

ADDRESS	Opinion/ Party Leader	Legislative Leader	ROLES Chief Executive	Chief Diplomat	Commander in Chief
FIRST January 8, 1790			need for uniform rules for naturalization, currency, weights and measures, and creation of roads; promoting education, science, and literature through a national university	Indian hostilities	military defense
SECOND December 8, 1790			paying debt and credit; improving judicial system, mint, post offices, and post roads	Indian affairs; appointing foreign consuls in Europe	establishing a militia

THIRD October 25, 1791		status of U.S. Bank; liquor tax; plans for District of Columbia; results of first census	security on western frontiers
FOURTH November 6, 1792	revise judicial system; mint coins; interstate commerce	foreign relations; loans in Holland	Indian hostilities
FIFTH December 3, 1793		war in Europe; Indian affairs	use of troops to secure territory
SIXTH November 19, 1794	Whiskey Rebellion	Whiskey Rebellion	Whiskey Rebellion
SEVENTH December 8, 1795		relations with Spain, Morocco, Great Britain, and Indian tribes	military and national defense
EIGHTH December 7, 1796	need for manufacturing, agriculture, and national university; pay of federal employees	Indian treaties; relations with Spain, Tunis, Algiers, Tripoli, Great Britain, and France	need for naval force and naval academy

there were few vetoes cast by any of the early presidents, since they all used the veto to judge constitutionality. This tradition of vetoing legislation only thought to be unconstitutional ended, of course, with Andrew Jackson, who vetoed 12 measures in order to strengthen his political programs.

Treaty Making. Treaty making posed a related concern as Washington attempted to include members of the Senate in the initial stages. Washington accompanied Secretary Knox to the Senate to seek its "advice and consent" on a treaty he had negotiated with the Creek Indians. When Washington read the treaty to the Senate, there was no response. This silence was followed by a confusing discussion by the senators. Finally, Senator Maclay indicated that there was no chance of a fair investigation with the president in the chamber, and the president's recommendation was submitted to a committee for further study. Washington was quite upset, indicating that "[t]his defeats every purpose of my coming here!"[51] Presidents thereafter never consulted with the Senate at the initial stage of the treaty process.

Executive Immunity. Washington also established the tradition of "executive immunity" when he held back information from the Congress concerning Indian victories over the U.S. military. Washington decided that it was not proper for Congress to have these dispatches that he controlled.[52] The president also followed this up by rejecting a second request by the Senate some years later, when Congress requested correspondence of Gouverneur Morris, then minister to France, to Washington that contained some negative commentary about the leaders of France. While Washington did turn over a number of these letters to the Congress, he chose to keep others from them, feeling it would be destructive to the national interest.[53] A final example occurred in 1796, when Washington again refused to turn over to the House papers concerning the negotiations of the controversial Jay Treaty. He indicated to Congress that "the nature of foreign negotiations requires caution; and their success often depends on secrecy." He felt that "full disclosure" in the House would violate that secrecy and overstep Constitutional boundaries fixed between departments of government and saw no essential need that the House would have in the use of the papers that he had already turned over to the Senate. He also made it clear that other countries understood our Constitutional procedure for processing treaties, and such a deviation would pose difficulties and have a negative effect on future negotiations.[54] A strong precedent was established by Washington's independence in the face of Congress.

Chief Executive

This role deals with the day-to-day operations of government. Each president organizes his own advisory system according to his own needs. Washington's goal was to establish a viable working government capable of enforcing the law. He hoped his presidency would become a symbol of national unity but recognized that the president could not do it alone. In a September 15, 1792, proclamation, Washington urged the courts to exert their power against violence that was threatening order within the country. As he stated in this proclamation: "I do moreover charge and require all courts, magistrates, and offices whom it may concern, according to the duties of their several offices, to exert the powers in them respectively vested by law for the purposes aforesaid."[55]

Washington was protective of the national government and stressed its dominance whenever possible. He worked to build the national government into a position so that it was greater than any particular state's government. He fully supported the passage of the Eleventh Amendment, which stressed federal precedence over state authority.[56] In this spirit Washington handed down his first Thanksgiving Proclamation, which should have been free from controversy. Because he asked for a blessing for the Constitution and the national government but failed to ask for one for the states, he was soundly criticized by states' advocates.[57]

Washington was sensitive to this relationship between national government and state government and made sure that the national government was always in the prominent position. He even went so far, when touring the northern states, to refuse to visit John Hancock, then governor of Massachusetts, unless Hancock would agree to call on him first. He was afraid that if he had to contact Hancock, this would show a weakness on the part of the national government, acquiescing to the state government.[58]

Washington was not adverse to handing down rulings based on presidential authority alone. Table 1.2 indicates the official proclamations issued by Washington during his years in office, avoiding having to await congressional delay. As indicated in this table, the new government of George Washington was anything but passive. Washington saw this activity as a means of ensuring order and stability in the nation.

New States and New Functions of Government. During Washington's administration, three states came into the Union: Vermont in 1791, Kentucky in 1792, and Tennessee in 1796. Kentucky's and Tennessee's entrance has been seen as "a complement to Washington's perseverance in coping with the instability along the fringes of his country."[59] Not only was it an addition to the administration's prestige, but it also furthered a "sense of nationalism," as Frank Reuter argues.[60]

The Appointment Power

In making his appointments, Washington at first stayed away from too much partisanship. He looked first at the qualifications for the office and the candidate, demanding that his appointees show loyalty to the Constitution. Former Tories, for example, were not appointed to the Washington

Table 1.2
Partial Listing of George Washington's Official Proclamations and Executive
Orders, 1789–1797

Date	Description
June 8, 1789	Creation of the Department of Foreign Affairs by executive order
October 3, 1789/ January 1, 1795	Thanksgiving Day Proclamation
August 14, 1790	Proclamation announcing ratification of treaty with the Creek Nation
August 26, 1790/ March 19, 1791	Proclamation warning U.S. citizens against violations of Indian treaties
January 24, 1791/ March 30, 1791	Establishment of a federal city (District of Columbia)
September 15, 1792	Proclamation warning citizens to refrain and desist from insurrections concerning distilled spirits (Whiskey Rebellion)
December 12, 1792	Proclamation encouraging law officials to bring to justice those who had destroyed Cherokee Nation villages
April 22, 1793	Proclamation of Neutrality in the war between Great Britain and France
March 24, 1794	Proclamation warning citizens in Kentucky not to take part in rebellions against the United States
August 7, 1794	Proclamation warning citizens in western Pennsylvania not to take part in the Whiskey Rebellion
September 25, 1794	Proclamation warning citizens not to participate in the Whiskey Rebellion
October 9, 1794	Executive Order to General Knox to send military supplies to Bedford, Pennsylvania
July 10, 1795	Proclamation of full pardon for those in the Whiskey Rebellion

administration.[61] He took his responsibility as chief executive seriously. In a letter to Thomas Jefferson dated January 21, 1790, Washington wrote: "I consider the successful Administration of the general Government as an object of almost infinite consequence to the present and future happiness of the Citizens of the United States."[62]

Minor Appointments. It was at the lower levels that Washington made most of his appointments. According to Leonard White, during his time in office Washington nominated "over 350 civil officials, not including the Supreme Court justices and heads of departments." In addition, White pointed out that by 1792 there were in the civil service "about 780 employees (excluding the deputy post masters, of whom approximately 660 were employed in the Treasury Department)."[63] He was a fully involved chief executive. As one observer suggested, "[N]o collector of customs, captain of a cutter, keeper of a lighthouse, or surveyor of revenue was appointed except after specific consideration by the President."[64]

One of those lower-ranking appointments also became the first presidential appointment rejected by the Senate. Benjamin Fishburn, who had been nominated as a naval officer of the port of Savannah, was rejected by the Senate. Washington accepted the Senate's decision. But he filed a statement with the Senate on August 6, 1789, stating all of the reasons he had nominated Fishburn. Washington indicated that in the future if the Senate wanted to know the reasons for his certain appointments, he would make sure he first consulted with Senate members and share the necessary documents with them before any other nominees were recommended. This instance may have begun the tradition of "senatorial courtesy."[65]

Cabinet and Staff. Washington's cabinet could be pointed to as the first one based on "equality," a model cabinet involving both Federalists and Republicans. There was even a geographic balance in the cabinet, with Jefferson and Randolph coming from Virginia, Hamilton from New York, and Knox from Massachusetts.[66] Quite a diverse group of persons served in the cabinet over Washington's two terms. As Secretary of State, for example, besides Thomas Jefferson, who served from 1790 to 1793, Edmund Jennings Randolph served from 1794 to 1795, while Timothy Pickering was Secretary of State from 1795 until 1800. Alexander Hamilton served the longest as Secretary of the Treasury, serving from 1789 to 1795. Oliver Wolcott served the last five years as Secretary of the Treasury from 1795 to 1800. The War Department saw three secretaries beginning with Henry Knox (service from 1789 to 1794), followed by Thomas Pickering, who was there for one year (1795), and James McHenry, who was the last to serve, from 1796 to 1800. The final position in the cabinet was the attorney general, which saw three persons serving—Edmund Jennings Randolph, serving from 1789 to 1794, William Bradford from 1794 to 1795, and Charles Lee, finishing out the Washington years, serving from 1795 to 1801.[67]

While Washington consulted constantly with his department heads in both personal consultation and written communiqués, he also met occasionally with them as a body to discuss certain issues, departmental concerns, and other national matters. On an individual basis, he kept in close contact with them.[68] Cabinet members also helped to prepare his public papers.[69] Washington attempted to reduce conflict and encourage cooperation within the cabinet. In a letter to Jefferson about a disagreement Jefferson was having with Hamilton, Washington wrote:

I regret, deeply regret, the difference in opinions which have arisen, and divided you and another principal Officer of the Government; and wish, devoutly, there could be an accommodation of them by mutual yieldings. A Measure of this sort would produce harmony, and consequent good in our public Councils; the contrary will, inevitably, introduce confusion, and serious mischiefs; and for what? Because mankind cannot think alike, but would adopt different means to attain the same end. For I will frankly, and solemnly declare that, I believe the views of both of you.[70]

Court Appointments. Some of a president's most important appointments are those he makes to the Supreme Court. Often these appointments assure the president's judicial legacy long after he has retired from office. By the time Washington's two terms had been completed, the president had appointed 10 members to the Supreme Court—more than any other president appointed, though none of the 10 Court members have been rated higher than "average" in competence.[71] Washington looked for men who had had some Revolutionary War experience or had rendered some service to the nation. Seven had been delegates to the Constitutional Convention, 1 had been a member of the Second Continental Congress, 3 had signed the Declaration of Independence, and 8 of the 10 had had judicial experience. All were loyal Federalists.[72] Included among the 10 were John Jay[73] and Oliver Ellsworth, who both served as chief Justice, as well as Associate Justices John Rutledge, William Cushing, James Wilson, John Blair, James Iredell, Thomas Johnson, William Paterson, and the controversial Samuel Chase, who was impeached by the House but was not convicted in the Senate and who thus was able to keep up his constant Federalist attacks against Thomas Jefferson.

Removal Power

No mention is made of a president's removal power in the Constitution, except for impeachment, but Hamilton argued in *Federalist* No. 77 that this removal power should be presumed to be the president's based on the president's appointment power. Madison, on the other hand, indicated that this power could be implied from the president's power to "take care that the laws be faithfully executed."[74] While Washington did not remove any person from his administration, he did assert the right of a president to do so, without Senate concurrence.[75]

The Pardon

On July 10, 1797, Washington issued his first pardon for those who had taken part in the Whiskey Rebellion. This was a "full pardon" to those who might have been guilty of treason or other offenses of consequence against the United States.[76] Since this pardon, of course, presidents have used this power to free individuals from incarceration and, in effect, held check over the courts.

The Civil Service

One might also argue that George Washington was first responsible for the growth of the bureaucracy at the federal level since he oversaw the creation and continuation of the Civil Service from 1789 until 1801. By 1792 there were nearly 780 Civil Service employees. Of these, about 660 persons were employed in the Treasury Department.[77]

Chief Diplomat

Foreign affairs are considered by most presidents to be most important, yet few presidents come into office with sufficient experience to be conversant with world politics. George Washington was in this position, but he was convinced that the stability of the nation really depended on the nation's established visibility in the world. Jefferson observed, on arriving back in the United States from Paris to take up his new position as Secretary of State, that Washington "considered foreign affairs so over-riding to the success of the administration that he had assumed the responsibility for foreign policy himself. In actual practice he is his own foreign minister."[78]

Authority in the Area of Foreign Affairs. Not everyone felt as George Washington did about this, and Washington's authority in the area of foreign affairs was challenged several times. A major crisis erupted over Washington's Proclamation of Neutrality on April 22, 1793, a proclamation that would establish U.S. neutrality in the war between Great Britain, its allies—Austria, Prussia, Sardinia—and the opposing forces in France. This caused Alexander Hamilton to challenge James Madison to a debate over neutrality where each found himself on opposite sides of the issue. In a series of articles appearing in *The Gazette of the United States* Hamilton, writing under the pseudonym of Pacificus (Lover of Peace), argued that authority in foreign affairs was "inherently" the president's and that a president is within his rights as Commander in Chief to declare neutrality for the United States. Madison, writing as Helvidius (Lover of Liberty), charged the president with assuming a power similar to the British monarch's "royal" prerogative, since he believed that only Congress had the right to declare war and make foreign policy, based on Article I powers.[79] In the long run, of course, the United States has come to adopt the argument of Hamilton in this debate.

Isolation. Even though Washington recognized the importance of establishing America in the world, he was insistent that most progress in this country would be made only if America were at peace. As he pointed out in 1798, "If this country can steer clear of European politics, stand firm on its bottom, and be wise and temperate in government, it bids fair to be one of the greatest and happiest nations in the world."[80] He argued that peace should be maintained at all costs. Thus, he cautioned against becoming involved in other countries' affairs.

His isolationist approach was revealed in the previously mentioned 1793 Neutrality Proclamation. Francophiles in America were eager for Washington to side with France against Britain and the other nations, while others in the country hoped Washington would support Britain. Despite these pressures, George Washington insisted in his proclamation that the United States would pursue a path "friendly and impartial towards the belligerent powers" and cautioned citizens of this country to "avoid all acts and proceedings whatsoever, which may in any manner tend to contravene such disposition." If citizens were unwilling to do this, Washington warned that

whosoever of the citizens of the United States shall render himself liable to punishment of forfeiture under the law of nations, by committing, aiding or abetting hostilities against any of the said powers, or by carrying to any of them, those articles which are deemed contraband . . . will not receive the protection of the United States against such punishment or forfeiture.

Moreover, he promised that prosecutions would be instituted against those who would "violate the law of nations, with respect to the power at war, or any of them."[81]

Washington's isolationism was reiterated in his 1796 Farewell Address. In this classic address, he warned against foreign alliances and entanglements, suggesting,

[T]he great rule of conduct for us, in regard to foreign Nations, is, in extending our commercial relations to have with them as little *political* connection as possible. . . . 'Tis our true policy to steer clear of permanent Alliances with any portion of the foreign world; . . . Taking care always to keep ourselves, by suitable establishments, on a respectable defensive posture, we may safely trust to temporary alliances for extraordinary emergencies.[82]

This policy of political isolationism would remain a part of the United States for at least 100 years.[83]

Recognizing Countries. In many ways, Washington established a precedent of recognition when he first used executive authority to recognize the new Republic of France after its Revolution. In doing this he immediately established a formal relationship with France, giving the country the legitimacy it desired. Washington felt the president should do this and not the Congress.[84] Washington also sent other emissaries to European countries establishing similar relations with Spain and Portugal.[85]

Treaty Making. Washington wanted everything done in the area of foreign affairs to speak well of the United States, even treaty making. In one statement to the Senate, on September 17, 1789, Washington indicated: "It doubtless is important that all treaties and compacts formed by the United States with other nations, whether civilized or not, should be made with caution and executed with fidelity."[86] The Jay Treaty of 1795, which attracted such criticism, established our primary relations with Great Britain. This treaty was controversial since it gave Britain more concessions than most would have liked to give it. For example, along the Canadian border, the British were able to continue their fur trade with the Indians, despite the fact it was within American territory. The French objected to the treaty since it gave them little protection and undermined some previous treaty obligations France had with the United States. Perhaps the greatest damage done by the Jay Treaty was what was done to the southern states, which depended more than other states on exports to other countries. Under the Jay provisions, American ships would not carry a number of goods from the South, including cotton. On the positive side, the treaty did keep the United States out of war, which was Washington's strong desire.[87]

Washington treated relations with Native Americans as foreign relations. He saw that Britain and Spain were encouraging the Indians to continue to pressure Americans along the frontier.[88] As a result, Washington saw that it was necessary, if progress were to be made, to work with Britain at the same time as he negotiated with the Indians. The high point in his work with the Indians was perhaps the treaty that was signed in New York in August 1790 with 30 Creek chiefs.[89] After renewed attacks by Indians in 1791, however, Washington found it necessary to sever relations with Britain, convinced that Britain had not adhered to the provisions of the Treaty of Peace. Relations were not reestablished until the end of 1792, when Thomas Pinckney was sent to Britain as the administration's first resident "minister plenipotentiary."

For domestic peace to be sustained, Washington saw it necessary to plead with Congress and all Americans to cease their warlike nature against the American Indian. In his Fourth Annual Address to Congress on November 6, 1792, Washington recommended that the Congress give "energy to the laws throughout our interior frontier" and be restrained in committing the "outrages upon the Indians; without which all pacific plans must prove nugatory." He also urged Congress to compensate "trustworthy" citizens, encouraging them to "reside among them [Indians], as agents" as a way to encourage peace efforts. A final suggestion was made for the Congress to come up with plans for promoting civilization among the friendly tribes, and for carrying on trade with them, upon a scale equal to their wants, and under regulations calculated to protect them from imposition and extortion. . . . its influence in cementing their interests with our's could not but be considerable.[90]

By 1795 Washington advised Congress that the best way to see justice done among the Indians is to

render justice to them. If these means can be devised by the wisdom of Congress; and especially if there can be added an adequate provision for supplying the necessities of the Indians on reasonable terms . . . I should not hesitate to entertain a strong hope, of rendering our tranquility permanent.[91]

Table 1.3 indicates the activity of George Washington as chief diplomat. U.S. treaties were signed with Algiers, Great Britain, Morocco, Spain, Tripoli, and Tunis, as well as with the following Indian tribes: Wyandot, Delawares, Shawanees, Ottawas, Chippewas, Pottawatamies, Miamis, Eel-river, Weeas, Kickapoos, Piankeshaws, Kaskaskias, Cherokees, Creeks, and the Oneida tribe.

Commander in Chief

The Commander in Chief role is a president's most visible role and the one where presidents can exhibit the greatest strength. The role was not always as powerful as it is today, since it was exclusively a military title when Washington assumed it in 1783 from the Continental Congress. It was transformed from a relatively unimportant title to one that Supreme Court justice Robert Jackson once referred to as "the most dangerous one to free government in the whole catalogue of powers"[92]; and later stated that it was a power to "do anything, anywhere, that can be done with an army or navy."[93]

Part of this change in the role we can blame on George Washington himself. The power of this role was broadened when Washington chose, as Commander in Chief, to ride into Pennsylvania, accompanying the state militia to restore order during the Whiskey Rebellion of 1793.

Congress also increased the power of this role when it granted Washington authority in 1789 to call out the militia to protect the frontiers from Indians[94] and again in 1791, when Congress granted Washington authority to enlist additional troops to protect citizens from Indian tribes. In 1792 still more authority was given by Congress to the president to organize the militia, while Congress gave the authority in 1795 to call the militia to suppress insurrections and to repel invasions.

The budget also focused attention on the Commander in Chief's activities through the expenses allowed in the 1790 budget. Washington writes in his

Table 1.3
U.S. Treaties with Foreign Countries and Native Americans from 1789 to 1797

Country	Subject	Date Ratified
Morocco	Assignment of Council	1791
Great Britain	Amity, Commerce, Navigation (Jay Treaty)	1795
Spain	Friendship, Boundaries, Commerce, Navigation	1795
Algiers	Peace and Amity	1796
Great Britain	Explanatory of Article III of Treaty of 1795	1796
Tripoli	Peace and Friendship	1796
Tunis	Amity, Commerce, Navigation	1797

Tribes	Subject	Date Ratified
Wyandot	Removing controversy, regulating trade, and settling boundaries	1789
Creek	Peace and Friendship treaty	1790
Cherokee	Treaty of Peace and Friendship (Holston Treaty)	1791
Five Indian Nations	Treaty of Peace	1792
Cherokee	Settling boundaries, compensation for land, fines for stolen horses	1794
Oneida, Tuscorora, Stockbridge	Compensation to tribe, saw mills, building churches	1794
Six Nations of Indians	Treaty of friendship and peace	1795
Cherokee	Treaty involving public lands	1795
Wyandot, Delawares, Shawanees, Ottawas, Chippewas, Pottawatamies, Miamis, Eel-river, Weeas, Kickapoos, Piankeshaws, and Kaskaskias	Peace Treaty (Treaty of Ft. Greenville)	1795
Seven Nations of Canada	Cession of Lands to New York	1797
Cherokee	Peace and friendship, settling boundaries	1798

diary on March 25, 1790, that he had received the following budget estimates from a "Commee. (sp.) Of Congress." Affairs of the Commander in Chief clearly are the most expensive:

dollrs(sp). Cents

141,492.73	for the Civil list
155,537.72	War Department
96,979.72	Invalid persons
10,000.	President—for Contingent Services of Government
147,169.54	For demands enumerated by the Secrety (sp). Of the Treaty. On wch (sp). The light Ho. On Cape Henry is includd (sp.)
120.	To Jehoiakim McToksin
96.	James Mathers
96.	Gifford Dally.
551,491.71	Total Amount[95]

General Desire for Peace Through Strength. Washington made clear in his Third Annual Message in 1791 and his Fifth Annual Message to Congress on December 3, 1793, that he intended to use his Commander in Chief role to preserve the peace with the Indians. As he stated in his Third Message:

It is sincerely to be desired that all need of coercion in the future may cease; and that an intimate intercourse may succeed, calculated to advance the happiness of the Indians, and to attach them firmly to the United States.[96]

Washington in his Fifth Annual Message made it quite clear to Congress that the best way to maintain the peace in the country was to be prepared for war. As he indicated:

If we desire to avoid insult, we must be able to repel it; if we desire to secure peace, one of the most powerful instruments of our rising prosperity, it must be known, that we are at all times ready for War.[97]

To do this Washington encouraged the passage of bills to strengthen the military establishment, including the raising of a 25,000-person army, the recruiting of an 800-member Corps of Artillerymen, and the procuring of an 80,000-member militia.[98]

Desire for Peace: The Indians. Few challenges to Washington's efforts toward peace were more immediate than the threats posed by the American Indian. Indeed, his greatest concerns were the western boundaries protecting them from Indian attack. Washington was particularly concerned with the violence on both sides. As he pointed out to the chiefs of the Seneca Nation in 1790: "The murders that have been committed upon some of your people, by the bad white men I sincerely lament and reprobate, and I earnestly hope that the real murderers will be secured, and punished as they deserve." He then added:

I shall inform you, that some bad Indians, and the outcast of several tribes who reside at the Miamee Village, have long continued their murders and depredations upon the frontiers, living along the Ohio. That they have not only refused to listen to my voice inviting them to peace, but that upon receiving it, they renewed their incursions and murders with greater violence than ever.

He ended by saying to the chiefs: "Remember my words Senecas, continue to be strong in your friendship for the United States, as the only rational ground of your future happiness."[99]

To the Cherokees, Washington's concern was to teach them the skills of agriculture. As he wrote:

My beloved Cherokees. . . . I have directed Mr. Dinsmoor, to procure all necessary apparatus for spinning and weaving, and to hire a woman to teach the use of them. He will also procure some plows and other implements of husbandry, with which to begin the improved cultivation of the ground which I recommend, and employ a fit person to shew you how they are to be used. I have further directed him to procure some cattle and sheep for the most prudent and industrious men, who shall be willing to exert themselves in tilling the ground and raising those useful animals.

Washington then added: "But the cares of the United States are not confined to your single nation. They extend to all the Indians dwelling on their borders."[100] Washington felt as if he had done all in his power to bring peace between the Indians and the government. As he stated in his Fifth Annual Address to Congress: "When we contemplate the war on frontiers, it may be truly affirmed that every reasonable effort has been made to adjust the causes of dissension with the Indians North of the Ohio."[101]

Desire for Peace: The Whiskey Rebellion of 1794. With the exception of Indian skirmishes, the Whiskey Rebellion was the only other warfare that Washington experienced, but it proved to be very important warfare since it was an example of domestic insurgency. The difficulties began when George Washington approved an excise tax on liquor to help pay off the national debt and bolster the economy. Farmers in Pennsylvania in 1794 who converted their crops of corn into alcohol, rather than pay the excessive transportation costs to send the corn to markets out of state, refused to pay the tax. The tax seemed to be popular only among the rich. Opponents of the tax in Congress had predicted dire results. Senator William Maclay's feeling was that the tax was "the most execrable system that ever was framed against the liberty of a people. . . . War and bloodshed are the most likely consequence of all this."[102] The rebellion centered in the four western counties in the state. These farmers had been encouraged by the Mingo Creek Society, a local Democratic–Republican organization.[103]

Washington was very concerned that if this rebellion got out of hand, it would make it difficult for the nation as a whole to achieve respect both at home and abroad. Washington's response at first was to issue a proclamation on September 15, 1792, indicating he was aware of the "violent and unwarrantable proceedings" that had gone on relative to the raising of revenue from distilled spirits. He also "admonished" and "exhorted" all of those who were involved to "refrain and desist from all unlawful combinations and proceedings whatsoever" that would obstruct the law, and then required that "all Courts, Magistrates and Officers" enforce the Proclamation.[104]

Opposition continued for the next two years. A second proclamation of August 7, 1794, handed down by Washington, insisted that those involved in the rebellion should "disperse and retire peaceably to their respective abodes." He also warned others about the consequences of "aiding, abetting or comforting the perpetrators of the . . . treasonable acts."[105] In addition to the proclamation, a group of three federal commissioners was appointed and instructed to actively talk with groups and individuals involved to learn if a resolution could come about short of coercion. Those involved were promised full pardon for their actions if they would submit to the law.[106]

One further action took place when Washington issued a final proclamation indicating that he would call for the militia, since all other measures had failed to achieve the desired results. As Washington stated in the proclamation:

[W]hen . . . Government is set at defiance, the contest being whether a small portion of the United States shall dictate to the whole Union, and, at the expense of those who desire peace, indulge a desperate ambition: Now therefore I, George Washington, President of the United States . . . exhort all individuals, officers, and bodies of men to contemplate with abhorrence the measures leading directly or indirectly to those crimes which produce this resort to military coercion; . . . And, lastly, I again warn all persons, whomsoever and wheresoever not to abet, aid, or comfort the insurgents aforesaid, as they will answer the contrary at their peril.[107]

Washington contacted the governors of Pennsylvania, New Jersey, Virginia, and Maryland to send militias into Pennsylvania to bring a halt to the rebellion. The governors cooperated and had themselves already called out the militia in the various states through state proclamation. Between 12,000 and 15,000 troops made an appearance.[108] Most importantly, George Washington rode to Bedford, Pennsylvania, and made his presence known inspecting the troops in the field.

As a result of Washington's presence and efforts, the rebellion soon came to an end. Washington had succeeded in emphasizing that national priorities must prevail over any local grievance.[109] Of this episode, Henry Cabot

Lodge, a George Washington biographer, wrote that the Whiskey Rebellion was the

first direct challenge to the new government. . . . the action of government vindicated the right of the United States to live, because they had proved themselves able to keep order. It proved to the American people that their government was a reality of force and power.[110]

Building of a Navy. President Bill Clinton on May 21, 1998, in a commemoration of the National Maritime Day Proclamation indicated, "The United States is and has always been a maritime Nation. Our history is tied to the sea . . . and our development as a Nation has paralleled the growth of our waterborne commerce."[111] This fascination with the sea began with George Washington as he urged the Congress to "look to the means to set about the gradual creation of a navy." Washington proposed that Congress should begin to "lay up the materials for the building and equipping of ships of war, and to proceed in the work by degrees, in proportion as our resources shall render it practicable without inconvenience."[112] Washington felt that this would be a way to provide for our national security, particularly if Europe in the future sensed America's weakness. In his Eighth Annual Address to Congress he indicated that

[t]o secure respect to a Neutral Flag, requires a naval force, organized, and ready to vindicate it, from insult or aggression. This may even prevent the necessity of going to war, by discouraging belligerent Powers from committing such violations of the right of the neutral party, as may first or last, leave no other option. . . . These considerations invite the United States, to look to the means, and to set about the gradual creation of a navy. The increasing progress of their navigation, promises them, at no distant period, the requisite supply of Seamen; and their means, in other respects, favour the undertaking. It is encouragement, likewise, that their particular situation, will give weight and influence to a moderate naval force in their hands.[113]

CONCLUSION

The question posed at the beginning of this chapter was, *Can we learn anything about the modern presidency by examining the presidency of George Washington, or will the net effect be negligible?*

Washington clearly took precautions in his presidency so that he would *not* be an uncertain model. He was well aware of what being the first president meant. As he wrote:

Many things which appear of little importance in themselves and at the beginning, may have great and durable consequences from their having been established at the commencement of a new general government. It will be much easier to commence the administration, upon a well adjusted system, built on tenable grounds, than to correct errors to alter inconveniences after they shall have been confirmed by habit.[114]

In 1790 Washington wrote to Catherine Macaulay Graham: "I walk on untrodden ground. There is scarcely any part of my conduct wch (sp.) may not hereafter be drawn into precedent."[115]

To determine Washington's lasting contributions to the shaping of the presidency, I suggested an analysis of each major role would be in order. It was discovered that as *chief executive*, Washington was concerned with building the structure of government, staffing it, filling vacancies when they occurred, and overseeing government's operation. In addition, the issue of removal was raised during his presidency, with Washington determining this was also a power of the presidency. His strong leadership as chief executive compensated for the lack of resources attending this role.

As *chief diplomat*, he was most aware of what needed to be done to stabilize this fledgling government. He was insistent that we maintain peace at any cost to allow the government to take hold. Those treaties listed in Table 1.3 were in effect to do just that. He was criticized for his isolationist stance, but such criticism did not dissuade him from doing what he felt was best for the country in the eyes of the world at large. Frank T. Reuter's assessment of Washington's importance in foreign affairs was that he

gained sufficient time for his country to establish its government, strengthen its unity, secure its borders, and promote its commerce. He had gained this time through patient diplomacy that neutralized the threats from England and Spain in the Northwest and the Southwest, pacified the Indians, and minimized regionalism by opening the West for protected and prosperous settlement.[116]

As *Commander in Chief* he exerted strong leadership. The Whiskey Rebellion was his primary test showing him as strong in this role. Probably, his major contribution to this role was what Seymour Martin Lipset pointed to when he noted, "It is not a natural thing for the military or other powerful stratas to obey when they see their interests or status threatened, but Washington, who led the army, recognized the tremendous importance of subordination to civil authority."[117] As president, Washington wrote specific instructions for such military leaders as General "Mad Anthony" Wayne, which immediately showed that he recognized this principle,[118] while at the same time showing that he was the person in charge of the military.

Even though he was most uncomfortable in expressing himself in this role, Washington as an *opinion/party leader* recognized the importance of maintaining a connection with the public. He made a particular effort to reach out to the people through his tours and social events. What may have distinguished Washington as an opinion/party leader from his modern-day counterparts, as David K. Nichols forcefully argues, was that George Washington and the United States were more intertwined in the minds of the people than any twentieth-century president has ever been.[119] As far as the other focus of this combined role is concerned, however, there are probably limited insights we can draw on from his "one-party leadership." He was of two minds regarding party. He both distanced himself from personal leadership of his party yet submitted himself to Hamilton's greater devotion to Federalist principles. At the end of his second term he could see nothing but difficulties emerging in the development of a two-party system for the United States.

The role that Washington seemingly contributed least to was that of *legislative leader*. It wasn't that he ignored his responsibilities in this role, since he gave the required speeches to Congress. Yet what he did he often did in conflict with the Congress. He was frequently irritated with its members; he stayed relatively aloof from them, even though members of Congress were invited to his residence for levees, dinners, and teas. He showed a real distance from the Congress when he became the first president to rely on "executive immunity," refusing to turn over to the House of Representatives the needed documents regarding the Jay Treaty, as well as holding back special dispatches detailing Indian skirmishes. Washington also vetoed two measures he felt were unconstitutional. For Washington, the role of legislative leader suggested more conflict than cooperation. The role had to await the presidency of Thomas Jefferson before it saw a president fully develop it.

Washington's accomplishments, including full development of three of the five presidential roles, established important precedents for later presidents to follow. Of the two roles that Washington made fewer contributions to, he joins a majority of succeeding presidents. Only a limited number of presidents have succeeded as opinion/party leaders and legislative leaders.

Final Summary. Scholars who have examined the Washington presidency have disagreed as to his lasting impact on the presidency. Forrest McDonald, for example, questioned Washington's long-term contributions, suggesting he was more symbol than substance. At the end of his book on Washington, McDonald indicated that

George Washington was indispensable, but only for what he was, not for what he did. He was the symbol of the presidency, the epitome of propriety in government, the means by which Americans accommodated the change from monarchy to republicanism, and the instrument by which an inconsequential people took its first steps toward becoming a great nation. [But then he concludes] No one who followed Washington in the presidency could escape the legends that surrounded his tenure in the office, but the more perceptive among them shared a secret: Washington had done little in his own right, had often opposed the best measures of his subordinates, and had taken credit for achievements that he had not shared in bringing about. . . . They kept the secret to themselves.[120]

Washington's achievements came closer to the assessments offered by Michael Riccards, George W. Nordham, and Seymour Martin Lipset. Riccards suggested of Washington that "[h]e began with a collection of clauses and an unformed office and crafted them into an institution."[121] Nordham added that "George Washington . . . made the presidency a workable, credible concept."[122] Lipset stated that Washington was a founder who "helped the country formulate an identity and institutionalize a competitive electoral democracy." Again, Lipset asserted that Washington "facilitated the formation of the culture and institutions that were necessary for a stable and . . . effective democratic system."[123]

To be sure, nations take on the characteristics of its leaders. Washington's insistence on peace at any price was important in providing critical time for a fledgling nation to stabilize. First persons are always important to the history of a nation or any organization, whether they are weak or strong. First persons the caliber of a Washington are essential for nations to grow strong and develop fully. Washington shaped the office he served in as well as the nation he served. Elements of power and presidency were forged into shape by a strong, competent leader with vision and direction who stayed the course despite opposition. Yes, political scientists would do well to study carefully the Washington presidency.

NOTES

1. Larry Gordon reminds us that Washington gave up power twice when he returned to civilian life after the war and then refused to run for a third term as president. See "*Column One*: Fresh Look at the First President," *Los Angeles Times*, February 16, 1998, p. A22.

2. In December 1788 Washington wrote to Arthur Young: "I can only say for myself, that I have endeavored in a state of tranquil retirement to keep myself as much from the eye of the world as I possibly could. . . . I wish most devoutly to glide silently and unnoticed through the remainder of life. This is my heart felt wish; and these are my undisguised feelings." John C. Fitzpatrick, ed., *The Writings of George Washington*, 39 vols. (Washington, DC: U.S. Government Printing Office, 1931–1944), 35:153–154.

3. Washington in 1789 wrote that becoming president could be compared to "—a culprit who is going to the place of his execution." See Gordon, "*Column One*," p. A22.

4. Being a *model*, of course, did not mean this president was beyond criticism of his peers. Thomas Paine, for example, indicated of George Washington that "[t]he character which Mr. Washington has attempted to act in this world is a sort of nondescribable, chameleon-colored thing, called prudence. It is, in many cases, a substitute for principle, and is so nearly allied to hypocrisy, that it easily slides into it." See William A. DeGregorio, *The Complete Book of U.S. Presidents*, 5th ed. (New York: Wings Books, 1997), p. 15.

5. Especially see *Federalist Paper* No. 72; also see *Federalist Papers* Nos. 68–78

for a complete examination of the type of president that Alexander Hamilton anticipated for this government. Alexander Hamilton, James Madison, and John Jay, *The Federalist Papers* (New York: New American Library, 1961), pp. 435–440 for No. 72, and pp. 411–472 for Nos. 68–78.

6. See, for example, Theodore J. Lowi and Benjamin Ginsberg, *American Government: Freedom and Power* (New York: W. W. Norton, 1996), p. 211.

7. See Fred I. Greenstein, *The Hidden-Hand Presidency* (New York: Basic Books, 1982).

8. See David K. Nichols, *The Myth of the Modern Presidency* (University Park: Pennsylvania State University Press, 1994), pp. 6–9, 13.

9. Arthur Schlesinger Sr., "The U.S. Presidents," *Life* (November 1, 1948), p. 65; and "Our Presidents: A Rating by 75 Historians," *New York Times Magazine* (July 29, 1962), pp. 12ff.

10. Gary Maranell and Richard Dodder, "Political Orientation and Evaluation of Presidential Prestige: A Study of American Historians," *Social Science Quarterly* 51 (September 1970), p. 418.

11. See Robert Murray and Tim Blessing, "The Presidential Performance Study: A Progress Report," *Journal of American History* (December 1982), pp. 540–541; Arthur M. Schlesinger Jr., "The Ultimate Approval Rating," *New York Times Magazine* (December 15, 1996), pp. 46–51.

12. Byron W. Daynes, Raymond Tatalovich, and Dennis Soden have argued that any president placed by scholars in a "great" or "near great" category reveals traits of "exceptional leadership, particularly during times of crisis." See their *To Govern a Nation: Presidential Power and Politics* (New York: St. Martin's Press, 1998), p. 24.

13. See James David Barber, *The Presidential Character*, 4th ed. (Englewood Cliffs, NJ: Prentice-Hall, 1992), p. 10.

14. These five roles were first defined by Raymond Tatalovich and Byron W. Daynes in their 1984 book on the presidency, *Presidential Power in the United States* (Monterey, CA: Brooks/Cole, 1984). They have since been used and refined by Daynes, Tatalovich, and Soden in *To Govern a Nation*. Many of the generalizations in this chapter regarding these roles come from the arguments in these two books.

15. See Daynes, Tatalovich, and Soden, *To Govern a Nation*, pp. 2–3.

16. When I use the reference "his" to refer to president, I in no way wish to suggest that at some time in the near future women may not occupy this position. The reference to "his" refers to past occupancy of the president and not future occupancy.

17. "Queries on a Line of Conduct to be Pursued by the President," May 10, 1789, in Fitzpatrick, *The Writings of George Washington*, 30:319–320. George Washington asked these same questions of John Jay and Alexander Hamilton as well.

18. Douglas Southall Freeman, *George Washington: A Biography*, vol. 6 (New York: Charles Scribner's Sons, 1954), p. 182n.

19. Quotation in Leonard D. White, *The Federalists: A Study in Administrative History, 1789–1801* (New York: Free Press, 1948), p. 108.

20. Michael Nelson, "History of the Presidency," in *Congressional Quarterly's Guide to the Presidency* (Washington, DC: Congressional Quarterly, 1989), p. 58.

21. See George W. Nordham, *The Age of Washington: George Washington's Presidency: 1789–1797* (Chicago: Adams Press, 1989), p. 59.

22. See Albert B. Hart, *Washington as President*, Pamphlet no. 8 (Washington, DC: Bicentennial Commission, 1931), pp. 37–38. Also see Nordham, *The Age of Washington*, pp. 87–88 for the complete itinerary of Washington on this trip.

23. Nordham, *The Age of Washington*, p. 61.

24. See Jeffrey K. Tulis, *The Rhetorical Presidency* (Princeton, NJ: Princeton University Press, 1987), p. 64.

25. Ibid., p. 138.

26. "Letter to Compte De Rochambeau," August 10, 1790, in Fitzpatrick, *The Writings of George Washington*, 35:83–84.

27. See Fitzpatrick, *The Writings of George Washington*, 35:37.

28. Statement of August 8, 1796, in Nordham, *The Age of Washington*, p. 262.

29. See the statement of Paul Leicester Ford in ibid., pp. 263–264.

30. Ibid., p. 264.

31. "To Governor Henry Lee (Private)," Philadelphia, July 21, 1793, in Fitzpatrick, *The Writings of George Washington*, 35:22–23.

32. "Letter to David Humphreys," June 12, 1796, in ibid., pp. 91–92.

33. Washington, *Writings*, 32, p. 189, in White, *The Federalists*, p. 111.

34. Nordham, *The Age of Washington*, p. 236.

35. Ibid., pp. 236–237.

36. See Forrest McDonald, *The Presidency of George Washington* (Lawrence: University Press of Kansas, 1974), p. 129.

37. See Nordham, *The Age of Washington*, p. 235.

38. Ibid., p. 237.

39. Washington to Edmund Randolph, October 16, 1794, in John Roger Sharp, *American Politics in the Early Republic: The New Nation in Crisis* (New Haven, CT: Yale University Press, 1993), p. 100.

40. See Robert F. Jones, *George Washington*, rev. ed. (New York: Fordham University Press, 1986), p. 123.

41. "Farewell Address." see W. B. Allen, comp. and ed., *George Washington: A Collection* (Indianapolis: Liberty Fund, 1988), pp. 519–520.

42. Edward C. Corwin and Louis W. Koenig, *The Presidency Today* (New York: New York University Press, 1956), p. 83.

43. David K. Nichols, *The Myth of the Modern Presidency* (University Park: Pennsylvania State University Press, 1994), p. 29.

44. "To John Francis Mercer," Mount Vernon, September 26, 1792, in Fitzpatrick, *The Writings of George Washington*, 32:165.

45. Glenn A. Phelps, "Washington the Precedent Setter," in Thomas E. Cronin, *Inventing the American Presidency* (Lawrence: University Press of Kansas, 1989), p. 266.

46. Freeman, *George Washington*, p. 221.

47. Ibid., p. 376.

48. See Donald Jackson and Dorothy Twohig, eds., *The Diaries of George Washington*, vol. 6 (Charlottesville: University Press of Virginia, 1979), p. 7.

49. See Table 7.3 in Daynes, Tatalovich, and Soden, *To Govern a Nation*, p. 153.

50. "Veto Message," April 5, 1792, in Nordham, *The Age of Washington*, p. 103.

51. William Maclay, *Sketches of Debate in the First Senate of the United States* (Harrisburg, PA: Lane S. Hart, 1880), pp. 122–126.

52. Michael P. Riccards, "George Washington," in K. Thompson, ed., *Great American Presidents*, vol. 1 (New York: University Press of America, 1995), pp. 47–48.

53. See Glenn A. Phelps, "Washington the Precedent Setter," in Cronin, *Inventing the American Presidency*, p. 274; "To the Senate," February 26, 1794, in Fitzpatrick, *The Writings of George Washington*, 33:282.

54. "To the House of Representatives," March 30, 1796, in Fitzpatrick, *The Writings of George Washington*, 35:2–3.

55. "Proclamation," September 15, 1792, in James D. Richardson, ed., *A Compilation of the Messages and Papers of the Presidents*, vol. 1 (New York: Bureau of National Literature, 1911), pp. 116–117.

56. DeGregorio, *The Complete Book of the U.S. Presidents*, p. 12.

57. See Glenn A. Phelps, "George Washington: Precedent Setter," in Cronin, *Inventing the American Presidency*, p. 276.

58. Ibid., p. 277.

59. Frank L. Reuter, *Trials and Triumphs: George Washington's Foreign Policy* (Fort Worth: Texas Christian University Press, 1983), p. 92.

60. Ibid.

61. Sidney M. Milkis and Michael Nelson, *The American Presidency: Origins and Development, 1776–1990* (Washington, DC: Congressional Quarterly Press, 1990), p. 77.

62. "To Thomas Jefferson," New York, January 21, 1790, in Fitzpatrick, *The Writings of George Washington*, 30:510.

63. Leonard D. White, *The Federalists: A Study in Administrative History 1789–1801* (New York: Free Press, 1948), pp. 254–255.

64. Ibid.

65. Nordham, *The Age of Washington*, p. 226.

66. Shirley Anne Warshaw, *Powersharing: White House–Cabinet Relations in the Modern Presidency* (Albany: State University of New York Press, 1996), pp. 15–16.

67. See DeGregorio, *The Complete Book of U.S. Presidents*, pp. 8–9.

68. See Warshaw, *Powersharing*, p. 16.

69. White, *The Federalists*, pp. 32–34.

70. "To the Secretary of State (Private)," Philadelphia, October 18, 1792, in Fitzpatrick, *The Writings of George Washington*, 35:185–186.

71. Nine of the 10 justices appointed by Washington rated as average, with Thomas Johnson rated as below average. See "Rating Supreme Court Justices," in Henry J. Abraham, *Justices and Presidents: A Political History of Appointments to the Supreme Court*, 2nd ed. (New York: Oxford University Press, 1985), pp. 377–379.

72. Ibid., pp. 71–79.

73. John Jay had first been asked to serve as Secretary of State but expressed his desire to become Chief Justice of the Supreme Court. Washington supported his request. See James Thomas Flexner, *George Washington and the New Nation* (Boston: Little, Brown, 1970), p. 225.

74. Two later Supreme Court decisions—*Myers, Administratrix v. U.S.* (1926) and *Humphrey's Executor (Rathbun) v. U.S.* (1935)—would give the president un-

limited removal power in 1926, only to have it modified in 1935 depending on the particular office in question.

75. See Riccards, "George Washington," p. 54.

76. "Proclamation," July 10, 1795, in Fitzpatrick, *The Writings of George Washington*, 34:232–234.

77. See White, *The Federalists*, p. 255.

78. Reuter, *Trials and Triumphs*, p. 50.

79. For the complete series of Pacificus essays see John C. Hamilton, ed., *The Works of Alexander Hamilton*, vol. 7 (New York: Charles S. Francis, 1851), pp. 76–117; for the complete series of Helvidius essays see Thomas A. Mason, Robert A. Rutland, and Jeanne K. Sisson, eds., *The Papers of James Madison*, vol. 15 (Charlottesville: University Press of Virginia 1985), pp. 64–120.

80. Statement by Washington, May 16, 1798, in Nordham, *The Age of Washington*, p. 271.

81. "Proclamation of Neutrality," April 22, 1793, in Allen, *George Washington*, pp. 585–586.

82. "Farewell Address," September 19, 1796, in ibid., pp. 524–525.

83. DeGregorio, *The Complete Book of the U.S. Presidents*, p. 12.

84. Daynes, Tatalovich, and Soden, *To Govern a Nation*, p. 233.

85. Elmer Pilschke, *Diplomat in Chief: The Presidency at the Summit* (New York: Praeger, 1986), p. 70.

86. "Statement to the Senate from the President," September 17, 1789, in Richardson, *A Compilation of the Messages and Papers of the Presidents*, pp. 53–54.

87. James Thomas Flexner, *Washington: The Indispensable Man* (Boston: Little, Brown, 1974), pp. 326–327.

88. Reuter, *Trials and Triumphs*, p. 74.

89. Ibid., pp. 75, 87.

90. See the "Fourth Annual Address," November 6, 1792, in Nordham, *The Age of Washington*, p. 109.

91. See the "Seventh Annual Message to Congress," December 8, 1795, in John Rhodehamel, *George Washington: Writings* (New York: Library of America, 1997), p. 923.

92. Warren W. Hassler Jr., *The President and Commander in Chief* (Menlo Park, CA: Addison-Wesley, 1971), p. 11.

93. See *Youngstown Sheet and Tube Co. v. Sawyer*, 342 U.S. 643 (1952).

94. "To Arthur St. Clair," October 6, 1789, in Rhodehamel, *George Washington*, p. 743.

95. "Thursday 25th [March]," in Jackson and Twohig, *The Diaries of George Washington*, p. 53.

96. "Third Annual Message," October 25, 1791, in Richardson, *Compilation of the Messages and Papers of the Presidents*, p. 475.

97. "Fifth Annual Message to Congress," December 3, 1793, in Rhodehamel, *George Washington*, p. 848.

98. "National Defence," History of Congress, March 1794, Debates and Proceedings in the Congress of the United States, *Annals of the Congress of the United States* (Washington, DC: Gales and Seaton, 1855), p. 534.

99. "To the Chiefs of the Seneca Nation," Philadelphia, December 29, 1790, in Rhodehamel, *George Washington*, pp. 774–775.

100. "Address to the Cherokee Nation," Philadelphia, August 29, 1796, in Rhodehamel, *George Washington*, pp. 957–959.

101. "The Fifth Annual Address to Congress," in Allen, *George Washington*, p. 489.

102. http://www.virginia.edu/~gwpapers/whiskey/index.html (accessed December 14, 1999).

103. Milkis and Nelson, *The American Presidency*, pp. 84–86.

104. "Proclamation," September 15, 1792 in Nordham, *The Age of Washington*, pp. 105–106.

105. "Final Warning of a Resort to Force," Proclamation of August 7, 1794, in William M. Goldsmith, ed., *Growth of Presidential Power: A Documented History*, vol. 1 (New York: Chelsea, 1974), pp. 246–248.

106. "Sixth Annual Address," November 10, 1794, in Nordham, *The Age of Washington*, pp. 159–161.

107. "By the President of the United States of America. A Proclamation," September 25, 1794, in Richardson, *A Compilation of the Messages and Papers of the Presidents*, pp. 153–154.

108. McDonald, in *The Presidency of George Washington*, p. 145, lists the number of troops at 12,950, whereas Gregorio, *The Complete Book of U.S. Presidents*, p. 10, and Hart, in "Washington as President," in *Washington as President*, p. 12, list the number at 15,000.

109. "Report to Congress on Success of Operation," November 19, 1794, in Goldsmith, *Growth of Presidential Power*, pp. 253–255.

110. Henry Cabot Lodge, *George Washington* (Houghton Mifflin, 1899), which appeared in Nordham, *The Age of Washington*, p. 159.

111. "A Proclamation" by the President of the United States, May 21, 1998; The White House, Publications-Admin@Pub.Pub.WhiteHouse.Gov.

112. See Nordham, *The Age of Washington*, p. 231. Also see the many references to Congress' activity in building up the navy under "Naval Armament" in 1794 (pp. 486–498) and in 1796 (pp. 234–236, 870–890) in Debates and Proceedings in the Congress of the United States, *Annals of the Congress of the United States*.

113. See the "Eighth Annual Message," in Allen, *George Washington*, pp. 507–508.

114. Washington, *Writings*, p. 321, in James Hart, *The American Presidency in Action, 1789* (New York: Macmillan, 1948), p. 12.

115. "To Catherine Macaulay Graham," New York, January 9, 1790 in Fitzpatrick, *The Writings of George Washington*, 30:496.

116. Reuter, *Trials and Triumphs*, p. 230.

117. Seymour Martin Lipset, "Excerpts from Three Lectures on Democracy: 1997 Julian J. Rothbaum Distinguished Lecture in Representative Government," *Extensions: A Journal of the Carl Albert Congressional Research and Studies Center* (Spring 1998), p. 11.

118. See "Special Messages," December 9, 1795; Richardson, *A Compilation of the Messages and Papers of the Presidents*, p. 181.

119. Nichols, *The Myth of the Modern Presidency*, p. 30.
120. McDonald, *The Presidency of George Washington*, p. 186.
121. Riccards, "George Washington," p. 44.
122. Nordham, *The Age of Washington*, p. 270.
123. Lipset, "Excerpts from Three Lectures on Democracy," pp. 9–13.

Chapter 2

George Washington: The First Modern President? A Reply to Nichols

THOMAS ENGEMAN AND
RAYMOND TATALOVICH

David K. Nichols (1994) has stirred interest among presidency scholars by arguing that the Founders intended a strong executive similar to that, in fact, created in the twentieth century. Moreover, the administration of George Washington—whom he calls the first "modern" president—realized in practice most of the essential features of the strong, modern executive.

Nichols is wise to draw attention to the actual, real executive power under Article II of the Constitution. As Hamilton wrote in *The Federalist*: "Energy in the executive is a leading character of good government." Moreover, Washington and Hamilton went very far in realizing the stated and the implied or prerogative powers of the Constitution. Indeed, the Washington administration should remain for us one of the great examples of the truly Constitutional use of executive powers. But there are problems connecting the Washington/Hamilton understanding of the strong executive with the modern understanding and reality.

Our rebuttal of Nichols' thesis is organized in three parts. In Part I we summarize the essentials of the Nichols thesis. In Part II we offer a theoretical counterargument that the "modern" understanding of the presidency originates not with the Constitutional Founding but from the Second American Constitution beginning with the Progressive critique and culminating in the mid-twentieth century. In Part III we give experiential and empirical support for our interpretation by revisiting four presidential roles discussed by Nichols: foreign policy making, legislative leadership, administrative responsibility, and personalized leadership. Only with respect to diplomacy can President Washington be rightfully considered the "first" modern president, because he did, in fact, establish all the vital precedents of that role. But the reasons underlying this unique impact of Washington have as much to do with the instruments of presidential power as with the scope of government activities in diplomacy.

PART I: THE NICHOLS THESIS

Most presidential scholars date the "modern" presidency as beginning with FDR, and Nichols (1994: 3) references Fred I. Greenstein (1978: 45–46) on four ways that Roosevelt brought about a "metamorphosis" in presidential power: his legislative leadership, his use of unilateral authority, his bureaucratizing the executive office, and his personalization of the office. Nichols (1994: 6) agrees that the compelling question is "whether something fundamental changed in the character of the office during Franklin Roosevelt's tenure," because, unlike Greenstein, he asserts that "the myth of the modern Presidency is incorrect in assuming that these [four] changes required a transformation of the constitutional office of the Presidency." Rather, Nichols argues that "[t]he increased activity of the President can be attributed to broad changes in the character of government and society, and not to a change in the balance of power between the President and the other branches." Going against presidential orthodoxy, Nichols asserts that

[n]ot only in 1932, but also in 1990, in 1890, and in 1790, the President was responsible for new legislative initiatives, for controlling the bureaucracy, for making unilateral executive decisions, and for serving as a symbol of national unity. The modern Presidency did not just burst on the scene in 1932; it arose much earlier in our history.

How early? Says Nichols (1994: 7):

All the elements of the modern Presidency were exhibited long before Franklin Roosevelt because their source is the Constitution. The truth behind the myth of the modern Presidency is that recent Presidents do more than previous Presidents, but that is traceable to the simple fact that modern American government as a whole does more. It is this broader change in the extent of government action, not a change in the constitutional balance of power among the branches, that provides some legitimacy to the myth of the modern Presidency. Relative to the tasks that government performs, modern Presidents do no more—and no less—than Presidents have done in the past.

This critical distinction has caused contemporary presidential scholars to be led astray. Nichols admits that notable historical figures—Wilson, Theodore Roosevelt, Lincoln (who "may legitimately claim to be the greatest modern President" [Nichols, 1994: 23]), and Jackson—exhibited attributes of the modern presidency but that George Washington ought to be considered the first "modern" president. Let us detail the specific points on which Nichols (1994: 28–30) lays his claim:

1. He asserts that Washington "took an active role in the legislative process. Through his Secretary of the Treasury, Alexander Hamilton, the Washington administration immediately sketched out a legislative agenda and began to lobby for its passage." As a consequence, "Washington established a precedent that the President would be actively engaged in legislative questions."

2. He asserts that "[t]he size and shape of the modern executive branch were determined during Washington's Presidency. The cabinet departments were created, and, more important, the relationship between the President and the executive branch began to take shape." Nichols claims that under Washington "the issue of the removal power first arose" and that Washington "first defended the idea of executive privilege as a necessary support for the integrity and independence of the executive branch."

3. He asserts that "[t]he question of unilateral presidential powers was most obvious in the debate over Washington's proclamation of neutrality" but that "in a broader sense Washington was staking a claim to a major source of unilateral authority. Through his proclamation he was unilaterally interpreting the U.S. treaty with France by deciding that it created no presumption of support for the French in their fight. Moreover, Washington was making policy. Congress had clearly not decided whether to act or on which side. By proclaiming neutrality in the midst of the policy debate in Congress, Washington created an overwhelming presumption in favor of inaction."

4. He asserts that "with the exception of Lincoln, no other Presidency was as dependent on personality as Washington's" because "[t]he father of his country, the man who had led the nation to victory and independence, was the quintessential heroic President."

Our position is that only with respect to Nichols' third point, unilateral authority in foreign affairs—but *not* specifically with regard to the proclamation—does Nichols' argument have merit. The key to understanding the historical development of the presidency is implied in Nichols' first point (though he does not adhere to it faithfully), namely, *the creation of "precedent(s)" by which his successors abided.* Other serious scholars of the presidency are similarly guided by historical antecedents of presidential power. Edward Corwin (1957: 30) reminds us that, although

what the presidency is at any particular moment depends in important measure on who is President . . . the accumulated tradition of the office is also of vast importance. Precedents established by a forceful or politically successful personality in the office are available to less gifted successors, and permanently so because of the difficulty with which the Constitution is amended.

Richard Pious makes that case even more forcefully, arguing that prerogative power is the essence (while any "political" influences operate at the margins) of presidential power: "Presidents who claim constitutional authority to unilaterally make the most important domestic and national security policies in effect institute *prerogative government*" (Pious, 1979: 47). Because any president can assert a prerogative power, the more important question is whether his assertion will survive long-term. Here Pious (1979: 50) draws a distinction between a "frontlash effect" and a "backlash effect" or an "overshoot and collapse effect." For our purposes the frontlash effect trumps the separation of powers because "Congress and the courts acquiesce in his actions and claims of authority, and the 'living presidency' of custom, usage, and precedent grows stronger. This outcome occurs most often when national security issues are involved" (Pious, 1979: 50). In contrast, the backlash effect finds that

the president's interpretation of his powers is challenged by other branches, events in the party system erode popular support for his initiatives, and his successors find their authority limited by laws, judicial decisions, or public opinion. This outcome is likely when prerogative powers are used to resolve domestic issues.

What "overshoot and collapse effect" produces is "a major constitutional crisis, his legitimacy as a national leader is ended, and he is censured or brought into the impeachment process" (Pious, 1979: 50).

Thus, following this logic, any argument that FDR is the first modern president implies not only that he fundamentally changed the nature of the office but that his example was followed by presidents from Truman through Clinton. To deny FDR's unique beginnings as the first modern president means that one would have to deny that his innovations had any long-standing impact on the office. Similarly, to argue that any earlier president showed attributes of modernity would require one to show that any particular precedent established by Jackson, Lincoln, the first Roosevelt, or Wilson continued and was incorporated into the presidential modus operandi. By this criterion, Washington may indeed be considered the first "modern" chief diplomat, but in Nichols' other areas Washington falls woefully short.

Why is that the case, and where did Nichols go astray? Nichols makes the point that a strong executive is not incompatible with small government (and we agree), but the reality is that we are governed by a modern Leviathan, surely not the socialistic regimes that inhabit Europe but a government *quantitatively* and *qualitatively* unlike the governmental apparatus that Washington faced in 1789. An entire philosophical tradition, beginning with the Progressives and later the New Dealers, championed activist government and a vigorous executive. But the problem is that the Progressives did not understand—no better than the Conservatives like Nichols—that unlimited government is fundamentally inconsistent with *personalized* presidential leadership. The rise of big government has disrupted the kind of executive–legislative and executive–bureaucratic relationships that emerged during the Washington administration, with the result that the presidential powers

Nichols grounded in our Constitution are not conducive to managing the modern Leviathan.

PART II: THEORETICAL ORIGINS OF HEGEMONIC GOVERNMENT

The "modern" presidential office was created de facto by the practical activities resulting from the Progressive criticism of the Founders for creating a weak government. According to the Progressives, whether intentional or not, the weakness of the national government made sure that it became an easy pawn of economic interests. In pathbreaking works by Woodrow Wilson (1885), Thomas Dewey (1927), and especially Herbert Croly (1909, 1914), the case for a vastly expanded and transformed executive was made. The Progressive views resonated in the speeches and in the actions of the "modern" presidential giants Teddy Roosevelt, Woodrow Wilson, and FDR. James P. Young argues that "at the least, the modern presidency began to emerge in the thought and practice of the Progressive presidents" (Young, 1996: 155). Indeed, Croly's thought may be said to have become the universal basis of "leading opinion" on both the Left and the Right about the conduct of the modern executive.

Since the Progressive doctrines were most fully realized in the administration of Franklin Roosevelt, and FDR chose to present himself as a pragmatist and not a "reformer" like the Progressives, the true dimension of the change in the modern presidency has largely gone unnoticed. Henry Steele Commager quotes his "Fireside Chat" of April 14, 1938, as defining FDR's consistent pragmatism: "We know in America that our own democratic institutions can be preserved. . . . But in order to preserve them we need . . . to prove that the practical operation of democratic government is equal to the task" (Commager, 1950: 342). Repeated by countless historians since the 1930s, this pragmatic view of institutional change has seemingly ensnared Professor Nichols into easily comparing the modern "imperial Presidents," FDR and LBJ, with such *great men, but institutionally weak presidents* as George Washington.

FDR argued that he had no theory or blueprint for fundamental change in the theory of American constitutionalism but merely made such incremental and pragmatic changes as were necessary to meet the continuing emergencies, domestic and foreign, of his generation's "rendezvous with destiny." Unlike the Progressives, who savaged the weakness and injustice of the Founders' Constitution, especially Thomas Jefferson's individualism, FDR embraced his presidential predecessors. Roosevelt especially admired those, like Thomas Jefferson and Abraham Lincoln, who in his creative eye used executive power expansively to solve problems decisively. He created national shrines in Washington to commemorate their greatness. Roosevelt embraced almost all aspects of American history as the necessary foundation for the national patriotism sought by the Progressives.

Roosevelt could offer his administration as merely pragmatic—not radical or revolutionary—because of the previous acceptance of Progressive ideas as the basis of "modern liberalism." The Progressives' critique of the conservatism of the traditional Constitutional system and their recommendation for a strong executive had gained such currency that FDR could sell his novel policies as merely pragmatic adaptions of a broad and beneficent American patriotic tradition.

If FDR was the happy warrior arguing there is nothing to fear but fear itself, the Progressive intellectuals saw themselves engaged in a dark struggle with the dark forces of Constitutional reaction. The most comprehensive of the Progressive Constitutional revisionists was Herbert Croly. E. J. Dionne is not alone in judging Croly "the Progressive Era's master thinker" (Dionne, 1996: 188). Croly synthesized the criticisms and reforms of his contemporaries and welded them into a Progressive program that did become accepted as the core principles of modern liberalism. As the leading Progressive intellectual and the adviser of the two Progressive—and "modern"—presidents, Teddy Roosevelt and Woodrow Wilson, Croly proposed the theory and program for a new political order. At the absolute center of Croly's Constitutional revisionism is a national American Republic in which an active and enlightened populace is stimulated and guided by a powerful president/executive to perfect modern industrial life. To achieve this new nation, Croly argued that every aspect of traditional Constitutional practice must be transformed, often radically so.

Constitutional Failure

In Croly's account, the Constitution sought to divide public opinion and substitute the rule of representatives, under natural and positive law, for true, direct democracy and the rule of public opinion. Prior to 1870, rural American life was not harmed by the weakness of its national institutions. But the Industrial Revolution, ignited by the Civil War, led to a national economy that co-opted the weak national government of the Founders. This concentration of economic power resulted in the corruption of state and national politics. When the early reformers sought to correct these abuses, they discovered that the Constitutional system resisted their every attempt. It resisted reform because the Constitution was designed to protect the wealthy few through a rule of law and of lawyers defending the natural right to property above all else. No matter how inflamed democratic public opinion became at the abuses of unregulated corporations and the malefactors of great wealth, the careful division of powers between states and nation and the three branches of the national government repelled reform.

Without elaborating on his agenda, Croly spoke against the principles enabling class oppression: the rule of law, especially organic and the "Higher Law," Federalism, separation of powers, individual rights, and the "great" document vivifying them all, the Founders' Constitution. All of these things led to the worst condition of all: "the human will in its collective aspect was made subservient to the mechanism of a legal system" (Croly, 1914: 39). "In dividing the government against itself by such high and rigid barriers, an equally substantial barrier was raised against the exercise by the people of any easy and sufficient control over their government" (Croly, 1914: 42). "The fundamental Law to which the American people entrusted their ultimate sovereign power unfortunately tended to become more than unusually inaccessible" (Croly, 1914: 43).

The Law in the shape of the Federal Constitution really came to be a monarchy of the Word. It had been imposed upon the popular will. . . . All that the American people had to do to insure their political salvation was vigilantly to safeguard the specific formulation of law and order which was found in the sacred writing. (Croly, 1914: 44, 45)

While a critical analysis of the Founders' Constitution was common by the end of the nineteenth century, Herbert Croly offers the most comprehensive and politically inspired formula for reform: a national (not a federal) and a democratic (not a republican or representative) state. The development of a true Progressive, direct democracy culminates in a national executive capable of mobilizing public opinion. Indeed, Croly's new constitutionalism is built on the twin pillars of public opinion and presidential power. His new understanding of public opinion is novel and far-reaching. To ensure a national, direct democracy, public opinion becomes the key to his numerous reform proposals.

Public Opinion

Croly believed the Federalists' fear of majority faction led them to create a Constitution totally impervious to popular government:

Every popular government should in the end, and after a necessarily prolonged deliberation, possess the power of taking any action, which, in the opinion of a decisive majority of the people, is demanded by public welfare. Such is not the case with the government organized under the Federal Constitution. . . . A very small percentage of the American people can in this respect permanently thwart the will of an enormous majority, and there can be no justification for such a condition on any possible theory of popular Sovereignty. . . . The time may come when the fulfillment of a justifiable democratic purpose may demand the limitation of certain rights, to which the Constitution affords such absolute guarantees; and in that case the American democracy might be forced to seek by revolutionary means the accomplishment of a result which should be attainable under the law. (Croly, 1914: 35–36)

In this rich paragraph Croly suggests that a new, national democracy will be based on national public opinion and national majorities and the "revolutionary" ability of initiating public policies extralegally or extraconstitutionally. The primary right limited by such "revolutionary" or extralegal means is the Fifth Amendment right to property. (The moderate, pragmatic formulation of Croly's bold theory argues that the Constitution is a "living" document. What generally appears as illegal or unconstitutional [according to Croly] is considered by the pragmatic theorists as a necessary and an inevitable Constitutional adaptation to new circumstances [or opinions].)

Croly's national majority is formed by those averse to the minority interests of corporate capitalism. In the language of the Founders, Croly sought to create a national "majority faction" for the purpose of economic redistribution. James Madison, as Publius, the author of *The Federalist Papers*, argued that majority faction was the chief evil of popular government. "When a majority is included in a faction, the form of popular government on the other hand enables it to sacrifice to its ruling passion or interest, both the public good and rights of other citizens" (Hamilton et al., 1788 [1961]: 60–61). Once a majority faction is formed, the auxiliary precautions—separation of powers, indirect elections or appointments, long elective terms, and life terms for the judiciary—cannot prevent the factional majority from carrying its unjust policies into law.

Indeed, Publius identified economic or class interest as the greatest source of majority factions, although he adds "a zeal for different opinions concerning religion, concerning Government and many other points, as well as speculation as of practice; an attachment to different leaders ambitiously contending for pre-eminence and power . . . has in turn divided mankind into parties" (Hamilton et al., 1788 [1961]: 59). The experience of many states after the Revolution confirmed the danger of class conflict in American politics: "[A] rage for paper money, for an abolition of debts, for an equal division of property" helped destroy the economy in many states (Hamilton et al., 1788 [1961]: 65). Writing 50 years later, Tocqueville expanded on Publius' analysis of majority faction by describing what he called the "tyranny of the majority" (Tocqueville, 1835 [1988]: 360ff.). Tocqueville saw a mediocrity of accomplishment and forced conformity, resulting in the exclusion of those violating the taste or opinions of the majority. While Tocqueville argued that under "Jeffersonian democracy" a general equality of conditions had largely eliminated economics as a serious cause of factions, he showed how noneconomic passions could cause a seemingly more tyrannical majority. The experience of slavery resulted in a hatred of blacks by the white majority. Therefore, even with the end of slavery, the white majority would invent means—like legal segregation—to exclude blacks. Only the end of popular government could quickly end the effects of prejudice, amounting to a majority faction or tyranny.

Let us return to Croly's support of direct democracy. In a modern industrial democracy, the majority will be averse to the interests of the wealthy—or be factional—because the rich have created a minority faction that has, through the Constitutional system, usurped the interests of the majority. To break the minority faction, the national executive needs to mobilize public opinion to force political officers (Congress and the courts) to follow the majority will. To ensure direct public rule, the executive introduces legislation favorable to the majority which, when joined with continuing public pressure, guarantees passage (and approval by the federal judiciary). "The executive is . . . an agency for leading and focusing public opinion and thus preparing it for decisive action" (Croly, 1914: 355). Finally, the actual business of governing is done by professional and expert administrators guided more by popular desire and professional judgment than by Constitutional law.

Although imperfect, Croly supported the initiative, referendum, and recall in state and local politics (Croly, 1909: 327). In conjunction with a dominant executive, an active, popular majority will set the agenda for the legislative "council" in the reformed state constitutions, Croly proposes.

The function of the representative body, needed under a system of direct legislation, is substantially that of a legislative and administrative council or commission. It is an experienced body of legal, administrative, and financial experts, comparatively limited in numbers, and selected in a manner to make them solicitous of the interests of the whole state. (Croly, 1909: 329; 1914: 284–302)

The "legislative council" adds expert deliberation to the policies suggested by the popular majorities (with the guidance of the powerful governor) and introduced by the governor to the council:

The governor should be empowered not merely to suggest legislation to the council, but to introduce it into the council. His right to introduce legislation need not be exclusive, but bills introduced by him should have a certain precedence and their consideration should claim a definite amount of the council's time. The council would possess, of course, full right of rejection or amendment. In the case of rejection or an amendment not acceptable to the governor the question at issue would be submitted to a popular vote. (Croly, 1909: 331)

The executive proposes and fights for his legislative agenda. To make him further responsible to the people, he should campaign on a "definite legislative policy" and be subject to popular recall if he fails to follow his campaign policy agenda after his election.

Here, as elsewhere, Croly condemns representative democracy. "One hundred district agents represent only one hundred districts and not the whole of the state" (Croly, 1909: 332).

Both the system of representation and the functions of the representative body have been admirably calculated to debase the quality of the representatives. . . . The state constitutions have gradually hedged them in with so many restrictions . . . that the legislatures have comparatively little to do.

The corruption of the state legislatures "began with the domination of the political machine," which completed the constriction of their powers (Croly, 1909: 321). In *Progressive Democracy* he observes:

It is just beginning to be understood that representative government of any type in actual practice becomes a species of class government. It cannot succeed except by virtue of a ruling class, which has earned the privilege of leadership and which has deserved and retained popular support. . . . It remains to be seen whether a representative system can be wrought for the benefit of a people who seek wholly to dispense with class leadership. (Croly, 1914: 262)

Again: "The particular function of representation by law in the traditional American system was to tie the hands of the majority and reduce it to insignificance in the management of public affairs" (Croly, 1914: 309). Because representation had not worked to promote democracy in America, Croly sought to initiate a version of national, direct democracy.

The New Executive

As we have seen, Croly's new nation is based on the twin pillars of national public opinion and a strong reformist executive. The new executive itself is composed of two parts: public cheerleading and legislative agenda setting and also a vastly expanded administrative state to do the actual governing. The national executive is the agent of change, the creator and guide of national public opinion, and the programmatic instigator of reform. In *The Promise of American Life*, Croly praises Lincoln as the first nationalist committed to democracy or equality. Theodore Roosevelt is cited as an exemplar of a strong executive fostering nationalism and business reform (Croly, 1909, Parts III, IV). The modern president should follow their example and the reforms Croly proposes to realize a national, direct democracy. But unlike the state constitutions, which proved easily changed in many cases, the national Constitution was proof against Progressive reform.

Croly supported the failed amendment to reform the Constitutional amendment process and other Constitutional reform proposals. These proposals proved incapable of breaking the Constitutional gridlock caused by the predominance of local and class interests. Croly's promotion of the Progressive Party led him to hope that the corrupt two-party system might be reformed by its influence. But his greatest hope for reform rested on the still-unrealized powers of the presidency to create a democracy capable of radical action. Both his writings and his actions as the Progressive reformer in the inner circle of advisers to both Theodore Roosevelt and Woodrow Wilson indicate that, in Croly's mind, the buck starts at the Oval Office.

Croly expected presidents to pass legislation empowering the executive to become the agent of democratic equality, social progress, and modernization, which would result in a unified, patriotic nation. The last two goals— economic and social progress and the new nationalism—were the easiest. The natural development of the American economy was national. But Croly was reticent about the radical changes necessary to make the federal Constitution direct and egalitarian.

Defining the relationship between the remaining federal features, the states and the local interests, and the powerful new nation above them, Croly adopts a version of the "two swords." Give to the new nation what is essentially national and democratic (i.e., most power and key activities) and to the states, what is not—very little of consequence. The majority of economic activity is now already national, as a result of the formation of national corporations and trusts. Oil, steel, rail, and such mail-order firms as Sears and Roebuck are the leading examples of national corporations. Moreover, magazines, many newspapers, the distribution of literature, professional societies (including religious ones, in particular), and major universities are also national in scope, while cities like Chicago and New York have become the new national capitals of commerce and culture. These national trends should not be constrained but strengthened through regulation. What can be left mainly to the states and society are the "local" issues. Croly is loath to say what these local responsibilities are. But he adds: "It can hardly be expected that American citizens will bring as much public spirit to their local public business as to the more stirring affairs of the whole nation" (Croly, 1909: 324).

Democratic Administration

In addition to his rhetorical power, Croly's modern president is the chief executive or the administrator in chief. Modern administration is the vehicle to create a modern society (and enhance executive power). If Congress is the breeding ground of local and economic interests, and the courts use Constitutional legalisms to emasculate change in the existing system, only administrative bureaucracies can reform a society impervious to reform in any other way. Croly argues that administrative officials will become the true representatives of the people, replacing Constitutional officeholders. Education in science enables the population to see the centrality of administration for the progress of society. "The best way to popularize scientific administration, *and to enable the democracy to consider highly educated officials as representative*, is to popularize the higher education" (Croly, 1914: 377).

Croly argues for the absolute, independent activity of the executive and his administrative agents. The executive's "primary business is that of organizing a temporary majority of the electorate, and of carrying its will into legal effect. He becomes primarily a law-giver and only secondarily an agency for carrying out existing law" (Croly, 1914: 355). The executive leaves the governing to a new, permanent administration. The importance of the scientific administrator to Croly's vision of a Progressive democratic republic is immense. The new administrator is a powerful leader and a visionary spokesman of the new society.

He is the custodian not merely of a particular law, but of a social purpose of which the law is only a fragmentary expression. . . . Thus with all his independence he is a promoter and propagandist. . . . He qualifies for his work as an administrator quite as much by his general good faith as by his specific competence. (Croly, 1914: 361–362)

The independence and power of Croly's new administrator are immense. First, he is protected by civil service appointment. Second, he is the "enforcer of law, in watching its operation and in advising its amendment or supplementation" (Croly, 1914: 361). Finally, Croly argues, the "administrator of an official social program" should have the "same kind of independence and authority in respect to public opinion as that which has been traditionally granted to a common law judge" (Croly, 1914: 361). As in the European nations, Croly argues that administrative officials should have large discretionary powers. Perhaps the most interesting characteristic of the new administrator is that his function is not to enforce a policy or law but to create a new society based on Progressive principles:

In the past the administration of the civil law, except through the agency of the courts, was of small importance, because the law was supposed merely to recognize and interpret customary ways of economic and social behavior. But when the chief object of legislation is to carry into effect an experimental social program, the administration of the law has a different and more responsible function. Legislation is being used as a means of modifying social behavior, not social behavior as an excuse for formulating legislation. The legislator has become an innovator. (Croly, 1914: 362)

The general principles of social legislation are so easily understood and will prove so popular that administrative government is more appropriate to true democracy than "representative" democracy.

Administrators not only create and enforce policy but, through administrative courts, are the judges of their own actions. Croly supports the autonomy of such courts, arguing that an administration court represents, it is true, an organization of the collective will for an accomplishment of a social program; and in this respect is not impartial in the sense that a regular court is supposed to be impartial. . . . [But] by uniting action in the interest of a binding and fruitful policy with the acquisition of the knowledge needed for some still more discriminating future actions . . . (they) are tending to accomplish what representative government has been supposed to accomplish: they are becoming an effective agency for extracting from the bosom of society the immediately available supply of social reason. (Croly, 1914: 367–368)

Administration "is representative without being elective" (Croly, 1914: 373) and "should borrow from the army the concept of a "general staff" (Croly, 1914: 374). While administrative government aims at improving "social reason" and equality, it clearly strengthens "executive leadership"— at the expense of the parties and of congressional government (Croly, 1914: 348). As Sidney A. Pearson notes, "The science of public administration was intended (by Croly) to serve executive leadership at the expense of legislative control of the public agenda" (Croly, 1914: Introduction, xxxvii).

The Modern President

Eric F. Goldman compares Croly's new nationalism to Mussolini's fascism. One does not look far to see why. Consider the following:

The modern nation, particularly insofar as it is constructively democratic, constitutes the best machinery as yet developed for raising the level of human association. It really teaches men how they must feel, what they must think, and what they must do, in order that they may live together amicably and profitably. (Croly, 1909: 284)

Although Goldman ultimately rejects this analogy, arguing that Croly was a genuine democrat and that his proposals were made in a thoroughly liberal society, the analogy is instructive (Goldman, 1960: 157). It is instructive in two respects. Goldman establishes that the greatest of the Progressive reformers sought far-reaching changes, not incremental or pragmatic adaptation to new circumstances. Nichols' inability to distinguish between FDR's pragmatic bromides and his use of Croly's thought to systematically subvert the Founders' Constitution can be seen in his too easy conflation of the limited executive of George Washington and the quasi monarchs of our century—those presidents able to mobilize public opinion to the degree Croly desired. Second, it shows Croly's commitment to a wholly new egalitarian society, with a post-constitutional political system requiring the ongoing assertion of presidential prerogative in every aspect of American life. All of these things were unimaginable to the Founders. Elton J. Eisenach speaks of Croly's leadership in creating a distinctly new Progressive political Constitution and regime, one "that contested and displaced another regime" (i.e., the Founders' Constitution). "Progressives . . . were attacking ideas and institutions on which many of their fellow Americans located their identities." Through "alternative resources, alternative institutions . . . they created an alternative public doctrine" (Eisenach, 1994: 22).

To illustrate: when FDR focused public opinion behind the "New Deal," he acted not only to win a policy dispute with Congress but to create a presidential bureaucratic state whose ultimate goal was social transformation, for example, Social Security and a guarantee of full employment (Goldman, 1960: 253, 262, 267, 288–289). His liberation from the ends and purposes and the forms of the original Constitution found him in Croly's shadow. At various times FDR used his hard-won popular mandate not only to persuade Congress and the courts to accept his program but to *permanently* reduce their political and Constitutional power to oppose himself as chief executive (Goldman, 1960: 277–280). Of course, even more than Croly, FDR poured his new wine of executive hegemony, based on popular opinion, into the old bottles of respect for American traditions and patriotism. His Progressive innovations, he said, were only temporary or pragmatic adaptions, not the fundamental regime replacement Eisenach describes. But FDR's success reflected Croly's wisdom even more profoundly. FDR's ability to adopt Progressive principles, enhanced by the Great Depression, allowed him to recast the "moribund" two-party system in order to reach the goal so long sought by Croly: a national Progressive Party. FDR was able to mobilize the prestige and power of the Democrats, the country's oldest party—still rooted in an unreformed South—to organize public opinion for the kinds of radical national reforms Croly envisioned only 20 years before.

Roosevelt's popularity and power over the federal bureaucracy he created and controlled allowed him to mobilize political support throughout the country. Intellectuals, labor, business, and social Progressives of all kinds supported liberal reform. So strong was this fusion of ideology, patriotism, and politics that Roosevelt was able to lead his reluctant new nation into a world war and postwar hegemony greater than anything envisioned by the new nationalism of Teddy Roosevelt and Herbert Croly. It was certainly more than anything envisioned by George Washington—who warned against, and avoided, entangling foreign alliances. Truman's election, largely an election fought as a referendum on Roosevelt's new liberalism (Progressive nationalism in new bottles), guaranteed the life of FDR's new Progressive executive through five terms and 20 years. But Croly and Roosevelt's final accomplishment was to bring the Republican opposition into its own Progressive/liberal orbit in the 1950s. Their total hegemony continued for several decades, a period often described as the era of the "end of ideology."

President Roosevelt almost perfectly realized Herbert Croly's New Republic. A Progressive legislative agenda led to high opinion polls. Popularity permitted vastly greater expenditures, which, appropriately spent, solidified the Democratic Party into a Progressive Party. Harry Hopkins enthused: "Tax tax, spend spend, elect elect." Dominating Congress, FDR created the alphabet administrative programs that legitimated his populist agenda and expanded his political reach into the cities and villages of the hinterland. He sought Progressive Supreme Court justices and, when that proved unavailing, threatened to pack the Court, making them bow to his politically powerful Constitutional positions. Wishing more than mere Progressive reform and national presidential power, FDR spent his wealth turning Washington into a shrine and place of pilgrimage for American patriots. Mainly through the Works Progress Administration (WPA), he founded a patriotic people's art in folk songs, photography, government films, and general support of artists and historians of all kinds. He created an historical patriotism, rooted in Progressive ideals of democracy, which proved nearly universal in appeal. The heroic, golden land belonged to one and all: "This land is your land, this land is my land."

While Nichols argues that the Progressives suggested "the possibility of unlimited expansion of government power," that vision did not determine the American political experience in the twentieth century. Indeed, he continues, "with or without the Progressives' theory of national community, the twentieth century would inevitably have seen tremendous growth in activity on the part of the national government in general and the President in particular" (Nichols, 1994: 171). Moreover, "in a government whose activities are as wide-ranging as ours, there is no substitute for the modern Presidency as it exists" (Nichols, 1994: 172). In embracing the inevitability of Leviathan, Nichols appears overly charmed by FDR's pragmatic version of Hegelian historical inevitability: "That which is, is right."

While Nichols seems correct that the exigencies of the twentieth century required an accretion of national power, the form of that national development would undoubtedly have been different if it had not followed the radical vision of the Progressives. (As Eisenach, [1994: 99–100] demonstrated, the Progressives were remarkably consistent in preferring a European, Hegelian statism to the strong Republic of the Founders.) One could point out a score of likely areas of difference between the Progressive agenda and that of a strong nation and executive based on non-Progressive principles. Such a constitutionally renewed nation would be closer to the Founders' view of strong, but limited, government. At the very least, a non-Progressive, or Constitutional, New Republic would vary from the Progressive norm in the areas of Federalism, labor, economic regulation, and entitlements. One could speak of Hamiltonian policies without Croly's radicalization of the Constitution in pursuit of "Jeffersonian" ends: Croly's radicalization of Hamilton for the sake of a new equality and a new society or, that is, Croly's famous formula of Hamiltonian means for Jeffersonian ends. Thus, if there had been a renewal of Hamiltonianism without Croly's Jeffersonianism, George Washington, not Franklin D. Roosevelt, would truly be our first "modern" president.

PART III: REALITIES OF DIPLOMATIC, ADMINISTRATIVE, LEGISLATIVE, AND PERSONALIZED LEADERSHIP

In his "cyclical" interpretation of American political development, Steven Skowronek (1993) argues that, while different presidents at different historical junctures represent similar positions vis-à-vis the ideological regime (what he calls "political" time), there is the additional element of "secular" time that yields what he calls institutional "thickness" in the ability of presidents to decisively shape the policy process and the permanent government of the United States. By that Skowronek seems to mean that the simple, one-to-one nexus between presidential power and governmental impacts has been lost to passing generations of chief executives because the size and complexity of government coupled with the growth of interests fragmentation within the polity have resulted in a more complex and nuanced relationship between presidential leadership and public policy. Skowronek's insight lies at the heart of our critique of Nichols. The existence of the modern Leviathan has required presidential leadership to develop in ways that would be entirely alien to the Framers and thoroughly unanticipated by President Washington. In making our case, for each role we delineate President Washington's leadership style and then, shifting to the modern era, draw upon presidential scholarship to outline how truly "modern" presidents face those tasks of leadership.

Washington's Diplomatic Role

Foreign affairs is where Washington properly may be regarded as the first "modern" president. It is the one area of governance where virtually all the original precedents by President Washington have held true for future presidents, largely because the bureaucratization within the U.S. government has least affected the diplomatic establishment, and, looking abroad, leadership between our country and other nations more or less reflects a relatively straightforward, one-to-one power relationship, with the president at its center. At the very beginning White (1948: 128) observed that

[t]he conduct of foreign negotiations was a matter so delicate and so concentrated that it fell to the personal attention of the Secretary of State. Nowhere in the Department was there a single person other than the Secretary who had experience or training in foreign affairs. Nothing beyond the necessary paper work and routine could consequently be delegated. To none of the four Secretaries who held office from 1790 to 1801 did it apparently occur to share with an experienced associate the tasks of deliberation, consultation, and consideration of policy. The product of the State Department *was not organizational but individual.* (emphasis added)

The State Department faced a much simpler world than today's. In 1792 its "field staff" abroad "was still very small—ministers or charges de'affaires at Paris, London, Lisbon, The Hague, and Madrid."

The Secretary of State—unlike the Secretary of the Treasury—had no independent relationship to the legislative branch. "In the act creating the Department of State, Congress placed full control of the Secretary of State in the President, four times repeating his subordination to the Chief Executive" (White, 1948: 130). "Nor did Congress retain any specific means of exerting its authority over the business of the Department; for example, it required no annual or special reports. Only two offices were created: that of Secretary and chief clerk." Thus, American diplomacy was highly personalized, since "[t]he conduct of foreign negotiations and the selection of American ministers remained under the close personal supervision and direction of both Washington and [John] Adams." In selecting his ministers and diplomatic agents, moreover, Washington made those decisions "after careful consideration of all the circumstances of each case. He regularly conferred with a small circle, principally of Federalist leaders . . . [but] [i]t does not appear that he relied especially on his Secretaries of State for recommendations" (White, 1948: 131).

In terms of

the conduct of foreign affairs, the administration of the State Department was little more than directing an office of correspondence and performing the ceremonies of international intercourse. These operations are of so little significance, administratively, that the central business of the Department has perforce been passed over in comparative silence. (White, 1948: 136)

Indeed, at that time the primary administrative workload of the department was domestic—census-taking, patents and copyright protection, supervising the Mint, recording land patents, protecting seamen, and granting ship passports!

Because the Framers divided diplomatic powers between the executive and legislative branches, argues Corwin (1957: 171), the Constitution "is an invitation to struggle for the privilege of directing American foreign policy." Nonetheless, the president has certain advantages. Corwin points to several presidential "precedents" begun by George Washington that have adhered to the office since that time.

First, the case of Citizen Genet illustrates President Washington as "sole organ" of the nation in diplomacy. When Genet addressed his request directly to Congress for an exequatur as a consul for France, Secretary of State Thomas Jefferson replied that

[a]s the President is the only channel of communication between the United States and foreign nations, it is from him alone that foreign nations or their agents are to

learn what is or has been the will of the nation, and whatever he communicates as such they have a right and are bound to consider as the expression of the nation, and no foreign agent can be allowed to question it. (quoted in Corwin, 1957: 178)

In defending this presidential prerogative, Congress in 1798 enacted the Logan Act "to Prevent Usurpation of Executive Functions" by private citizens (Corwin, 1957: 183). But the "sole organ" potentially involved more than simply being the nation's mouthpiece, according to Alexander Hamilton's view, and a larger struggle over presidential prerogative was provoked by Washington's Proclamation of Neutrality, which did *not* represent the win-win outcome posited by Nichols.

According to Corwin (1957: 181), "[T]he practical fruits of victory were divided between the parties to it. In 1794 Congress passed our first neutrality act, and *ever since then the subject of neutrality has been conceded to live within its jurisdiction*" (emphasis added). Yet the president gained even more from "the 'executive power' clause as an always available peg on which to hang any and all unassigned powers in respect to foreign intercourse" and the practice "of treating these and all other presidential powers in the diplomatic field as potentially *policy-forming* powers, and constitutionally independent of direction by Congress, though capable of being checked by it." However potent the force of customary practice, the debate between Hamilton's loose and Madison's strict construction of the Constitution was not legally resolved by the Supreme Court until its ruling in *United States v. Curtiss-Wright Export Corp.*, 299 U.S. 304 (1936).

Second, the power to "receive" ambassadors and public ministers became de jure recognition of their governments (Corwin, 1957: 182):

Actually, the reception of Genet involved this very issue, and yet it was decided by Washington without consulting Congress. Nor did Washington consult Congress when some months later he demanded Genet's recall, thereby establishing a precedent followed by later Presidents again and again.

Moreover, "[a]nother precedent of great significance from Washington's administration was the first president's refusal in 1796 to comply with a call from the House of Representatives for papers relative to the negotiation of the Jay Treaty." That doctrine became known as executive privilege, which conservative scholar Raoul Berger (1974) argued had no Constitutional grounding whatsoever.

A more balanced account comes from Rozell (1994), who looks beyond Constitutional text to its use by Washington, Adams, and several nineteenth-century presidents: Jefferson, Madison, Monroe, Jackson, Tyler, Polk, Fillmore, Buchanan, Lincoln, Johnson, Grant, Cleveland, and Benjamin Harrison. It is noteworthy that President Washington claimed executive privilege in foreign affairs—not domestic affairs—and that precedent guided virtually every invocation by his successors until Dwight D. Eisenhower: "The actual use of the term 'executive privilege' originated in the Eisenhower Administration. President Eisenhower's administration invoked that doctrine on more than forty occasions . . . [the most important being] the army–McCarthy hearings" (Rozell, 1994: 44). As such, "[i]t is most important to recognize that Eisenhower's 17 May 1954 letter [that Defense Department personnel not testify before Senator McCarthy] established a precedent for the exercise of executive privilege in the modern presidency." When Nixon tried to expand executive privilege to cover up Watergate, that assertion was disallowed by the Supreme Court in *United States v. Nixon*, 418 U.S. 683 (1974). But the ruling explicitly stated that President Nixon advanced no national security claim for executive privilege and that, had he done so, the outcome of this litigation might have been different. In other words, the High Court sided with Washington's precedent of using executive privilege in foreign affairs.

Third, the use of special, personal, or secret agents "in whose designation the Senate has no voice," rather than ambassadors who are subject to Senate confirmation, began when

[o]n February 14, 1791 the President informed the Senate that he had 'employed Mr. Gouverneur Morris, who was on the spot,' to confer with the British government concerning their further carrying out of the Treaty of Peace . . . and four days later he reported having sent his friend Colonel David Humphreys to Madrid and Lisbon on a similar mission. These precedents have since been multiplied many times. (Corwin, 1957: 206)

Fourth, almost immediately the Senate was precluded from its "advice" if not consent role in treaty making. On Saturday, August 22, 1789, President Washington went to the Senate asking their advice on Indian treaties, but parliamentary confusion soon erupted, and the matter was postponed until Monday, whereupon Washington returned to the Senate,

and while the ensuing colloquy seems to have moved along without any of the earlier jars, no President of the United States has since that day ever darkened the doors of the Senate for the purpose of personal consultation with it concerning the advisability of a desired negotiation. (Corwin, 1957: 210)

Law professor Arthur S. Miller (1977: 138) holds that

[i]n the Convention of 1787 the original idea was to give the Senate power to negotiate treaties and to appoint ambassadors. . . . That view was dropped, however, for the provision that seems to say that the President and the Senate will be closely associated throughout the treaty-making process. President Washington, who had presided during the Convention, so thought [and tried to consult about the Indian treaties, but since that time the plain meaning of the Constitution has not been

followed. No President has gone to the Senate's chambers, there to attempt to consult personally with the Senators as a formal body. . . . Thus early on the Senate lost forever the right to be an executive council in foreign affairs.

Miller (an avowed critic of original intent) points to this episode to show how Washington altered the intentions of the Framers. Nichols fails to recognize that the "modern" precedent begun by Washington in treaty making was not precisely constitutionally mandated.

Modern Diplomatic Role

It is not simply that President Washington established legal and customary precedents in foreign affairs that survived 200 years later. It is also the fact that diplomacy remains a highly personalized enterprise, and Washington's hands-on presidential leadership has not been upended by the modern Leviathan. Diplomacy is an arena that is relatively immune from bureaucratization when compared to administrative management. Today the Department of State ranks 10th among the 14 departments in personnel, with around 25,000 employees, and 13th in its share of the budget. While huge by the standards of Washington's day, still the point is that State remains a relative pygmy within the federal bureaucracy. Only a few of its personnel are actually involved in diplomacy, moreover, which remains a top priority with most presidents.

Nor has the "institutionalization" of the modern presidency provided much additional layering. The National Security Act of 1947 established the National Security Council, which in 1949 was reorganized to include the president, vice president, Secretary of State, Secretary of Defense, and the chairman of the National Security Resources Board, and its statutory advisers are the Central Intelligence Agency (CIA) director, the chairman of the Joint Chiefs of Staff, and the director of the Arms Control and Disarmament Agency. Therefore, the National Security Council (NSC) remains a small advisory body with mostly members of the presidential cabinet. The NSC "was foisted upon Truman by Congress" (Pious, 1979: 362) partly as "Forrestal's revenge" because Admiral James Forrestal opposed President Truman's plans to unify the armed services. One more addition to the diplomatic establishment was the special assistant for national security affairs, first appointed by President Eisenhower, who normally heads the NSC staff.

Where Washington appointed Thomas Jefferson, a distinguished statesman and intellectual giant, as his Secretary of State, today this official often may not be a pivotal figure. According to Pious (1979: 358–359),

In modern times the problem is the weakness of the secretary and his department in the government. Presidents often choose secretaries whom they can dominate or

ignore, [and, consequently,] [t]he atypical pattern is for the president to pick someone of experience and ability to work with closely: Truman and Marshall, Eisenhower
and Dulles, Nixon and Kissinger, Carter and Vance.

Somewhat more complexity in the diplomatic establishment resulted when
the special assistant for national security affairs was established by President
Eisenhower. His appointee, however, operated behind the scenes and clearly
was dwarfed in influence by Secretary of State John Foster Dulles. On the
other hand, Nixon deliberately chose a relative unknown (William Rogers)
as Secretary of State so that he and National Security Adviser Henry Kissinger (who later became a "two-hatter" by being appointed also Secretary of
State) monopolized foreign policy making in their own hands. Lesser-known
individuals served under Reagan as national security advisers, yet the "modern" era also has witnessed serious competition between these two foreign
policy makers; the Vance–Brzezinski feud under Carter eventually led Secretary of State Vance to resign because President Carter followed Brzezinski's advice to attempt the ill-fated military rescue of Americans held hostage
by militant Iranians.

These episodes are relatively mild and do not preclude strong presidential
leadership in foreign affairs:

While presidents often rely on secretaries of state for advice, they rarely permit them
to manage foreign relations. Presidents in the post–World War II period have ignored
the recommendations of no less than seven study groups that have urged a "state-
centered" foreign policy apparatus. (Pious, 1979: 359)

Yet the growth of the NSC apparatus did pose a command-and-control
problem for Reagan that Washington never had to confront. The Iran-
Contra scandal may have resulted from President Reagan's inattention to
detail rather than his direct culpability, but, whatever the immediate cause,
the Tower Commission concluded that the national security adviser and his
NSC staffers enjoyed too much discretion and autonomy.

Washington's Administrative Responsibility

The first Congress lodged administrative responsibility squarely on the
president, not his subordinates. According to White (1948: 18–19),

Congress took care to maintain the unity of the executive branch by vesting the great
bulk of administrative authority in the President and by placing him in a position to
direct the affairs of every subordinate officer. The laws required *all major and many
minor decisions* to be made by the President himself, his agency was involved at every
turn. (emphasis added)

To illustrate, White noted that "[a]ll loan and debt transactions were made subject to his approval" and that "[h]e was required to sign patents for inventions" and "had to approve each contract for building a lighthouse." "He established and modified many administrative districts," "made regulations governing trade with the Indians," and "prescribed rules for the distribution of prize money among officers and crew." The delegation of direct authority did not stop there:

Thus he was required to devise a form of a land patent, and a passport for vessels. He was authorized to lay an embargo, to make individual exceptions, and to revoke the embargo in his discretion. He was authorized to order aliens to leave the country, or to license them to remain; and in case they returned after deportation, to keep them in prison at his discretion. He approved a contract for the purchase of copper for the Mint, and was directed to collect information on the copper mines south of Lake Superior. He was authorized to erect two docks. He was directed to prohibit travel on the trace from Knoxville to Price's settlement if the Indians objected. These, too, are only examples of a host of *ad hoc* administrative authorities placed in the President's office. Congress vested duties large and small in the single office of Chief Executive rather than in the offices subordinate to him. Their execution he might delegate to one or another of his "assistants," but not his ultimate responsibility. (White, 1948: 19)

Washington kept his "assistants" on a short leash:

The President looked upon the [departmental] Secretaries . . . as *assistants*, not as rivals or as substitutes [insofar as] [n]o department head, not even Hamilton, settled any matter of importance without consulting the President and securing his approval. All of them referred to the President numerous matters of detail as well as large and many small issues of administrative policy. [The result:] Washington accepted full responsibility as a matter of course, and throughout the eight years of his service there is no indication of a tendency to consider department heads other than dependent agencies of the Chief Executive. (White, 1948: 27)

In his recruitment efforts, Washington "searched diligently for men of stature as Secretaries" (White, 1948: 30) in order to abide by his "general rule of noninterference in departmental business." He allowed his secretaries to appoint their clerks, but "[t]he appointment of such important officials as the Comptroller, the Postmaster General, and the Director of the Mint . . . he settled himself, after consultation with his advisers." Concludes White (1948: 31): "Washington did not reach down into departmental operations, although much departmental business rose from subordinate levels to his desk." At the level of policy, Washington seemingly forged a "cabinet government" system:

Contacts between the President and his department heads were close and unremitting. In the official correspondence there remain hundreds of written communications and records of oral consultation. Washington invited Jefferson, Hamilton, and others to have breakfast with him to discuss matters which often he had transmitted to them on the previous day. We went to his Secretaries' offices to consult them. He was accustomed to send a file to any one of his Secretaries with the request that he come to the President's house on the following day at ten o'clock, or eleven o'clock, with a written or oral opinion. In due course of time these meetings with the heads of departments grew into the Cabinet. (White, 1948: 32)

Such meetings in late 1791, 1792, and 1793 "were genuine Cabinet meetings," and by the end of 1793 White (1948: 40) concludes that "the Cabinet as an institution for consultation and advice was firmly established." However, "*matters of administration* [that] were almost entirely departmental in nature and those that came to the attention of the Chief Executive were settled between the President and the heads of departments individually." Unfortunately, Washington

was more clear in principle about the necessity of avoiding detail than he was successful in practice [insofar as] [t]he interchange of correspondence between Hamilton, Jefferson, Knox, and the President reveals a mass of business which the heads of departments thought it essential to clear with the Chief Executive, and which Washington continued to accept throughout his two terms. Appointments, great and small, were of direct concern to Washington, and no collector of customs, captain of a cutter, keeper of a lighthouse, or surveyor of revenue was appointed except after specific consideration by the President. In signing contracts for the construction of a lighthouse, the President took time to enjoin economy in the selection of materials. Leaves of absence of important officials were requested from and approved by the Present himself. (White, 1948: 106)

In sum, while President Washington did not allow his cabinet to develop collectively an independent base of power,

[t]he Cabinet, nevertheless, assumed considerable importance as a frequently convening advisory council, dealing with matters of high policy, especially in relation to the conduct of foreign policy. The power of the President to require "opinions in writing" had grown into an institution. (White, 1948: 41)

To give Nichols his due and to affirm our own understanding of regime building, the emergence of a cabinet is one aspect of Washington's administrative role that we accept as indicative of "modern" presidents, simply because he established a "precedent" (our preferred terminology is customary practice) that *every one of his successors in the White House continued*. This point is explicitly made by Corwin (1957: 82–83), who noted two transformations in the consultative process, namely, that "[t]he Cabinet may be said to have emerged as a definite institution of the national government from the diplomatic crisis of 1973" and, second, that

as a result of Secretary of State Randolph's equivocal attitude in the fight over the Jay Treaty, [Washington] proceeded to reconstruct his Cabinet on the avowed basis of loyalty to his own policies, and in so doing *created a precedent that . . . has guided Presidents in their choice of departmental heads ever since then.* (emphasis added)

On this score, one cannot identify the cabinet as an attribute of the post-FDR "modern" presidency. Yet, as we shall see, the cabinet is virtually the only aspect of Washington's administrative role that survived the passage of time.

The primary reason that Washington's administrative legacy has not survived is that the size of government was incomparably "tiny" as compared to the modern bureaucratic state. White (1948: 101) argues that Washington's

competent performance in administration grew out of two separate aspects of his experience—his life as a plantation manager and his life as a military commander, [and, in fact,] the number of persons whom Washington supervised directly at Mount Vernon was greater than the number required to carry on the functions of any of the departments of state in New York or Philadelphia (omitting their embryonic field services); and the lessons which he learned in plantation management he applied to public affairs.

In other words, the size of the managerial task in the private sector compared favorably with public administration, a stark contrast to what a president would confront today. No private organization is as large as the U.S. Department of Defense, let alone the entire federal government.

It is estimated that the Department of Treasury—by far most important among the original cabinet offices—employed 39 persons, rising to 70 in 1790 and to 90 in 1792 (White, 1948: 122). The attorney general was a part-time position, since he was paid an annual retainer by the U.S. government, and his duties

were simple and closely contained. Upon request of the President, or of heads of departments, he was directed to give opinions on matters of law. That was all. He was not placed in supervisory charge of the attorneys of the United States. . . . He had no establishment, not even a single clerk. His private law office was the seat of his official duties. (White, 1948: 166)

At the outset, the War Department consisted of Henry Knox and one clerk but grew eventually to 80 officials and employees by 1801 (White, 1948: 147). In administrative terms, White (1948: 128) describes the State Department as "a relative pygmy throughout the Federalist period. The task imposed upon the Secretary of State in his central office was negligible, amounting at the utmost to the direction of the work of a half dozen clerks." In 1792 legislation authorizing a postmaster general "remained a very modest one, despite the growth of business. [Timothy] Pickering performed all the business of the agency in 1792 with the aid of an assistant and one clerk in two rooms of his dwelling house" (White, 1948: 177). These departments were supported by a civil service that "grew substantially in size between 1789 and 1801. By 1792 it was in full working order. There were then about 780 employees (excluding the deputy postmasters), of whom approximately 660 were employed in the Treasury Department" (White, 1948: 255).

President Washington sat atop a three-tiered bureaucracy.

At the top was a handful of immediate representatives of the authority and dignity of the government: heads of departments, territorial governors and officials, Indian commissioners and superintendents, and ministers at foreign posts. A second group comprised an important class of officials responsible for the operation of the administrative machine along the lines of established policy. This group included the principal Treasury officials . . . the chief clerks, the Director and Treasurer of the Mint, the Purveyor, the accountants in the War and Navy Departments, the War Department paymaster, the loan commissioners, the collectors of customs, the surveyors of revenue, the receivers and registers of the land officers, and the district attorneys. The third group, relatively numerous, comprised a wide variety of subordinate personnel, such as clerks, deputy postmasters, customs and excise employees, marshals, surveyors, Indian agents, officers and seamen on the cutters, lighthouse keepers, "door keepers" (messengers), and others.

All told, of the 3,000 federal employees in 1801, only about 150 were in departmental service, and the rest were in the field (White, 1948: 255–256).

Modern Administrative Responsibility

While Washington is credited for utilizing implied powers to fashion the first cabinet of his four principal advisers, the style of Washington's cabinet did not survive the modern era. His cabinet was small; his cabinet operated as a collectivity (though there was no "collective responsibility" as such); his cabinet debated the full range of policy issues; his cabinet comprised prestigious associates; and it was the *only* advisory group supporting President Washington. Warshaw (1996: 23) observes that during the eighteenth and nineteenth centuries

the Cabinet remained the president's primary source of policy advice, [mainly] due to an absence of viable alternatives for policy development. While several presidents relied on "kitchen cabinets" for policy advice, their members did not have the range of technical expertise to match that of the executive departments.

Andrew Jackson was the first president to create a "kitchen cabinet" of his informal advisers (who were not subject to the confirmation process), but every president since, and before, had personal confidants from whom they got advice. However, Jackson's innovation was not institutionalized until the 1930s. Says Warshaw (1996: 23): "The creation of the Executive Office of the President [EOP] and the White House staff under Franklin Delano Roosevelt began to change the traditional role of the Cabinet as the president's primary counselors." Now EOP has gained the upper hand over the cabinet as an advisory forum. So extensive has the EOP become since 1939 that Hart (1995) refers to it as the "presidential branch" of government, a minibureaucracy that is headed by a chief of staff.

None of the features of Washington's cabinet would characterize the cabinet today. The cause and effect for this fundamental transformation in the cabinet resulted from the marked increase in the size and scope of government in the "modern" era, which ironically has undermined the cabinet as an advisory and managerial tool. No "modern" president strove to achieve the goal of "cabinet government" except President Eisenhower, whereas most chief executives rely more heavily on individual cabinet members or on subgroups of the cabinet (Reagan's use of cabinet councils). There are now 14 departments, but the cabinet is even larger, as presidents generally accord cabinet "rank" to the vice president and the United Nations representative (plus others). So large and unwieldy is the "modern" cabinet that today we regularly differentiate between the "inner" cabinet, which dates back to Washington (State, Treasury, Defense, and attorney general), and the "outer" cabinet, with strong ties to departmental "clientele" groups (Labor, Agriculture, Interior). Thus, Nichols fails to appreciate that President Washington relied on a very simple advisory system, whereas today there are competing and varied sources of "institutional" as well as "personal" advisers to the chief executive. The "span of control" under Washington was direct; today it is complex and convoluted.

Now the federal bureaucracy has about 3 million civilian employees, of whom 87 percent are located outside Washington, D.C., and over 90 percent are covered by civil service. (There was no civil service under Washington; it did not begin until the Pendleton Act of 1883, and then its coverage reached only 10 percent of federal employees.) Nor did President Washington have to confront the "headless fourth branch" of government consisting of 60 "independent" agencies, corporations, regulatory commissions, and foundations that are organizationally separate from the presidential chain of command and doubly accountable to the president and Congress. To supervise the permanent government, there are around 3,300 appointive positions available to the president, which means that presidents must rely on the judgment of their cabinet, subcabinet, and White House staffers in those recruitment efforts. It takes the chief executive increasingly more time to fill those positions: 2.4 months under Kennedy, 3.3 under Nixon, 4.6 under Carter, 5.3 under Reagan, and 8.1 under Bush (*Washington Post*, 1993).

George Washington formed a government of "friends," but the modern counterpart is a government of "strangers" (Heclo, 1977). It is not simply that no modern president personally knows every cabinet appointee; the deeper problem is that "unlike the situation in most private organizations, in the U.S. executive branch those in the top positions of formal authority are likely to be substantially less familiar with their working environment than both their civil service and political subordinates" (Heclo, 1977: 101). Despite the assumptions of democratic accountability, taming the bureaucratic Leviathan is no easy task. Says Heclo (1977: 10): "Even under the most favorable circumstances (typically at the beginning of a new administration), a modern chief executive and his personal aides face severe constraints in trying to breathe new life into the executive branch."

In one sense, however, Washington and Roosevelt are analogous. Washington had to create a "new" federal government from scratch, just as FDR established a host of regulatory and welfare agencies and appointed to them committed New Dealers. Later presidents, notably Republicans, without the opportunity to wholly rebuild the bureaucracy believed—and with good reason (see Aberbach and Rockman, 1976)—that they had inherited a decidedly "liberal" government hostile to their own electoral mandates. All kinds of administrative tactics were used in an effort to take control of the permanent government. Eisenhower had Congress create a "Schedule C" category of exempt positions for political appointment; Nixon tried an "administrative strategy" (Nathan, 1983) through White House operatives to politicize agencies, like the Office of Management and Budget (OMB); Carter successfully lobbied Congress to enact the Civil Service Reform Act of 1978 to allow more presidential discretion over top-level careerists; and Reagan relied upon his regular appointment powers, augmented with the most intense ideological screening procedures of any recent president.

Washington's Legislative Leadership

The linchpin of Nichols' argument that Washington's legislative leadership presaged modern developments rests with Alexander Hamilton's unique legal and political relationship with Congress. Only with respect to the Treasury Department "did Congress work out the essential elements of internal organization" (White, 1948: 116). In the enabling statute of 1789

[t]he control of the President was noticed only in the words recognizing his constitutional power of removal. In contrast, a type of responsibility to Congress was clearly provided in the clause requiring the Secretary "to make report, and give information to either branch of the legislature, in person or in writing . . . respecting all matters referred to him by the Senate or House of Representatives, or which shall appertain

to his office." [Moreover it stipulated the] Secretary's duty to "digest and prepare" plans for the improvement and management of the revenue, and for the support of the public credit, and in his duty to "prepare and report" estimates of revenue and expenditure. The Treasurer, too, was required to make an annual report to Congress. (White, 1948: 116)

The roots of Hamilton's legislative activism lay in his own conception of his proper relationship to President Washington:

Hamilton contemplated an American adaptation of the British scheme of things—with Washington as George II and himself as Sir Robert Walpole. But, like Washington, he had to await the event, for no overtures on his part would have been proper. (McDonald, 1979: 126)

We cannot assume that Washington directed Hamilton's efforts, because White (1978: 28–29, n.7) suggests that Hamilton's "cultivation of requests from the House directly to the Secretary for reports on public policy . . . was fought by Jefferson and apparently was disliked by Washington."

One incident may suffice. On November 19, 1794, President Washington gave his Sixth Annual Address to Congress, calling for "a definitive plan for the redemption of the public debt," and two days later the House of Representatives appointed a committee, chaired by William Loughton Smith of South Carolina (a friend of Alexander Hamilton), to report such a plan. After struggling with this proposal, Smith's committee, "as previous Congresses had done, . . . asked Hamilton to supply it with well-organized and definitive answers to many large questions. Hamilton obliged," and so "masterful" were the "tactics and timing of Hamilton's submission" that "[t]he disgruntlement it caused Madison and Jefferson is an index of its significance" (Hendrickson, 1985: 422). Apparently, Madison never read Hamilton's *Final Report on the Public Credit* before it was enacted, just as the House was about to adjourn. So it seems that Washington's role in self-promoting this major enactment was, at best, minimal and deferential to the legislative branch.

A long suppressed (and severely mutilated) 73-page document that President Washington prepared for delivery as his First Inaugural Address (for speculation on why it was abandoned, see Flexner, 1970: 163) gives extremely important insights, according to historian James Flexner (1970: 163): "If the sections that remain are combined with passages from various of Washington's letters, a good idea may be achieved of the ideas he carried with him to the Presidency." Among them was his passive view of the executive–legislative relationship. Flexner (1970: 168) states that Washington

did make it clear that he did not visualize the President as an initiator of policy, a prime mover: "The election of the different branches of Congress by the freemen, either directly or indirectly, is the pivot on which turns the first wheel of the government, a wheel which communicates motion to all the rest."

Richard Loss (whose philosophical leanings seem entirely consistent with those of Nichols) tries to discredit Flexner's interpretation by claiming that

[o]n important matters, such as his proposal for a national university, President Washington was prepared to go over the head of Congress to the people, [and, therefore,] [f]or President Washington the people were the ultimate tribunal when Congress stalled a measure of importance for the common good. (Loss, 1990: 64)

As evidence, Loss (1990: 64) cites this commentary from Washington to Hamilton:

But to be candid, I much question whether a recommendation of this measure to the Legislature will have a better effect *now* than *formerly*. It may show indeed my sense of its importance, and that is a sufficient inducement with *me* to bring the matter before the public in some shape or other, at the closing scenes of my political exit. My object for preparing to insert it where I did . . . was to set the people ruminating on the importance of the measure, [and the] most likely means of bringing it to pass.

It is surely curious—and hardly a precedent for "modern" legislative leadership—that Washington believed it more efficacious to "lobby" Congress for the national university at the end of his tenure than at the beginning or during his terms. Indeed, one could imagine that what Washington meant by this passage is that legislative lobbying was inappropriate for a sitting president but not unacceptable for a retired chief executive. Nor would any benign interpretation allow us to even hint that Washington had a "going public" strategy in mind, since there is scholarship (Tulis, 1987) documenting how political communications by the Founding generation was elite-to-elite and not elite-to-mass. Besides, to provoke "public" discussion about his national university is one thing, but to advocate a contemporary "going public" strategy, where presidents tell voters to directly pressure their representatives to support presidential initiatives, is quite another. This political stratagem (see later) even postdates Franklin D. Roosevelt.

In terms of the precedential value of Hamilton's legislative initiatives, it may not be coincidental that neither Pious (1978: 176–210) nor Corwin (1957: 263–305) makes mention of Washington or Hamilton in his discussion of legislative leadership. Corwin (1957: 265) believes that "[t]he present-day role of the President as policy determiner in the legislative field is largely the creation of the two Roosevelts and Woodrow Wilson," because, as he recollects elsewhere, the potential for Hamiltonian precedents in this sphere was blocked by the Jeffersonians. Hamilton's "financial measures exemplified the legislative leadership of the executive," though "[t]his leadership Hamilton was encouraged to assume by the very terms of the act of Congress by which the Department of the Treasury was established." However:

Indeed, had it not been for the pedantry of Madison and the jealousy of Jefferson, Hamilton would probably have been asked to report to the House in person—a precedent that might in time have blossomed into something approximating the cabinet system. As it was, the ever alert suspicion of Jefferson discovered that Hamilton's connection with Congress, whereby "the whole action of the Legislature was . . . under the direction of the Treasury," tended definitely toward the overthrow of republican institutions; and it was on this fundamental ground . . . that he erected against Hamilton's measures the opposition from which the Jeffersonian party in due course took its rise. (Corwin, 1957: 17–18)

Other practices that are directly attributable to Washington did not survive to become precedents in the "modern" era. One was the Annual Address (Pious, 1978: 158):

In the nineteenth century, presidents followed the custom Washington established and simply listed in their annual message to Congress subjects on which new legislation might be required, without offering an administration position. [But] [t]wentieth-century presidents follow the precedent established by Theodore Roosevelt and make the message . . . into a major statement of foreign and domestic goals.

Moreover, Washington's practice of personally delivering the Annual Address to Congress was adopted by nobody except his immediate successor until "Wilson revived the custom that Jefferson had abandoned of addressing Congress in person, and in his first address requested that Congress pass his banking bill." The Jeffersonians clung to more Whiggish views of legislative supremacy. According to Corwin (1957: 18),

The President [Washington] gave his annual "address" in person, and it was answered by formal "addresses" from the two houses, and to each of these was returned in due course an equally formal "reply"—all of which "trappings of monarchy" were incontinently consigned to the trash basket by "the Revolution of 1800."

The veto, finally, was normally used by Washington and his immediate successors in accordance with original intent, a situation that is rare today. According to Corwin (1957: 279), the veto "was solely a self-defensive weapon of the President" for "carrying out his oath to 'preserve, protect and defend the Constitution' and was not validly usable for any other purpose," and, accordingly, he summarized the early history of veto usage: "Washington exercised the power twice, once on constitutional grounds, once on grounds of expediency. Neither Adams nor Jefferson exercised it at all. Of Madison's six vetoes, four urged constitutional objections to the measure involved, two objections of policy." Then Corwin cites the scholarship of Mason (1891: 120) that "[f]rom Jackson's administration to the Civil War vetoes on grounds of expediency became more frequent, but they were still in a decided minority. Since the [Civil] War constitutional arguments in a veto message have been almost unknown."

Washington's assessment of the veto, says Spitzer (1988: 29), was

a reflection of his restrained view of the presidency as a whole. He was not inclined to veto any given bill simply because he disagreed with it, in part or whole. Nor did he consider his wisdom and judgment to be inherently above that of Congress. Yet the functional constraints he observes on the veto are not of a Constitutional nature but rather those which emphasize his own values of propriety and restraint. Nevertheless, as Washington's second veto shows, he considered the president's policy judgment to be an acceptable rationale for use of the veto.

Yet a comparison of first and second vetoes led Phelps (1993: 150) to argue that Washington "already had a constitutional conception of the presidency that anticipated [Aaron] Wildavsky's [1966] observation [on the "two presidencies"]." The first veto involved domestic policy; the second, military policy. After mentioning several instances where Washington chose *not* to veto suspect legislation, Phelps (1993: 152–153) concludes that Washington

believed the policy preferences of Congress on domestic matters should prevail unless a clear constitutional provision commanded his intervention not only because he chose to take a strictly literalist view of the Constitution, but because to do otherwise would arouse the suspicions and jealousies of those who saw monarchist tendencies lurking in the new constitutional arrangements.

But Washington did veto a bill to reduce the size and cost of the military establishment because he objected to one specific provision that dismissed two companies of light cavalry. His argument

was based purely on practical (policy) considerations that he felt confident in asserting, [and] Congress agreed and immediately passed a new bill without the objectionable item. Congress had found it difficult to resist a firmly convinced president on military and diplomatic matters ever since. (Phelps, 1993: 154)

All this begs the question of who established the "modern" precedent for veto use. Watson (1993: 15) believes

[i]t was when Jackson assumed the presidency that the use of the executive veto power changed radically. He vetoed 12 bills in his eight years in office, more than all his predecessors combined. Jackson did not hesitate to substitute his judgment

on policy matters for that of the Congress. [But] [s]ubsequent presidents continued to differ on the proper reasons for casting a veto. Several who held office prior to the Civil War continued the early tradition [but] [f]or the most part, however, what Kallenbach [1966] terms Jackson's "tribunative" view of the veto authority, ultimately prevailed. (Watson, 1993: 16)

After the Civil War, Watson (1993: 19) agreed with Spitzer that "it was generally conceded that the president could negate any legislation he considered inappropriate for whatever reason." Spitzer (1988: 59) summarized that development this way:

Few of the many vetoes applied by presidents from Grant on aroused a level of controversy comparable to that surrounding controversial vetoes before the Civil War. And in the controversies that did arise there was a critical difference: Interpretations of the veto power rarely questioned the right of the president to veto any given bill if he considered it inappropriate to be a law. Presidential judgment continued to be questioned but not the power that gave rise to the judgment.

In sum, the precedent for the "modern" veto was established by Andrew Jackson, not George Washington.

Modern Legislative Leadership

Surely modern legislative leadership cannot be traced back—without serious interruption—to Washington with respect to his use of the veto, his personal presentation of the Annual Address to Congress, or his acquiescence of Hamilton's direct liaison with the legislative branch. Today the Secretary of Treasury is *not* charged with the responsibility of cultivating legislative support in Congress for presidential programs. But the problem of historical antecedents runs deeper. Trying to define "modern" legislative leadership is like trying to fix in time and space a moving target. Any historic benchmarks in the development of legislative leadership do not necessarily hold precedential value, and that applies equally to Franklin D. Roosevelt and George Washington.

To recall, one criterion used by Fred Greenstein to characterize FDR as the first "modern" president was legislative leadership. While one cannot deny the significance of enactments during his tenure, the modus operandi used by FDR and the conditions for his legislative success were more unique to him (or analogous to Washington at the Founding) than generalizable to his successors. First, although Sam Kernell (1986) argues that "going public" is the dominant form of executive–legislative interaction today, nonetheless, he characterized Franklin Roosevelt (16) as one who adhered to the traditional "bargaining" system of personalized communications with congressional leaders. Bargaining was the appropriate response by FDR for a politics grounded in what Kernell calls "institutionalized pluralism," whereas the emerging politics of "individualized pluralism" encouraged Ronald Reagan to personify "going public" in his efforts to influence Congress. Thus, FDR may have used "fireside chats," but their purpose was aimed more at reassuring public opinion rather mobilizing the voters against Congress.

Second, FDR also made history because of the impressive amount of legislation enacted during his first "Hundred Days" of 1933. It was the stuff from which myths are made, as when Hodgson (1980: 60) declared that the 73rd Congress "did not so much debate the bills it passed . . . as salute them as they went sailing by." But myths they are, because presidency scholars overlooked the few studies that closely examined lawmaking during the Hundred Days of 1933. One who did was E. Pendleton Herring (1934: 83):

For its sanction, it relied in large measure upon the popular fear during an emergency and upon the political patronage flowing from an electoral victory. The sessions [of Congress] made clear the urgent necessity of responsible political leadership, but it afforded little light as to how this authority can be effectively retained under other conditions.

Seemingly, the conditions were ripe for "responsible partyism" under FDR, but Snowiss (1971: 60) also debunks that mythology:

That the Democratic administration could *not* elicit sufficient partisan support to implement a program designed to meet the commonly perceived crisis without being compelled to resort to cross-party support or extensive legislative bargaining provides strong grounds for discarding the party government model for one that emphasizes the president's role as a leader of cross-party majorities. (emphasis added)

Nor does the FDR Hundred Days benchmark hold much meaning for today. Systematic analysis of Hundred Days legislation since 1896 (Tatalovich, Frendreis, and Schaff, 1998) found a sharp decline since the late 1940s. No "modern" president has had the degree of Hundred Days success approaching that of FDR—or *any* of his successors since McKinley.

In other words, one suspects that the success of President Washington's policy agenda was likely *more* dependent on Federalist solidarity in Congress—as compared to FDR's or any of his successor's. Of course, Washington operated under conditions approximating one-party government, whereas the emergence of a two-party system electorally and legislatively has complicated the legislative leadership role. While party may be the most reliable "cue" to congressional voting behavior, it is not all that reliable. The standard used by congressional scholars to measure a "party vote" (majority of Republicans opposing a majority of Democrats) means that 49 percent of the presidential party in Congress can vote *against* his legislative agenda. Because party is so unpredictable and presidential skills of persuasion so uneven and dependent on the exigencies of the moment, the prevailing view among presidential scholars is that executive leadership operates "at the margins" of the lawmaking process (Edwards, 1989; Bond and Fleisher, 1990).

This point is made most forcefully by Charles Jones (1994), whose case-by-case analysis of legislative enactments revealed so many permutations in the legislative process and such variability in presidential leadership that he offered this summary judgment:

The United States has the most intricate lawmaking system in the world. It will not be made better through simplification. Preponderance of one branch over the other should be a cause for concern, not celebration. Presidents are well advised to appreciate the advantages of the separated system and to define their role in it. Most do not have to be counseled on the legitimacy of Congress, but some do. Most know instinctively that their advantages are in certifying the agenda and persuading others to accept their proposals as a basis for compromise, but some have grander conceptions of presidential power. Most understand that they are temporary leaders of a convention of policy choice already in session, but some lack the skills to define the limits or realize the advantages of that status. Most realize that patience, persistence, and sharing are required for effective work in the separated system, but some are overly anxious to take immediate credit for change. And most grasp the purposes of a diffused-responsibility system of mixed representation and shared powers, but some believe that the president is the presidency, the presidency is the government, and ours is a presidential system. Those who believe these things may even have convinced themselves that they are right. They will be proven to be wrong. (Jones, 1994: 297–298)

Washington's Personalized Leadership

To assert the simple truth that beloved George Washington was the "Father of our Nation" is not simply validation for Nichols' implicit hypothesis that "routinization of charisma" resulted after Washington. Not only may Washington's public persona have been one of a kind, but the manner of its being is fundamentally different from how "cults of personality" are presidentially manufactured in the modern era. Washington was loved by the people but was not of the people, nor did he attempt to mobilize the populace around his personage. The Framers feared "demagogic" leadership, which they understood as "direct" appeals to the masses, and Washington shared those concerns and acted accordingly. Indeed, Washington's restraint vis-à-vis the populace was exhibited by most of his nineteenth-century successors (the notable exception being Andrew Johnson)—so argues the definitive study by Jeffrey Tulis (1987).

While Tulis (1987: 7) asserts (as would Nichols) that many changes attributed to the "modern" presidency "do not constitute metamorphoses of the institution . . . the rhetorical presidency *does* represent a true transformation of the presidency." Tulis (1987: 47) argues that "George Washington was particularly sensitive to the need to establish constitutionally informed, useful precedents—so much so that he devoted considerable time during his first year as president to decisions regarding the symbolic dimension of his office." At the first inaugural ceremony Washington "was groping for a model of speech and ceremony that would establish the dignity of his office but not appear monarchical" (Tulis, 1987: 48), and Tulis approvingly quotes Glen Thurow with respect to how Washington resolved the dilemma. Thurow's point was that President Washington chose to lead by "example" because

[i]t is only through the force of his example that he could be said to have a direct relationship to the people in the speech. His outstanding qualities provide a model for other politicians, and attracts the people at large to their government. This model helps to infuse the Constitution with the proper spirit. But Washington's relationship to the people is not the grounds of either his powers or his duties. (quoted in Tulis, 1987: 48–48)

That is the distinctive difference between Washington and the "moderns" that Nichols fails to appreciate.

Similarly, when Washington "established the practice of 'going on tour' " through New England and the South, "public speaking was not as important as public appearances—'seeing and being seen,' as Washington called them" (Tulis, 1987: 69). Viewed in the context of Washington's restrained, "personalized" leadership, President Andrew Johnson

violated virtually all of the nineteenth-century norms encompassed by the doctrine. He stands as the stark exception to general practice in that century, so demagogic in his appeals to the people that he seems not so much a forerunner of twentieth-century practice as a parody of popular leadership. (Tulis, 1987: 87–88)

However, demagogic appeals soon became a mainstay of the personalized presidency, and that development can be attributed to Woodrow Wilson, our "first" modern rhetorical leader.

Modern Personalized Leadership

Whereas Washington typified the "old way" of elite-to-elite communications, and Theodore Roosevelt accommodated the turn-of-the-century "crisis" of industrialization with his "middle way" of popular rhetoric within the bounds of constitutionalism, there was no stopping Wilson's advocacy of a "new way" for personalized presidential leadership. President

Washington saw his example of character and statesmanship as setting constitutional precedents, but Wilson believed that the public could judge presidential character and, according to Tulis (1987: 131–132), "that public understanding of the leader's character would come from his oratory rather than from a history of his political activity or from direct contact with him. The public's understanding of character might be based solely on words." Thus, Wilson casts aside the Framers' concerns about demagoguery (Tulis, 1987: 130) by differentiating between a demagogue and "the leader [who] appeals to 'true' and durable majority sentiment" (rather than whimsical popular moods) and who "is more interested in fostering the permanent interests of the community" (rather than personal power per se).

This exalted statement by Wilson shows that he most fully conceptualized a personalized presidential leadership grounded in public opinion and political party:

[The president] cannot escape being the leader of his party except by incapacity and lack of personal force, because he is at once the choice of the party and the nation. He is the party nominee, and the only party nominee for whom the whole nation votes. . . . There is no national party choice except that of President. No one else represents the people as a whole exercising a national choice . . . the President represents not so much the party's governing efficiency as its ideals and principles. He is not so much a part of its organization as its vital link of connection with the thinking nation. He can dominate his party by being spokesman for the real sentiment and purpose of the country, by giving direction to opinion, by giving the country at once the information and the statements of policy which will enable it to form judgments alike of parties and of men. (cited in Egger, 1972: 172)

Wilson made good on his conception of personalized leadership. He began the practice—now commonly accepted—for a president to campaign actively for his party's candidates during the midterm congressional elections (though Wilson failed in 1918 with the GOP takeover of Congress).

But it was the second Roosevelt who attempted a radical extension of Wilson's campaign "precedent" with his failed 1938 "purge" of conservative Democrats in the *primary* elections. That unprecedented action was precipitated when Congress defeated Roosevelt's "court-packing" plan of 1937, and FDR explained its justification in a radio broadcast to the nation:

As the head of the Democratic party . . . charged with the responsibility of the definitely liberal declaration of principles set forth in the 1936 Democratic platform, I feel that I have every right to speak in those few instances where there may be a clear issue between candidates for a Democratic nomination involving these principles, or involving a clear misuse of my own name. (cited in Koenig, 1975: 132)

The transformation of personalized leadership has not stopped with electioneering, as envisioned by the Progressive and New Dealers, since the advent of instantaneous communications, opinion polling, and electronic mass media enables any president—even ordinary politicians not remotely comparable to George Washington—to gain celebrity status. Where the goal of personalized power for the Progressives and New Dealers was to enhance "representative" government, its growth today signifies an entirely different rationale for the Leviathan: delivery of services. The president is held personally accountable for the major duties of government—peace and prosperity—and for the multitude of minor claims against the state. Says Theodore J. Lowi (1985: 151), "[S]ince the rhetoric that flows from the office so magnifies the personal responsibility and so surrounds the power with mystique, it is only natural that the American people would produce or embrace myths about presidential power."

FINAL OBSERVATIONS

The entire logic of our argument is based on what public administrationists call the "span of control" problem: there are a limited number of subordinates who can be managed effectively by one supervisor. In absolute and relative terms the government that President Washington created beginning in 1789 was small, both in ends and means, which allowed him to exert one-to-one control over literally the entire diplomatic, administrative, and (had he desired) legislative arenas. Clearly, the size of the modern Leviathan precludes Washington's kind of hands-on presidential control over the bureaucracy. The problem now is to exert *any* degree of personal control because there are so many subordinates involved. On the other hand, how could the Washington example of legislative leadership through his Treasury Secretary establish "precedents" for modernity when, in fact, the concept of legislative leadership itself is called into question by so many presidency scholars? The myth that presidents propose but Congress disposes should be rephrased: presidents (may or may not) propose, but Congress disposes (and proposes)! None of the legislative precedents that President Washington began survived him, and even Greenstein's assertion of FDR's "modern" legacy of legislative leadership ought to be challenged. If anything, there may be more critical variables linking Roosevelt to Washington, rather than either man to his White House successors.

Only with respect to diplomacy was Nichols correct in identifying George Washington as the first "modern" president, because he did establish the legal precedents and customary practices that guided his successors. That his example can be followed today simply attests to the fact that diplomacy remains highly personalized, with one-to-one exchanges between our president and his foreign counterparts as standard operating procedure. There is also a relatively small bureaucracy in foreign affairs, but no Leviathan. On the other hand, the Framers' fear of demagoguery cannot be squared with the kind of highly "personalized" (and partisan) presidential leadership of the modern era. Tulis correctly points to the intellectual chasm that divided the Framers, particularly Washington, and Woodrow Wilson. No point better illustrates that the Progressives conceptualized a regime fundamentally at odds with Constitutional republicanism.

Yet despite their grave differences of opinion on the "ends" of government, conservatives like Nichols and Progressives like Croly also underestimated the impact of the Leviathan on personalized presidential leadership. But surely the conservatives intellectually got it more right than wrong, because the "means" of personalized leadership as envisioned by Nichols and embodied in Washington could not have survived had not the "ends" of government grown quantitatively and qualitatively so much. The Progressives, however, naively insisted that the growth of positive government and its inevitable bureaucratic Leviathan are entirely compatible with—indeed, are dependent on—personalized, heroic leadership by the president. They have achieved their ends, but the means have been lost. Progressives like Woodrow Wilson celebrated presidential rhetoric to mobilize public opinion behind social change and, thereby, overcome the inadequacies of our separated system. But today's generation of presidency scholars are more concerned about system collapse resulting from the "expectations gap" of inflated rhetoric versus inept performance, not from the separation of powers (Yenor, Cook, and Tatalovich, 1998: 16–17).

REFERENCES

Aberbach, Joel D. and Bert A. Rockman. 1976. "Clashing Beliefs within the Executive Branch: The Nixon Administration Bureaucracy." *American Political Science Review* 70 (June), pp. 456–468.

Berger, Raoul. 1974. *Executive Privilege: A Constitutional Myth.* Cambridge, MA: Harvard University Press.

Bond, Jon R. and Richard Fleisher. 1990. *The President in the Legislative Arena.* Chicago: University of Chicago Press.

Commager, Henry Steele. 1950. *The American Mind: An Interpretation of American Thought and Character since the 1880's.* New Haven, CT: Yale University Press.

Corwin, Edward S. 1957. *The President: Office and Powers.* New York: New York University Press.

Croly, Herbert. 1909. *The Promise of American Life.* Reprint, Boston: Northeastern University Press, 1989.

———. 1914. *Progressive Democracy.* Reprint, New Brunswick, NJ: Transaction, 1998.

Dewey, Thomas. 1927. *The Public and Its Problems.* New York: Henry Holt.

Dionne, E. J. 1996. *They Only Look Dead: Why Progressives Will Dominate the Next Political Era.* New York: Simon & Schuster.

Edwards, George. 1989. *At the Margins: Presidential Leadership of Congress.* New Haven, CT: Yale University Press.

Egger, Rowland. 1972. *The President of the United States*. New York: McGraw-Hill.

Eisenach, Eldon J. 1994. *The Lost Promise of Progressivism*. Lawrence: University Press of Kansas.

Flexner, James Thomas. 1970. *George Washington and the New Nation, 1783–1793*. Boston: Little, Brown.

Goldman, Eric F. 1960. *Rendezvous with Destiny: A History of Modern American Reform*. New York: Vintage.

Greenstein, Fred I. 1978. "Change and Continuity in the Modern Presidency." In Anthony King, ed., *The New American Political System*. Washington, DC: American Enterprise Institute, pp. 45–85.

Hamilton, Alexander, James Madison, and John Jay. 1788. *The Federalist Papers*. Middletown, CT: Wesleyan University Press, 1961.

Hart, John. 1995. *The Presidential Branch: Executive Office of the President*. Chatham, NJ: Chatham House.

Heclo, Hugh. 1977. *A Government of Strangers: Executive Politics in Washington*. Washington, DC: Brookings Institution.

Hendrickson, Robert A. 1985. *The Rise and Fall of Alexander Hamilton*. New York: Dodd, Mead.

Herring, E. Pendleton. 1934. "American Government and Politics: First Session of the Seventy-Third Congress, March 9, 1933 to June 16, 1933." *American Political Science Review* 28 (February), pp. 65–83.

Hodgson, Godfrey. 1980. *All Things to All Men: The False Promise of the Modern American Presidency*. New York: Simon & Schuster.

Jones, Charles O. 1994. *The Presidency in a Separated System*. Washington, DC: Brookings Institution.

Kallenbach, Joseph. 1966. *The American Chief Executive: The Presidency and the Governorship*. New York: Harper and Row.

Kernell, Samuel. 1986. *Going Public: New Strategies of Presidential Leadership*. Washington, DC: Congressional Quarterly Press.

Koenig, Louis W. 1975. *The Chief Executive*, 3rd ed. New York: Harcourt Brace Jovanovich.

Loss, Richard. 1990. *The Modern Theory of Presidential Power: Alexander Hamilton and the Corwin Thesis*. Westport, CT: Greenwood Press.

Lowi, Theodore J. 1985. *The Personal President: Power Invested, Promise Unfulfilled*. Ithaca, NY: Cornell University Press.

Mason, Edward C. 1891. *The Veto Power*. Boston: Ginn and Co.

McDonald, Forrest. 1979. *Alexander Hamilton: A Biography*. New York: W. W. Norton.

Miller, Arthur S. 1977. *Presidential Power*. St. Paul, MN: West.

Nathan, Richard P. 1983. *The Administrative Presidency*. New York: Wiley.

Nichols, David K. 1994. *The Myth of the Modern Presidency*. University Park: Pennsylvania State University Press.

Phelps, Glenn A. 1993. *George Washington and American Constitutionalism*. Lawrence: University Press of Kansas.

Pious, Richard M. 1979. *The American Presidency*. New York: Basic Books.

Rozell, Mark J. 1994. *Executive Privilege*. Baltimore: Johns Hopkins University Press.

Skowronek, Steven. 1993. *The Politics Presidents Make*. Cambridge, MA: Harvard University Press.

Snowiss, Sylvia. 1971. "Presidential Leadership of Congress: An Analysis of Roosevelt's First Hundred Days." *Publius* 1(1), pp. 59–87.

Spitzer, Robert J. 1988. *The Presidential Veto: Touchstone of the American Presidency.* Albany: State University of New York Press.

Stettner, Edward A. 1993. *Shaping Modern Liberalism: Herbert Croly and Progressive Thought.* Lawrence: University Press of Kansas.

Tatalovich, Raymond, John Frendreis, and Jon Schaff. 1998. "Predicting Legislative Output in the First '100 Days,' 1897–1995." Paper delivered to the Annual Meeting of the American Political Science Association, Boston.

Tocqueville, Alexis de. 1835. *Democracy in America.* Garden City, NJ: Doubleday, 1988.

Tulis, Jeffrey K. 1987. *The Rhetorical Presidency.* Princeton, NJ: Princeton University Press.

Warshaw, Shirley Anne. 1996. *Powersharing: White House–Cabinet Relations in the Modern Presidency.* Albany: State University of New York Press.

Washington Post. 1993. March 2, p. A1.

Watson, Richard A. 1993. *Presidential Vetoes and Public Policy.* Lawrence: University Press of Kansas.

White, Leonard D. 1948. *The Federalists: A Study in Administrative History.* New York: Macmillan.

Wildavsky, Aaron. 1966. "The Two Presidencies." *Trans-Action,* 4, pp. 7–14.

Wilson, Woodrow. 1885. *Congressional Government.* New York: Meridian Books, 1956.

Yenor, Scott E., Travis S. Cook, and Raymond Tatalovich. 1998. "The Normative Study of the Presidency." In Ryan J. Barilleaux, ed., *Presidential Frontiers: Underexplored Issues in White House Politics.* Westport, CT: Praeger, pp. 3–21.

Young, James P. 1996. *Reconsidering American Liberalism: The Troubled Odyssey of the Liberal Idea.* Boulder, CO: Westview Press.

Chapter 3

Family Imagery and Revolutionary Spirit: Washington's Creative Leadership

ELIZABETH W. MARVICK

> It is less difficult to discover the Northwest passage than to create a people, as you have done.
>
> —F.-R. Chateaubriand[1]

Early in the 1850s there seems to have been a general belief that "any one could be President, and some very shady characters were likely to be." This is what Henry Adams, the grandson and great-grandson of presidents, discovered as a boy living in Washington, D.C. He learned that "no sort of glory hedged Presidents, and, in the whole country, one could hardly have met with an admission of respect for any office or name, unless it were George Washington." That name, exceptionally, was "sincerely . . . respected." George Washington, the young Adams was told by his father, "stood alone."[2]

A century and a half later, George Washington still stands alone. It is hard to think about him or to study him without getting the notion that the history of this continent would have been very different without him. Undoubtedly, he helped significantly to shape our political institutions and practices in their formative years.

What seems most extraordinary about Washington is that the very important differences he intended to make in our country's history are the ones he actually did make. This leader of the American Revolution, this creator of a new nation, this Founder and first president of the American Republic under its federal Constitution, had dreamed of a newly independent nation whose people had in common a sense of themselves as Americans. He actively strove to transform that dream into reality. Intending to see liberty and justice established for his fellow citizens, he helped to give the new nation its laws and then presided over it. From the time he entered national politics in 1774 until he died at the very end of his century, his influence on the course of history tended in the direction of his aims. In these respects, by most standards, Washington must be counted as a highly creative or transforming leader.[3]

Few other leaders in the history of the West in modern times fit this pattern. Perhaps Charles de Gaulle of France, creator first of "Free France" and then of the Fifth Republic, comes to mind. Or Mustapha Kemal, the founder of modern Turkey, or Nelson Mandela of South Africa. But among American leaders Washington stands alone.

Abraham Lincoln, for example, does not fill this particular bill. A recent biography of the Civil War president by David Donald stresses Lincoln's rejection of the great man theory of history—at least, as far as it applied to himself: "I claim not to have controlled events," Lincoln wrote toward the end of the Civil War, "but confess plainly that events have controlled me."

Such a thing could not be said about Washington's influence on events. Furthermore, no one could have said of Washington, as Donald says of Lincoln, that he had an "essentially passive personality."[4] Indeed, *activity*, not passivity, was one of Washington's most conspicuous characteristics. An intimate friend of the first president wrote of him,

Few men of such steady persevering industry every existed. . . . He could at the dictate of reason control his will and command himself to act. . . . Who [else] could like Washington completely, at any moment, command the energies of his mind to a cheerful exertion[?][5]

Leaders who seem to stand higher than most and from their high places even to shape the destinies of nations may in their own time be idols of the crowd, but their godlike qualities discourage us from seeking an understanding of what is at work in their personalities that allowed them to play their notable roles.

Compare the interest in Washington's character with that in Lincoln's, for example. Lincoln's true nature has perhaps interested psychologists and historians more than any other American's. He was a man many feel they can empathize with. Often sad, conflicted, and indecisive, sometimes beset by feelings of anguish and helplessness, he was eventually martyred. No wonder that this leader's character continues to fascinate: most of us can recognize ourselves in some aspect of his all-too-human personality. He embodies our fears as well as our aspirations, our failings as well as our abilities. Again, Thomas Jefferson—another American hero—has rarely been seen as a perfect model of leadership. Words that are often used to describe him are "deeply flawed" and "ambivalent." A recent biographer calls him "sphinxlike"—a more sympathetic term for what his enemies, then and now, preferred to call "two-faced." Even those who most admired Jefferson's great qualities had to admit that he was sometimes deceitful, vengeful, hypocritical, unjust and—psychologically speaking—narcissistically self-serving. These contradictions have made his personality and how it was shaped the objects of lively interest to psychopolitical analysts ever since he emerged on the public stage.[6]

Since about 1920, the searchlight of depth psychology has been turned upon most notable presidents from John Adams to Bill Clinton. Americans have seen the intimate histories of many of their most admired leaders subjected to close investigation in attempts to explain the personal dynamics that animated and shaped their political performances. Yet Washington, preeminent in every role that distinguished American political history in the last quarter of the eighteenth century, has largely eluded such scrutiny.

Up until quite recently, Washington was largely treated as an icon—a character cast in marble rather than a dynamic figure of flesh and blood, prone to ordinary human passions and weaknesses. He was represented as molded all of one piece; without the seams and cracks endemic to ordinary people and certainly without their internal struggles and unconscious conflicts. Indeed, Chief Justice John Marshall, who knew Washington well, declared "his real and avowed motives were the same."[7] Since what you saw was what there was, there could be no purpose in probing more deeply.

Beginning in the 1930s, with the publication of John C. Fitzpatrick's massive edition of Washington's writings, ever-better-documented biographies began to appear that were far less reverential than their predecessors. Some of these pointed to Washington's early limitations as a military leader and to his occasional failures of insight and skill as a politician. As a result of new information and an antiheroic trend in American culture, many of what might be deemed Washington's character flaws have been exposed. The young Washington's passionate ambition for glory has been stressed, as has his lust for real estate and other wealth. It has been shown that he did not always tell the truth about such matters. It has been pointed out that he had a taste for women and for gambling and possibly indulged both tastes somewhat promiscuously. Evidence has been produced that his suspicion of plots against his authority in the Revolution bordered on the paranoid. He has been charged with tolerating, if not actively initiating, cruel and unusual punishment of delinquent soldiers. It has been suggested that, as a Virginia planter, his management of slaves was at best businesslike and at worst no better than average for his milieu. The allegation has even been made that as Commander in Chief during the Revolutionary War he habitually padded his expense accounts.[8]

Yet even if all these imputations were justified, they would fail to connect Washington the man with Washington the historical figure. How did this devalued Washington become the Washington who led the vanguard of the independence movement, helped to steer the Revolution to a successful outcome, and personally symbolized the new nation? How did he become the military leader who refused to extend his powers beyond the laws, who rejected opportunities to gather political authority in his own hands, and who instead helped to sponsor and shape a new political system? How were his personal resources brought to bear in forming a new administration under new laws into an institution that was authoritative yet strictly limited in powers?

Devalued or idealized, there seems a baffling inconsistency between the personality of the man and these roles he played. Perhaps there never has been a less likely revolutionary or a more unusual republican politician than Washington. His aversion to risk, his profoundly conservative respect for tradition, for formality, and, specifically, for English institutions give few clues to the personal sources of the innovative part he would take in forging the "First New Nation." His dislike of self-exposure and his preference for domestic over public life seem to belie the self-dramatizing flair, the high energy, single-minded concentration, and consummate skill with which he helped to guide the American state through its perilous first few years.

When there is so much to explain about Washington, what accounts for the fact that so little attention has been given to how his developmental history resulted in the personality dynamics that characterized the adult leader?

The modern scholar does not accept Marshall's picture of Washington's seamless personality. Today's historian is aware that the most serene equilibrium is likely to have been won through resolving intense conflicts. Behind any "finished" character are traces of inner struggles that date to the earliest stages of life. As the infant meets obstacles to gratification and develops means of coping with them, patterns are laid down in the unconscious as well as the conscious mind that later characterize the mature personality.

Thus, today's biographers initially seek insight into a public character's performance by looking for evidence on the experience of the child in forming links to the outside world. Such links, in the first instance, are to family members, and it is to George Washington's early family relationships that we turn here in search of information on how his experience of childhood may be related to his development as a political leader.

Primary among sources of such information are the words and actions of Washington himself. Fortunately for our inquiry, the monumental new edition, now in progress, of Washington's writings, together with much other recent scholarly research, improves the possibility of discovering patterns in his reactions to events.[9] With the help of insights from depth psychology, close attention to the details of such evidence promises to disclose latent meanings in his imagery and emphasis. Oversights, inconsistencies, repetitions, and errors of fact may hint at unconscious tendencies to deny or repress motives that are felt as unacceptable. When direct evidence on personal experience is scarce, it becomes a "question of paying attention to each phrase, of following out each faint clue."[10] This is a slow and laborious process, however, and in this short time we can expect to make only a little progress.

For the most part, the sources of the clues we need are the widely scattered occasional passages from Washington's correspondence and diaries that contain allusions to his early, intimate experience or that seem, unguardedly, to express his deeper emotions. Among the more interesting of these is a short group of written comments the general himself made on a draft of what was to have been an authorized biography by his friend and former aide-de-camp, David Humphreys, a poet-diplomat who lived at Mount Vernon from 1786 to 1788. Fragmentary as they are, the various manuscripts that constitute Humphreys' unfinished "Life of General Washington," together with Washington's annotations, are a good point of departure to illustrate the kind of careful analysis that seems necessary.

The biographical sketch that Humphreys began to prepare while he was Washington's guest profited not only from prolonged and intimate daily contact with the national hero but also from "copyediting" by its subject. Washington himself made corrections and elaborations of the narrative as Humphreys composed it. The fact that the short sketch depends heavily on Washington's own communications gives the work autobiographical value. He himself seems to have feared that his written comments revealed too much, since he enjoined Humphreys to return or burn them after he read them. Fortunately, Humphreys did neither; hence, we can study his text together with Washington's annotations for hints on what Washington inadvertently may have disclosed.[11]

Although Rosemarie Zagarri, editor of the newly synthesized manuscripts, deals most vividly with Washington's feelings about experiences in the French and Indian War,[12] it is Washington's references to his much earlier experience that are in question here.

Humphreys' account begins with Washington's ancestry and refers to the brothers John and Lawrence as the first family members to settle in Virginia, in 1657. At this point Washington appends the remark that they "transferred a considerable inheritance . . . to their adoptive country." In fact, however, the English father of these two immigrants, the Reverend Lawrence Washington, had been driven out of his comfortable church living in 1643 by the influence of those Puritans who would later sponsor what Washington would call "the usurpation of Oliver Cromwell."[13] This unfortunate ancestor had been accused of being a "common frequenter of Alehouses," of "daily tippling," and of having "oft been drunk." He had been forced to take a living so "poor and miserable" that it was difficult to persuade anyone to accept it.[14] "Financially," one historian concludes, "he must have been a ruined man."[15] The impoverished Reverend Washington died in 1652, a few years before his two sons found their way to the New World. What seems significant in George Washington's addition to this history is that, whatever these first Washington emigrants brought to the American mainland, it was not likely to have been a "considerable inheritance," unless by a lucky stroke they had since benefited from the death of some other family connection. Furthermore, their father, the rector, had been disadvantaged from the start: he had descended from the modest junior branch of a family whose more prosperous lines included titled members intermarried with persons bearing such distinguished names as Guise, Pargiter, and Villiers.[16]

Another interesting feature of George Washington's account of his American origins is that he implies that "pull" rather than "push" brought his great-grandfather and great-granduncle from across the sea. According to him, these first American Washingtons were not constrained to come to our shores in search of a fortune that they lacked in their native land. Instead, we are to understand, America was their freely chosen destination, and they brought, along with high social status, sizable inherited resources to invest in the country of their choice.

Humphreys continues, without his hero's demurral, that "almost every branch of their offspring still possesses a considerable portion of property and respectability."[17] The expectations of the two brothers who were the original migrants, it seems, were validated: the Washingtons multiplied and prospered in the New World.

The fact was, however, that George Washington was descended from the younger son of the senior immigrant brother. The line of the elder brother seems to have died out early, although he was the father of three sons. Of course, neither George Washington himself nor his half brother Lawrence had any descendants.

Thus far, the emphases and omissions that Washington induced his biographer to make give an interesting twist to the myth of the hero-founder of a new nation. Then, as now, the picture of America as the land of opportunity for dispossessed and persecuted victims of Old World injustice had its charm. Washington could certainly have represented his own forebears as driven by intolerance to a new land, there to achieve success despite obstacles. His preference for depicting them as continuously superior in affluence and respectability may hint at defensiveness. This quintessentially achieving hero did not wish to be known as a self-made man. He preferred to represent fortune as smiling upon his ancestors before as well as after they were called to the scene of the hero's later distinction.

Even given prosperous ancestors, the American myth requires that the hero fulfill his personal destiny by dint of his own efforts, against the odds. In this, George Washington's history and his version of it conform to the myth. The death of his father, Augustine Washington, while George was still a child is one event that forced early self-reliance and striving for achievement upon the future leader.

Here it is in order to recapitulate some of the established facts concerning the family situation of George Washington from the time of his birth to his father's death.

Like a disproportionate number of ambitious, successful leaders, George Washington was the firstborn son of his mother.[18] Yet Mary Ball Washington also conferred a handicap on Washington. Her husband had another, older family by his first wife, Jane Butler. Thus, as the second wife of Augustine Washington, Mary may be said to have made her eldest son the head of the five children that constituted the "B team." Furthermore, while the first Mrs. Washington was the daughter of a prosperous Virginia landowner and brought a considerable fortune to her marriage, Mary Ball, like her son George, was a child of her father's second family. Joseph Ball had settled his most substantial assets on the children of his first marriage before he married Mary Johnson, Mary Ball's mother.

When George Washington was born, therefore, he was subordinate in rank, as his father's third son, to two older half brothers, Augustine and Lawrence. It seems significant, too, especially since it is not mentioned in Humphrey's account of George Washington's ancestry, that Augustine senior was himself a younger son of his father and had suffered serious disadvantages as the result of that father's death.[19] Indeed, the fact that neither Washington nor Humphreys makes any allusion to Augustine's way of life, other than to his legacies of land, may also mask unadmitted feelings of relative deprivation.

George Washington's father, Augustine, had not been a typical Virginia plantation-dwelling patriarch. A man of mediocre fortune, his main occupation was as manager of an iron works. This factory, at a considerable distance from the various houses to which he moved his family in George's childhood, often required his absence from home. Furthermore, when George was four years old, business took Augustine to England. There he could visit his two oldest boys, who were being educated at the same elite school the father had been forced to leave at the age of nine. On that visit Augustine was away from home for at least six months. It is little wonder that George was "heard to say that he knew little of his father, other than a remembrance of his person"—Augustine was a tall and powerful man—"and of his parental fondness."[20]

To identify childhood deprivations is one thing; to determine the feelings about them of the one who experienced them is another. It, therefore, seems important to notice that, real as Washington's deprivation was, he exaggerates the loss imposed on him by his father's death. He changes an important fact about it by telling Humphreys, "My father died when I was only ten years old." The truth is that when his father died on April 12, 1743, George had already passed his 11th birthday.

The loss of a parent by death or other cause is apt to arouse anger (among other emotions) in a child. The fact that George Washington backdated by a year the handicap placed on himself by his father's death is suggestive of unexpressed resentment at the disadvantage he had suffered.

A study of the will of George Washington's father shows that while he intended to provide for all his sons from both marriages, he divided his estate among them roughly on the basis of priority of birth. Thus, Lawrence, the eldest, who had already received the Mount Vernon estate, was also bequeathed his father's share in the Principio Iron works (which Lawrence later bequeathed to his brother Austin or his heirs). Most of the remaining tracts of real property were allocated, in descending order of size, choiceness, and certainty of title, among the six sons of both marriages, giving the eldest the right of refusing his legacy in exchange for one of his brother's should he prefer it, a similar right of choice being given to each of the younger brothers in turn—again, in order of birth. References are also made in this will to property belonging to the three older children through their mother, in which the younger children had no share. Thus, George received only the best legacy of the "second team," and even the few modifications he has made so far in Humphrey's draft suggest that he felt the disadvantage keenly.

George Washington does not, in Humphreys' account, express directly any sentiments about his relatively low position in the family order. That he was sensitive to such matters, however, is suggested by a letter that he had written several years before to his nephew and principal heir, Bushrod Washington. In it, he admonishes this elder son of his younger brother to moderate his financial demands on his father, John Augustine Washington, whom he was pushing into debt. "Prudence," wrote George Washington, "and every other consideration is opposed to your requiring more than his conveniency and a regard to his other children will enable him to pay."[21] Clearly, George was attuned to the rights of younger siblings, among whom he probably counted not only his own younger brothers and those of his nephews but himself as well.[22]

Priorities of inheritance were not the only ways in which George Washington was disadvantaged as a result of his relatively low birth order and the early death of his father. Deficiencies in his education could also be attributed to these handicaps—and Washington did so, showing himself to be very aware of having got the short end of the stick on this point. Augustine compensated for his own schooling deficiencies by providing his first two sons with the education of English gentlemen.[23] But, George suggests, he missed receiving a similar advantage by his father's premature death. He tells Humphreys of himself: "His father and two oldest brothers had received their education in England, whither he would have been sent for the same purpose had it not been for the death of the former."[24]

How keenly Washington felt this disadvantage is shown by one of his letters. Humphreys had written him that he thought it would better for Washington to write an autobiography, than for Humphreys to undertake a biography of the general. Washington demurs that he has neither the leisure nor the talents for it: "I am conscious of a defective education and want of capacity to fit me for such an undertaking."[25] Nor was such self-consciousness mere modesty, for while Washington was certainly gifted with an unusual talent for writing, his schoolbooks and earliest letters show the many hours of laborious practice he had to put in to develop to the point that he ultimately reached as an adroit and expressive correspondent.

Humphreys' "life" goes on to claim that Washington was educated by "a domestic tutor." This may put a gloss on reality. Jonathan Boucher, who knew Washington well, reports that Augustine Washington hired a "convict servant bought as a schoolmaster" to educate the firstborn of his second family.[26] Certainly, this practice was common, even among families better off than the Washingtons.[27] George eventually attended the Fredericksburg classes of the Huguenot minister James Marye, where he shared his teacher's services with several schoolmates. Possibly Washington's education was even less privileged than he represented it. A suggestion that this was so may lie in an observation that he made in a later letter concerning the education of a young nephew: consulted on whether the youth should be sent to a certain college, he advises with somewhat unusual emphasis that this depends in part "upon the number of Boys; for I lay it down as a maxim, that if the number of the pupils is too great for the tutors, justice cannot be done, be the abilities of the latter what they will." What the minimal proportion is cannot be told, but "an extreme must be obvious to all."[28] It is plausible that he speaks from experience of such an extreme.

If there are indications that George Washington suffered from his position of comparative disadvantage as a child, such feelings may have been augmented by certain features of his mother's family. Mary Ball Washington's elder half brother, Joseph Ball, had the advantage of an English education that made him eligible for a prestigious professional career in the mother country. Judging from surviving portions of Mary Washington's correspondence with this half brother, an English barrister, her son George must early have been made aware that he and his widowed mother were "poor relations" in her family—deferential petitioners not only for advice but also for gifts from their superior connections abroad. Joseph Ball himself did not definitively migrate to England until 1743, the year of Augustine's death. It is even possible that the departure of this affluent, powerful relative augmented a sense of paternal abandonment on George Washington's part.

Another correction by Washington is suggestive. When Humphreys notes that the preparation of Washington for a career in the navy was a "design of his father," Washington corrects him with, "It was rather the wish of my eldest brother." It may not be stretching a point to suggest that this observation is unfavorable to his half brother Lawrence. At the time George was about to join the navy, the worldly Joseph Ball warned George's mother that if he did so, he would be treated little better than a "Negro," lacking as he did any influence or connections that would give him preferment. In the event, Humphreys adds, it was by his mother's "earnest entreaties" as well as "tears" that her son was led to desist from boarding the ship to which his baggage had already been dispatched.[29] As Washington later became the foremost figure in his country largely by dint of his military leadership, his correction of Humphreys may imply that George had received bad advice from his half brother. Had it been followed, it would have landed him at sea in the Royal Navy instead of commander of his own country's forces.[30] In this light the intervention by his mother seems less ill placed than some have considered it.

In like manner, when Washington had joined Braddock's army over his mother's objections, his reassurances to her that he was treated as one of the family imply that his mother's worries on this score were as much that he might be socially denigrated and bereft of protection as for the more self-interested concerns that have sometimes been attributed to her. These are, indeed, the very concerns that Joseph Ball urged on Mary Washington to cause her to prevent George from joining the British navy.

That this description to Humphreys of his mother's role in "retrieving" him from the navy is meant to be one of timely rescue rather than unwelcome interference is confirmed by the fact that in later years Washington publicly described Mary Ball Washington as the "revered Mother by whose Maternal hand (early deprived of a Father) I was led to Manhood." In the final version this phrase has been changed by Washington himself from "led from Childhood" to the published official version. Thus did the first American president credit his mother with guiding him through the age during which he made the choice of a career.[31]

In addition to the financial and educational disadvantages George Washington saw as imposed upon him by the too-early death of his father, the sense of a moral handicap is revealed by Humphreys' text. By being kept at home instead of sent to England, the youthful Washington was exposed to temptation in Virginia. Humphreys explains, perhaps echoing his subject's words, that most of the "opulent class" who were brought up at home were in danger of becoming

indolent and helpless from the usual indulgence of giving a horse and a servant to attend them as soon as they could ride, if not imperious and dissipated from the habit of commanding slaves and living in a measure without control.[32]

Prominent among the temptations to which the young slave master felt himself exposed was that of sloth. As recent scholarship has elaborated, the ambitious planter's son had constantly to struggle against the opportunities for laziness presented by his situation. A man was "expected to be sober, courageous and hardworking . . . [but] received advice that subtly stressed his unique opportunities for self-ruin . . . idleness . . . extravagance and dissipation."[33]

Humphreys, a New Englander, may be paraphrasing his southern informant when he generalizes: "Those Virginians educated in a domestic manner who had fortitude enough to resist the temptations to which they were exposed in their youth have commonly been distinguished by success in their various professions." Washington's behavior, in the light of this characterization of his milieu, is a clue to possible early struggles against such temptations. For example, Washington's lifelong, zealous, and systematic efforts to account for the way he spent his time, money, and other resources may well have been enhanced by his awareness of the temptation to do otherwise. That they were, indeed, in part such a defense against slothful impulses is suggested by his occasional lapses in the struggle.[34]

The excessive temptation to which he was exposed, the acuteness of his conflict in resisting it, and the significance of his triumph over it (as well, perhaps, as the excusability of sometimes succumbing to it)—George Washington here has Humphreys attribute these, in effect, to his position in the family that denied him the advantages of his elder half brothers.

What seems to be significant about this evidence is that Washington felt a sense of grievance—of having been deprived of his "birthright." Such a dynamic pattern of loss and resentment, combined with the pressures of an ambitious mother who may have felt herself similarly disadvantaged and deserted, could have stimulated the aspirations of this second-team captain and concentrated his energies on achievements that would redress the balance. George Washington's ability to focus on the goals he set himself with a single-mindedness that excluded all diversion was a characteristic that began to be noted by many witnesses early in his career as a military leader.

How did such a pattern translate into the political legacy of George Washington, the creative leader? First, I approach the conversion of the enthusiastic, ambitious servant of the British king into the ardent revolutionary.

From the beginning, Washington's experience in the army under British rule seemed to recapitulate earlier familial experience. He was to find that as an officer in the Virginia military contingent he and his cohorts would, by law, be systematically subordinated to their British counterparts. Moreover, they were to be paid far less at comparable ranks. This was the initial and compelling spur to his entry into the arena of political action. In letters to Governor Dinwiddie, the 22-year-old Washington described this discrimination as "ignoble," a

cancer that will grate some officers of this regiment beyond all measure to serve upon such different terms when their lives, their fortunes and their characters are equally, and I dare say as effectually, exposed as those who are happy enough to have King's Commissions.[35]

The reiteration of royal orders that confirmed this preference continually disappointed Washington's hopes that his military superiors would rectify the injustice.

That the king seemed to the young officer to repeat the part that his own father had played is conveyed by a letter Washington wrote to a friendly British officer:

I hope Captn McKay will have more sense than to insist upon any unreasonable distinction, though he and His [officers] have commissions from His Majesty. Let him consider that, though we are greatly inferior in respect to profitable advantages, yet we have the same Spirit to serve our Gracious King as they have.[36]

To his seniors Washington emphasized the positive: the loyalty of the colonial officers to their Crown. But years later, to David Humphreys, he spoke plainly of his outrage at the discrimination against him and his colleagues: "Advice was received. . . . [that] no officer who did not . . . derive his Commission from the King could command one who did—This was too degrading for George Washington to submit to; accordingly, he resigned his Military employment."[37]

It is hard to recognize in the importunate, youthful officer the later revolutionary commander who would studiously defer to the civilian leadership of Congress. Time after time young Washington would make demands upon royally appointed father figures with disillusioning results. First, Governor Dinwiddie of Virginia, whose early fatherly relationship to George was acknowledged by both, lost Washington's confidence and respect. Then Governor Shirley of Massachusetts, whom George had originally called a "fine gentleman and great politician" with "more enthusiasm than he ever had shown for a public official," proved disappointing to his ambitions.[38]

His hopes were again aroused by a new commander sent from Britain, whom he assured that if Braddock had survived, "I should have met with preferment equal to my wishes"—but he had not survived. "General Shirley was not unkind in His Promises," Washington admitted, "but—he is gone to England."[39] The deaths and absences of his patrons, like those of his father, resulted in an unfair share of recognition and recompense for their deserving young officer and his military brothers—his "family," as he always would call them.

Seeking further to understand the conversion of the British king's loyal young servant into a still more ardent champion of the revolutionary cause, we may follow Washington as he reentered public life in 1774. By that year it was the American colonial nation that was experiencing a "denial of its inherited rights, surrender of which, without a struggle, was unworthy of self-respecting men."[40] More nationalist in sentiment than any other Virginian, quicker than most revolutionists to talk of "America" as a unity, he had manifestly expanded his feelings of solidarity with his military brothers to the cause of winning the birthright of a far more extended family.[41]

In later years, he would often describe the new nation that he had helped create in terms that evoked the family he had experienced in early years. As he bemoaned the disorder under the Articles of Confederation, he depicted the situation in which he and his brothers found themselves "early deprived of a father." He fears that his newly fatherless country will, "like a young heir, come a little prematurely to a large inheritance . . . wanton and run riot until we have brought our reputation to the brink of ruin."[42] This may express an apprehension he had once had in observing his more prosperous older half brothers. He could have seen, too, in the rebelliousness of his fellow Americans passionate tendencies that he felt in himself and that he had suppressed with great effort.

But by then he had put aside expectations of finding a benevolent and powerful leader who would sternly render justice and rectify the wrongs of the past. The almost miraculous luck that had allowed his country to emerge victorious from its Revolution had persuaded him that the hand of Providence had repeatedly intervened on its behalf, just as he thought Providence had brought him, personally, safely through his earlier military travails. The war for independence of the new nation that he had helped to conceive and to bring into being had been validated by success. Now the former commander of the B-Team, already widely depicted as the Father of His Country, was ready to assume its leadership himself.

NOTES

1. F.-R. Chateaubriand, *Oeuvres complètes*, 6 (Paris: Garnier, 1861), 55–56.

2. Henry Adams, *The Education of Henry Adams* (New York: Random House, 1999), ch. 3.

3. Some of the literature on "transformational" or "creative" political leadership is reviewed in Betty Glad, "Passing the Baton: Transformational Political Leadership from Gorbachev to Yeltsin; from de Klerk to Mandela," *Political Psychology* 17 (1996), 1–28.

4. David H. Donald, *Lincoln* (New York: Simon & Schuster, 1996), 14f., 514.

5. Gouverneur Morris to John Marshall, June 26, 1807, in Herbert A. Johnson, ed., *The Papers of John Marshall*, 8 vols. (Chapel Hill: University of North Carolina Press, 1974–), 5:174.

6. Joseph J. Ellis, *American Sphinx: The Character of Thomas Jefferson* (New York: Knopf, 1997), Erik H. Erikson, *Dimensions of a New Identity: The 1973 Jefferson Lectures in the Humanities* (New York: W. W. Norton, 1974). For a review of psychological studies of Jefferson see Elizabeth W. Marvick, "Thomas Jefferson's Personality and His Politics," *Psychohistory Review* 25 (1997), 125–164.

7. John Marshall, *The Life of George Washington* (Philadelphia: Crissy & Markley, 1850 [1804–1807]), 2:447.

8. John C. Fitzpatrick, ed., *The Writings of George Washington*, 39 vols. (Wash-

ington, DC: U.S. Government Printing Office, 1931–1944); Douglas S. Freeman et al., *George Washington*, 7 vols. (New York: Scribner's, 1948–1957), 1:passim; Bernhard Knollenberg, *Washington and the Revolution: A Reappraisal* (New York: Macmillan, 1940), 30–77; Marvin Kitman, *George Washington's Expense Account* (New York: Ballantine, 1976 [1970]).

9. W.W. Abbot, Dorothy Twohig et al., eds., *The Papers of George Washington* (Charlottesville: University Press of Virginia, 1983–).

10. Geoffrey Gorer, *The Danger of Equality* (New York: Weybright & Talley, 1966), 249.

11. Rosemarie Zagarri, ed., *David Humphreys' "Life of General Washington" with George Washington's "Remarks"* (Athens: University of Georgia Press, 1991), 37–39. Held in three separate collections and only recently integrally published, the manuscripts in question have, until now, been accessible only to a few readers.

12. Zagarri, *Life*, xlii.

13. George Washington to Sir Isaac Heard, May 2, 1792, in Fitzpatrick, *Writings*, 32:31–33.

14. Worthington C. Ford, ed., *Writings of George Washington* (New York: Putnam's, 1893), 14:372–373, 378–379.

15. Freeman et al., *George Washington*, 1:528.

16. Evidence exists that John Washington, George Washington's immigrant ancestor, was in Barbados as early as 1654, possibly as an agent for his cousin, Thomas Pargiter, who obtained a license to export goods there in 1653. Ford, *Writings*, 14:386–387.

17. Zagarri, *Life*, 5.

18. Dean K. Simonton. *Genius, Creativity and Leadership, Historiometric Inquiries* (Cambridge, MA: Harvard University Press, 1984).

19. Interestingly, Humphreys does mention that George Washington's father was descended from the elder of the two immigrant brothers. Zagarri, *Life*, 5.

20. George W. P. Custis, *Recollections and Private Memoirs of Washington* (New York: Derby & Jacson, 1860).

21. January 15, 1783. Fitzpatrick, *Writings*, 26:39–40.

22. Ford thinks "not a little remarkable" a curious mistake in George Washington's will. In one bequest he calls the younger son of a nephew Augustine, instead of Charles Augustine. Charles Augustine Washington was the grandson and namesake of Washington's youngest brother. The effect of the mistake in terms of George Washington's own sibling array was to give the name of the eldest to the youngest. Ford, *Writings*, 14:292.

23. Both Lawrence and Austin Washington had benefited from a rather distinguished English education, and Lawrence seems to have pursued advanced studies in England, probably in the law. He left the Appleby preparatory school in December 1632 and remained abroad until 1643. It seems likely that the study of law was one of his pursuits. See "From 'Transactions of the Cumberland & Westmoreland Antiquarian & Archeological Society,'" *Virginia Magazine of History and Biography* 11 (1903–1904), 215.

24. Zagarri, *Life*, 6.

25. Humphreys to GW, July 17, 1785; GW to Humphreys, July 25, 1785. *Papers*, Confederate Series 3.

26. Jonathan Boucher, ed., *Reminiscences of an American Loyalist, 1738–1789* (Boston: Houghton Mifflin, 1925), 49.

27. "As [for] . . . poor scotch school masters . . . I can have a ship load now from Glasgow, Aberdeen or St. Andrews for 20£ to teach 8 scholars." Phillip L. Lee to William Lee, July 20, 1773, Lee Family Papers, Virginia Historical Society.

28. GW To Tobias Lear, November 7, 1790, Fitzpatrick, *Writings*, 31:149.

29. I am at a loss to understand why Zagarri, Freeman, and others express disbelief in Washington's clear assertion to this effect.

30. This is not the only instance in which George Washington acted contrary to the example, if not the advice, of his older half brother. See Peter R. Henriques, "Major Lawrence Washington versus the Reverend Charles Green, a Case Study of the Squire and the Parson," *Virginia Magazine of Biography and History* 100 (1992), 233–245. In George Washington's corrections to Humphreys he downgrades Lawrence's status at the time of his military service in the British navy and accents his youth. Zagarri, *Life*, 8.

31. Fredericksburg, February 14, 1784. *Papers*, Confederation Series, 1:123–124.

32. Zagarri, *Life*, 6.

33. Steven M. Stowe, *Intimacy & Power in the Old South: Ritual in the Lives of the Planters* (Baltimore: Johns Hopkins University Press, 1987), 131.

34. Freeman, for example, remarks that Washington's "bookkeeping never had been as good as it should have been . . . never as informative as he thought it was . . . Often there was confusion." *George Washington*, 3:244–245.

35. GW to Dinwiddie, May 18, June 10, 1754, *Papers*, Colonial Series 1:99, 130.

36. GW to McKay, June 10, 1754, ibid., 129f.

37. Zagarri, *Life*, 14.

38. Freeman, *George Washington*, 2:23.

39. GW to Lord Loudoun, January 10, 1757, ibid., 4:89.

40. Douglas S. Freeman, *Washington* (New York: Scribner's, 1968), 513.

41. For example, "The better genius of America has prevailed." G. W. to Philip Schuyler, July 1775, *Washington*, Freeman, 3:502.

42. GW to Benjamin Harrison, January 18, 1784, *Papers*, Confederation Series 1: 54–56.

Part II

Presidential Powers and the Washington Administration

Chapter 4

Washington, Hamilton, and the Establishment of the Dignified and Efficient Presidency

MALCOLM L. CROSS

INTRODUCTION

"I walk on untrodden ground," George Washington once said after becoming the first president of the United States. "There is scarcely any part of my conduct which may not hereafter be drawn into precedent."[1]

Washington knew that the vagueness and brevity of Article II of the Constitution, which created the American presidency, gave him considerable freedom to interpret his powers and responsibilities as he saw fit. But he also knew that how he discharged his duties would set precedents for future presidents to follow and standards by which they would be judged. "Many things which appear of little importance in themselves and at the beginning," he said, "may have great and durable consequences from their having been established at the commencement of a new general government."[2]

This chapter discusses a major precedent that George Washington established: that the president should be both the nation's chief of state and its government's active chief executive as well.

The chief of state functions as the nation's ceremonial leader and as the symbol of its customs, values, and traditions. The chief executive staffs and supervises the executive branch of government.[3]

The distinction between the two roles reflects a dichotomy in governmental institutions discussed by Walter Bagehot in his analysis of the English Constitution. Bagehot divided the institutions of government into two categories: the dignified and the efficient. The dignified institutions were "those which excite and preserve the reverence of the population."[4] By inspiring the population's loyalty to the government, they give the government "its motive force."[5] The government's efficient institutions were "those by which it, in fact, works and rules" with the power won by the dignified institutions.[6] Studying the government of England, Bagehot said the monarchy and the House of Lords were its dignified institutions, while the cabinet and the House of Commons were the efficient institutions. The people's loyalty to the monarchy and the House of Lords led them to accept the authority of the cabinet and the House of Commons.[7]

In Bagehot's terms, Washington wanted to make the American presidency both dignified and efficient. Washington wanted the president to be the chief of state who would inspire Americans' loyalty to their nation and their government, but he also wanted the president to use the loyalty he inspired to more effectively administer the executive branch as chief executive.

That the president should fill both roles may be taken for granted today. The public's mourning of the deaths of its presidents and its disgust with Watergate reflect its acceptance of the president as its chief of state. In the twentieth century, the Congress has created, or has permitted the president to create by executive order, the Executive Office, the White House Staff, the Office of Management and Budget, the Office of Personnel Management, the Senior Executive Service, and other offices and agencies whose incumbents help the president discharge his duties as America's chief executive.[8]

But the combination of these two roles in one office did not follow inexorably from the Constitution. The Constitution made no mention of the role of chief of state, and although Article II said that "the executive power shall be vested in a president of the United States,"[9] it said little about how he was to wield that power. For example, it said that the president could nominate executive department heads with the advice and consent of the Senate, but he could not appoint them on his own. The Constitution also said he could solicit written reports on their work, but it said nothing about whether he could actually supervise their work or dismiss them from office.[10] Washington knew that he, either alone or in conjunction with Congress, would have to fill in the gaps left by the Framers of the Constitution and that his decisions would shape the evolution of the American presidency for years to come.

Washington chose to interpret the Constitution as mandating both ceremonial leadership and administrative activism from the president, but given its ambiguities and omissions, he could have chosen differently. Indeed, his closest adviser, Alexander Hamilton, may have wanted him to do so. As Washington's first Secretary of the Treasury, Hamilton loyally accepted his leadership. But Hamilton frequently wrote and acted as if he wanted Washington to be the ceremonial chief of state while real executive leadership was exercised by his department heads functioning independently of him but coordinated by Hamilton as his de facto prime minister. The prevalence of Washington's belief in an activist presidency over Hamilton's belief in a passive presidency determined the pattern of evolution both for the American presidency and for the government of which it is a part.

To elaborate on this theme, this chapter compares and contrasts Hamilton's ideas on the presidency and the organization of executive power with Washington's and discusses the significance, for the success of the presidency and the new government created by the Constitution, of the triumph of Washington's views.

HAMILTON AND MINISTERIALISM

Despite their different views on the organization of executive power, Washington and Hamilton agreed on other important issues. They were both nationalists who regarded the United States under the Articles of Confederation with dismay and who favored the establishment of a stronger national government under which the new nation would achieve the greatness of which it was capable. In temporary retirement following the American Revolution, Washington said:

We have probably had too good an opinion of human nature in forming our confederation. Experience has taught us that men will not adopt and carry into execution measures best calculated for their own good, without the intervention of a coercive power. I do not conceive we can exist long as a nation without having lodged somewhere a power which will pervade the whole Union.[11]

Elsewhere, Washington elaborated on what sort of "coercive power" he had in mind and what benefits would accrue with its establishment. Describing the United States as "[t]hirteen sovereignties pulling against each other and all tugging at the federal head," he predicted that this

[w]ill soon bring ruin on the whole, whereas a liberal and energetic constitution, well guarded and closely watched to prevent encroachments might restore us to that degree of respectability and consequences to which we had a fair claim and the brightest prospect of attaining.[12]

Hamilton, likewise, believed:

There is something . . . diminutive and contemptible in the prospect of a number of petty states, with the appearance only of union, jarring, jealous and perverse, without any determined direction, fluctuating and unhappy at home, weak and insignificant by their dissensions in the eyes of other nations.[13]

He thought states should be mere subdivisions of the nation, administered by nationally appointed executives with the power to veto bills passed by state legislatures.[14]

Washington and Hamilton also believed that effective government re-

quired effective administration. Observing the apparent incompetence of administrators under the Articles of Confederation, Washington said:

The stupor, or listlessness with which our public measures seem to be pervaded is,
to me, [a] matter of deep regret. Indeed it has so strange an appearance that I cannot
but wonder how men who solicit public confidence or who are even prevailed upon
to accept of it can reconcile such conduct with their own feelings of propriety.
    The delay is inauspicious to say the best of it, and the World must condemn it.[15]

After he became president, Washington added: "I consider the successful
Administration of the general Government as an object of almost infinite
consequence to the present and future happiness of the Citizens of the
United States."[16]
    Hamilton agreed: In *The Federalist*, he wrote:

Energy in the executive is a leading character in the definition of good government.
It is essential to the protection of the community against foreign attacks; it is not
less essential to the steady administration of the laws; to the protection of property
against those irregular and high-handed combinations which sometimes interrupt the
ordinary course of justice; to the security of liberty against the enterprises and assaults
of the ambitious, of factions, and anarchy . . .
    . . . A feeble executive implies a feeble execution of government. A feeble execution
is but another plan for a bad execution, and a government ill executed, whatever else
it may be in theory, must be, in practice, a bad government.[17]

But who was to actually exercise presidential power? Department heads?
The president himself? Both? On this issue the views of Washington and
Hamilton diverged.
    Hamilton's words and deeds seem to indicate, on balance, his belief in
ministerialism—government in which executive leadership was to be exercised by department heads acting in the name of a chief of state but with
considerable independence and initiative and coordinated by himself as de
facto prime minister.[18] His beliefs reflected his admiration for Jacques
Necker, the French finance minister during the American Revolution whose
memoirs Hamilton studied and whom Hamilton may have adopted as a role
model.[19]
    A ministerial regime, as Hamilton conceived it, would have had similarities
to modern parliamentary regimes, which are two-headed and have fusion,
rather than separation, of powers. In the modern parliamentary system, the
chief of state may be a monarch or an elected president, but he or she acts
as the ceremonial leader and symbol of national unity, with little or no role
to play in day-to-day politics or governing. The true chief of government—
the prime minister, premier, or chancellor—is the leader of the majority
party or coalition of parties in the legislature, with a cabinet consisting of
other lawmakers who also head executive departments.[20]

Hamilton did not necessarily believe in all features of modern parliamentary government. He apparently accepted the constitutionally established principle that executive department heads could not simultaneously serve in the Congress. But he also advocated that department heads be answerable to Congress but function independently of the president, who, in turn, would function only as the chief of state, but not the chief executive.

As early as 1780, Hamilton had expressed his belief in the benefits of strong department heads when he wrote in opposition to Congress' plan to create a Treasury Board to supervise the country's finances. Hamilton argued:

A single man, in each department of the administration, would be greatly preferable. It would give us a chance of more knowledge, more activity, more responsibility, and, of course, more zeal and attention. . . . [Boards'] decisions are slower, their energy less, their responsibility more diffused. They will not have the same abilities and knowledge as an administration by single men. Men of the first pretensions will not so readily engage in them; because they will be less conspicuous, of less importance, have less opportunity of distinguishing themselves. The members of Boards will take less pains to inform themselves and arrive to eminence, because they have fewer motives to do it. All these reasons conspire to give a preference to the plan of vesting the great executive departments of the [United States] in the hands of individuals.[21]

It must be noted, however, that Hamilton did not consistently advocate ministerialism under all circumstances. At the Constitutional Convention of 1787 Hamilton advocated an executive branch dominated not by powerful department heads but by a single, powerful president. Hamilton said, according to Madison's paraphrasing, "that the British Govt. was the best in the world" because it was "the only Govt. in the world 'which unites public strength with individual security.' "[22] He proposed the creation of an American presidency based on the British monarchy and possessing the various powers he and the other delegates to the convention thought the British king exercised.[23]

Hamilton's affinity for British government, while extreme to some extent, nonetheless reflected the desire of most of the delegates to model America's Constitution on what they perceived to be Great Britain's. The delegates accepted Montesquieu's interpretation that the British Constitution was based on separation of powers, with the monarchy, Parliament, and courts exercising, respectively, the executive, legislative, and judicial powers.[24] In doing so, Hamilton and his colleagues failed to note a trend in the evolution of British government described by McDonald: during the reigns of English kings George I and George II (1714–1760)

[t]hose functions that had to do with the exercise of power—defending the nation against alien enemies, enforcing domestic order and justice, and formulating and

implementing governmental policy—became the province of the ministry, which was composed of members of Parliament and headed by the Chancellor of the Exchequer. The ritualistic and ceremonial functions remained the province of the Crown. Removed from the actual work of government, the English Crown became the symbol of the nation—its mystical embodiment—as such the object of reverence, awe, veneration, even love.[25]

Nonetheless, Hamilton proposed a presidency modeled after the monarchy as he and the other delegates understood it to be, that is, the chief executive office in a government based on separation of powers, not as it was becoming, that is, the office of chief of state in a parliamentary system. With respect to the president's executive power, Hamilton further proposed that he would also have the sole power to appoint "the principal or Chief officer of each of the departments of War, Naval Affairs, Finance, and Foreign Affairs," and he could nominate, subject to the consent of the Senate, other officials, too.[26]

In *The Federalist*, using hypothetical terms, Hamilton explained some of the features of a presidency whose incumbent would be a single person with the power to hire department heads. He wrote:

That unity is conducive to energy will not be disputed. Decision, activity, secrecy, and dispatch will generally characterize the proceedings of one man in a much more eminent degree than the proceedings of any greater number; and in proportion as the number is increased, these qualities will be diminished.[27]

On the relationship between the chief executive and his department heads, Hamilton added:

The actual conduct of foreign negotiations, the preparatory plans of finance, the application and disbursement of the public moneys in conformity to the general appropriations of the legislature, the arrangement of the army and navy, the direction of the operations of war—these, and other matters of a like nature, constitute what seems to be most properly understood by the administration of government. The persons, therefore, to whose immediate management these different matters are committed ought to be considered as the assistants or deputies of the Chief Magistrate, and on this account they ought to derive their offices from his appointment, at least his nomination, and ought to be subject to his superintendence.[28]

Whether Hamilton's remarks at the convention or in *The Federalist* represented an actual, if temporary, rejection of ministerialism is debatable. Hamilton's belief in a government headed by a powerful chief executive with the sole power to appoint department heads did not necessarily contradict his earlier belief in a government dominated by strong department heads. It is perfectly possible that Hamilton wanted an executive branch in which the chief executive had the power to appoint his department heads and direct their work, while they, in turn, had the power to effectively advise the chief executive while equally effectively carrying out his orders. Such a system would have a major characteristic of ministerialism—strong department heads, although their powers would still be overshadowed by the power of the president.

But Hamilton believed that the power the president had over his department heads should be based on the length of time the president could actually serve in office, and the Constitution's provisions on presidential power apparently revived Hamilton's belief in ministerialism, if, in fact, he had temporarily abandoned it at all. At the convention, Hamilton said that the president, once elected, should serve for life, that is, "during good behavior, removable only by conviction upon an impeachment for some crime or misdemeanor."[29] He explained that if the president began his duties with a guarantee of lifetime tenure, he would "be a safer depository for power,"[30] since he would be less likely to use those powers to promote corruption or intrigue to stay in office. He expressed the possibility that a president with a limited term who wanted to prolong it might exploit a war or emergency to unconstitutionally refuse to leave office when his term expired. He concluded that the shorter the term a president had, the less power he should be given. If, for example, the term of office for the president was seven years, then he "ought to have but little power."[31]

Despite Hamilton's arguments, his colleagues refused to guarantee lifetime tenure for the president. They decided, rather, to limit him to four-year terms.[32] In theory, a president could still serve for life, but only if he won re-election every four years, which was by no means guaranteed. Therefore, Hamilton concluded, the president's power, especially over his department heads, had to be significantly reduced in order to prevent presidential abuse of his power in an effort to win re-election and also to promote an additional concern: administrative stability in the absence of stability in the presidential office itself.

Hamilton believed there to be an "intimate connection between the duration of the executive magistrate in office and the stability of the system of administration."[33] The problem with allowing the president only a short term, said Hamilton, is that it could lead to too much turnover in the presidency, and the problem with too much turnover was that each incoming president might be too eager to reverse his predecessor's policies, however sound those policies might be:

To reverse and undo what has been done by a predecessor is very often considered by a successor as the best proof he can give of his own capacity . . . and in addition to this propensity, where the alteration has been the result of public choice, the person substituted [i.e., the incoming president] is warranted in supposing that the dismission of his predecessor has proceeded from a dislike to his measures; and that the less he resembles him, the more he will recommend himself to the favor of his constituents.[34]

The danger of this, said Hamilton, is that

These considerations, and the influence of personal confidences and attachments, would be likely to induce every new President to promote a change of men to fill the subordinate stations; and these causes together could not fail to occasion a disgraceful and ruinous mutability in the administration of the government.[35]

The solution to the problem lay not in a particular clause in the Constitution but on a point on which the Constitution was silent: the circumstances under which the president could dismiss another executive officer. Noting that the Constitution allowed the president not to appoint officials (as Hamilton had initially wanted) but only to nominate them with the advice and consent of the Senate, Hamilton said that the president could not remove an official without the Senate's approval either; that is, "the consent of that body would be necessary to displace as well as to appoint."[36] Hamilton explained that this "would contribute to the stability of the administration" by giving department heads the power to unite with the Senate to block a president's efforts to remove them.

A change of the Chief Magistrate, therefore, would not occasion so violent or so general a revolution in the officers of the government as might be expected if he were the sole disposer of offices. Where a man in any station had given satisfactory evidence of his fitness for it, a new President would be restrained from attempting a change in favor of a person more agreeable to him by the apprehension that a discountenance of the Senate might frustrate the attempt, and bring some degree of discredit upon himself. Those who can best estimate the value of a steady administration will be most disposed to prize a provision which connects the official existence of public men with the approbation or disapprobation of that body which from the greater permanency of its own composition, will in all probability be less subject to inconsistency than any other member of the government.[37]

Under this arrangement, department heads would have more independence from the president. The president himself, unable to hire or fire department heads without Senate consent, would have no effective means of directing or supervising their work. Therefore, he would be left with little to do other than serve as chief of state—a ceremonial leader and symbol of national unity but one without real executive power, in spite of the Constitution's statement that "executive power shall be vested in a President of the United States." Thus, Hamilton, who at the convention proposed a presidency stronger than his colleagues were willing to create, eventually advocated a presidency far weaker than his colleagues actually did create.

WASHINGTON AND THE STRENGTHENING OF THE PRESIDENCY

"With me," George Washington once said, "it has always been a maxim, rather to let my designs appear from my works than by my expressions."[38]

In saying so, Washington may have underestimated both the quantity of his writings and the value they have for students of his efforts to make the presidency both a ceremonial and an administrative office.

Yet Washington's statement nonetheless hinted at both a problem and its solution. The problem is that while Washington may have written more than he thought, he did not write as much as Hamilton did on his concept of the presidency; hence, it is more difficult to determine what Washington thought about it. The solution is to infer his thoughts from his actions, on the assumption that the latter accurately reflect the former, as Washington implied they would.

The significance George Washington attached to a strong executive branch within a strong central government as a means of promoting nationalism has already been discussed. At the Constitutional Convention of 1787 and as the first president of the United States, he continued to show, through word and deed, his determination to make the presidency both an office of administrative activism and a symbol of national unity.

At the convention Washington, as its president, spoke little, but he nonetheless voted for measures to create a strong presidency, albeit not one as strong as what Hamilton proposed. For example, the convention had seriously considered plans either to make the presidency a three-member committee with each member having the right to veto the actions of the others or to divide executive power between a president and an executive council. But Washington, apparently sharing Hamilton's view that "energy in the executive" required "unity in the executive," voted to make the president a single person. To strengthen the presidency further, Washington also voted against congressional election of the president and voted to raise the proportion of senators and representatives required to override the president's veto of proposed legislation from two-thirds to three-fourths.[39]

Washington's efforts to strengthen the presidency continued once he took office as first president of the United States under the new Constitution, and herein lies the fundamental difference between Hamilton's approach to the presidency and Washington's: Hamilton, having failed to create a presidency as strong as he wanted, therefore wanted to weaken the presidency even further, as his desire to prevent the president from unilaterally removing department heads apparently showed. Washington, taking the presidency actually created, worked to strengthen its powers as much as he thought the Constitution allowed.

To that end Washington strove to make the presidency "respectable," that is, to vest the president with a suitable title and surround the presidency with pomp and ceremony that would command the deference of not only Americans but foreigners as well. For example, Washington apparently seriously considered accepting the recommendation of the Senate that his title be "His Highness, the President of the United States of America, and Protector of Their Liberties," although in the end he accepted the more simple (and perhaps therefore more dignified) title of "President of the United States."[40]

Washington also sought luxurious living quarters for himself and his wife in America's temporary capitals of New York City and Philadelphia, which he staffed with servants and slaves in livery and where he lavishly entertained. He rode white horses adorned with saddle clothes of gold bunting and used them to draw his carriage.[41] Although Washington claimed to personally dislike "the glare which hovers around the external trappings of the elevated office," except for the "luster which may be reflected from its connection with a power promoting human felicity,"[42] he nonetheless sincerely believed that "if he behaved like an ordinary citizen he would damage the prestige needed to carry out the Presidential office."[43]

One of the most widely reported examples of Washington's efforts to enhance the prestige of the presidency occurred in Boston in the fall of 1789 while Washington was making the first of his tours throughout the country, ostensibly to learn more about the issues confronting the United States at the onset of his administration. In Boston he received an invitation to dine with Massachusetts governor John Hancock. He initially accepted Hancock's invitation, assuming Hancock would first call on him. But when Hancock sent word that he was too ill to visit Washington, Washington replied that he would not visit Hancock until Hancock first visited him. Hancock's health thereupon suddenly improved to the point where he could visit Washington in the latter's lodgings. Thus, Washington established the social priority of the nation's president over the state's governor.[44]

But while making the presidency "respectable" or dignified, Washington also sought to make it more efficient or powerful as an instrument for governance. One way Washington acted to strengthen the presidency was to support and sign legislation that rejected Hamilton's views on the president's powers to dismiss department heads. When the Congress created by the new Constitution first met in 1789, one of its first duties was to create new executive departments for the new government. In doing so it had to make what is known to history as the "Decision of 1789," that is, it had to determine how, when, and even if the president could dismiss their heads.

The issue provoked considerable debate. Many members of Congress, echoing Hamilton's concern with administrative stability, united with those who feared the president could become too tyrannical if he had the sole power to remove department heads. Typical of their views were those expressed by Theodorick Bland of Virginia, who combined fear of administrative instability with fear of executive tyranny to argue:

A new President might, by turning out the great officers, bring about a change of the ministry, and throw the affairs of the union into disorder; would not this, in fact, make the President a monarch, and give him absolute power over all the great departments of Government?[45]

Bland's fellow Virginian John Page, offering an interpretation of the consequences of "energy in the executive" that differed markedly from the conclusions of Washington and initially Hamilton, said:

The doctrine of energy in Government . . . is the true doctrine of tyrants. . . . Energy of Government may be the destruction of liberty; it should not, therefore, be too much cherished in a free country. A spirit of independence should be cultivated. . . .
The liberty and security of our fellow-citizens is our great object, and not the prompt execution of the laws. Indecision, delay, blunders, nay, villainous actions in the administration of Government, are trifles compared to legalizing the full exertion of a tyrannical despotism.[46]

But James Madison, rejecting his fellow Virginians' arguments, emphasized the necessity to be able to hold the president responsible for the conduct of his subordinates and stressed that giving him the sole power to fire them if necessary was the most effective way to do so: if the Senate shared the removal power with the president, the president could not fairly be held responsible for the conduct of executive officers. But

if the heads of the Executive departments are subjected to removal by the President alone, we have in him security for [their] good behavior. . . . If [a department head] does not conform to the judgment of the President in doing the executive duties of his office, he can be displaced. This makes him responsible to the great Executive power, and makes the President responsible to the public for the conduct of the person he has nominated and appointed to aid him in the administration of his department.[47]

Washington himself thought he should have the power to unilaterally dismiss department heads.[48] Although he apparently played no overt role in the debate, he, nonetheless, signed the legislation giving himself and subsequent presidents that power. Indeed, it is reasonable to assume that the fact that he was president made it easier for Congress to assign the president that power in the first place. Washington thereby helped "firmly anchor" the administrative system to the president, not the Senate, and thus helped make the president the chief executive in fact as well as in name.[49]

Washington's support of the Decision of 1789 reflected his basic attitude toward the departments created by the Congress, their heads, and his own administrative responsibilities. He assumed as a matter of course that he himself was responsible for the functioning of the executive branch of the government and that the Congress had created the departments and department heads to assist him, not to function independently of him:

The impossibility that one man should be able to perform all the great business of the State, I take to have been the reason for instituting the great Departments, and appointing officers therein, to assist the supreme Magistrate to discharging the duties of his trust.[50]

Having helped attain legal authority over his subordinates, Washington proceeded to exercise practical authority as well, by instructing his subordinates on how to perform their work and by actively supervising them to determine that they were conforming to his mandates.

White has collected numerous examples of Washington's instructions to his subordinates, from which one can infer his approach to administration. For example, Washington wrote: "System to all things is the soul of business. To deliberate maturely, and execute promptly is the way to conduct it to advantage."[51]

"To deliberate maturely" could be done only "upon the ground of well authenticated facts," rather than mere theories or opinions. Only on the basis of facts could one determine whether a conclusion "will be *right* or *wrong*, according to the actual state of things."[52]

To execute promptly, one could:

not . . . put things off until the Morrow which can be done, and require to be done today. Without an adherence to these details business never will be *well* done, or done in an easy manner; but will always be in arrears, with one thing treading upon the heals of another.[53]

Thomas Jefferson, Washington's first Secretary of State, in a lengthy passage quoted by White, recalled how Washington matched his words with deeds, actively supervising his department heads in the performance of their duties:

Letters of business came addressed sometimes to the President, but most frequently to the heads of departments. If addressed to himself, he referred them to the proper department to be acted on: If to one of the secretaries, the letter, if it required no answer, was communicated to the President, simply for his information. If an answer was requisite, the secretary of the department communicated the letter & his proposed answer to the President. Generally they were simply sent back after perusal, which signified his approbation. Sometimes he returned them with an informal note, suggesting an alteration or a query. If a doubt of any importance arose, he reserved it for conference. By this means, he was always in accurate possession of all facts and proceedings in every part of the Union, and to whatsoever department they related; he formed a central point for the different branches; preserved an unity of object and action among them; exercised that participation in the suggestion of affairs which his office made incumbent on him; and met himself the due responsibility for whatever was done.[54]

HAMILTON'S LAST EFFORT TO ESTABLISH MINISTERIALISM

Washington's efforts to establish administrative control did not prevent Alexander Hamilton from trying again to establish some semblance of ministerial government. Appointed by Washington to be America's first Secretary of the Treasury, Hamilton initially tried to use his department's central position in the government, as well as legally prescribed duties, organizational structure, and size, to act as Washington's de facto prime minister.

The exact role Hamilton played in creating the Treasury Department is unknown. Because he was not a member of Congress in 1789, he could not formally help draft or vote on the Treasury Department's organic act. But the act reflected Hamilton's belief in ministerialism and is assumed to have been written under his influence and in conformity to his will.[55] For example, the law placed at the head of the Treasury Department a single secretary. Congress thereby rejected the practice of financial administration by committee as practiced by the government under the Articles of Confederation and accepted Hamilton's demand, quoted earlier, that departments be headed by single individuals.[56]

The organic act directed the Secretary of the Treasury

[t]o digest and prepare plans for the improvement of the revenue, and for the support of the public credit; to prepare and report estimates of the public revenue, and the public expenditure; to make report and give information to either branch of the legislature, in person or in writing (as he may be required), respecting all matters referred to him by the Senate or House of Representatives, or which shall appertain to his office, and generally to perform all such services relative to the finances, as he shall be directed to perform.[57]

The act put the Treasury Secretary in a unique and potentially powerful position, especially in comparison to his fellow department heads, the Secretaries of State and War. The organic acts creating the State and War Departments had given the president the authority to appoint their secretaries subject to Senate confirmation, to supervise their work, and to dismiss them. But the Treasury Department's organic act made no mention of any presidential supervisory authority. As the excerpt shows, it spoke only of the supervisory authority of Congress.[58]

The act's intent may have been to make the Treasury Secretary the agent of Congress and thereby maintain congressional supremacy in public finance. But the practical effect of the act, consistent with Hamilton's belief in ministerialism, was to give the secretary the authority to communicate directly to Congress and not through the president. The Treasury Secretary could thereby exercise the dynamic leadership advocated by Hamilton's role model, Necker, or so Hamilton thought.

The potential for ministerial government was reinforced by the organizational structure and size of the Treasury Department as specified in the organic act. "Knowledge is power" may be a cliché, but a cliché based on truth. The more control over information one has, the more able one is to influence the decisions of others by shaping the information they acquire for decision making. The organization and size of the Treasury Department gave Alexander Hamilton access to better information and more of it than anyone else in government.[59]

In 1789 President Washington's staff consisted of one secretary.[60] An attorney general sat in the president's cabinet, but he was the president's legal adviser, not a department head: the Department of Justice would not be created until 1870.[61] The Secretary of War led America's 930-man army with only three clerks and a messenger. The Secretary of State's staff included a chief clerks, two additional clerks, an interpreter, and a messenger-doorkeeper, while the diplomatic corps abroad consisted of a minister, his clerk, and a consul-general in Paris, a chargé d'affaires in Madrid; and an agent at The Hague.[62]

The Treasury Department was the largest in terms of civilian personnel. The organic act provided for not only a secretary but an assistant secretary, a comptroller, a treasurer, an auditor, and a register. The secretary and his subordinate officers also had three chief clerks, 18 additional clerks, and a messenger. Hence, Hamilton, in effect, headed a staff of 27—a staff greater than those of the president and other department heads combined.[63]

Moreover, the Treasury Department, unlike the others, also had an extensive field service that strengthened to an even greater extent Hamilton's information resources while giving his department a central role in the affairs of the United States: the Treasury's tax collectors and postmasters—for the Post Office was initially run by the Treasury Department—were stationed throughout the country, bringing the Treasury Department into contact with every part of America. The cutters of the Treasury's Revenue Marine—the forerunner of today's Coast Guard and America's only maritime, uniformed service until the navy was revived in 1798—patrolled the seas, working with the Treasury's customs officers, stationed in America's ports, to enforce foreign trade regulations and hence promote American foreign economic policy. The Customs Service also worked with mercantile, fishing, and shipowning interests to regulate and develop their industries, while the Treasury's Bank of the United States brought it into contact with leading professional, business, and financial interests. The Treasury's purchasing agents supplied the army. By today's standards, the national government was small and detached, yet by the standards of eighteenth-century America, Alexander Hamilton's Treasury Department seemed to be everywhere and involved with everything.[64]

The Treasury Department's officers, staffs, and field service provided Alexander Hamilton with the human resources necessary to collect and analyze information for effective leadership through helping to shape the decisions of Congress. For example, Hamilton's records show that during the first year of his tenure as Secretary of the Treasury, he sent out over 40 circulars, or notices, to members of the Treasury's field service and other officials. Many circulars solicited information on money collected, the state of finances in different states, navigation conditions, shipbuilding shipping routes, and other matters relevant to commercial, industrial, and economic conditions throughout the country—information he used for his famous and congressionally mandated reports to Congress.

The reports themselves—on the public credit, on a national bank, on the Mint, and on manufacturing—are the most famous products of his information system. They are widely recognized for the research, the effort, the vision, and scope they show. Hamilton made them effective tools in his efforts to persuade Congress to adopt his policies.[65]

Hamilton's mastery of Congress is also reflected in the less dramatic, more obscure system of executive budgeting that his position allowed him to promote. Hamilton's office was pivotal. It was the channel through which information from and about the executive branch flowed to Congress, as well as the channel through which appropriations flowed from Congress to the executive branch.

The Congress was not organized to systematically review Hamilton's first budgets. The House of Representatives had created, on July 24, 1789, a Ways and Means Committee to supervise public finance. But Hamilton's supporters, who dominated both houses of the first Congress and who would form the nucleus of the Federalist Party, abolished the committee on September 17, 1789, just six days after Hamilton took office. With their leader as their fiscal agent, they saw no need for any oversight committee: a ways and means committee would only reduce Hamilton's efficiency. The disposition of the majority of both houses to accept Hamilton's recommendations, coupled with the inability of the minority Jeffersonian Republicans to challenge them, assured the acceptance of Hamilton's budgets with no significant changes and strengthened Hamilton's leadership role over Congress.[66]

Washington initially allowed Hamilton far more freedom of action than he allowed his other department heads, although not necessarily as much freedom as Hamilton may have wanted. Washington believed he knew enough about foreign and especially military policy to supervise the State and War Departments, but he did not think he knew enough about public finance to supervise Hamilton's efforts. Moreover, Washington thought that the special status the Treasury Department apparently attained through its organic act precluded him from supervising the formulation and transmittal of Hamilton's reports and budgets to Congress.[67]

However, Washington also drew a sharp distinction between the Treasury Department's financial planning functions and its other functions, such as collecting taxes, maintaining lighthouses, fighting smugglers, and running the Post Office. These he considered administrative rather than legislative matters, and on these issues he subjected Hamilton to the same supervision to which he subjected everyone else.[68]

Moreover, while Washington was eroding Hamilton's efforts at ministerialism through direct supervision, Congress was preparing to destroy Hamilton's ministerialism through revolt. Hamilton became a victim of his own early successes.

Hamilton's leadership on matters of budgeting and public finance pleased his Federalist followers in Congress. For example, Massachusetts Federalist Senator Theodore Sedgewick argued that, the Constitution notwithstanding, Hamilton should be allowed to draft all bills relevant to finance, since Congress was too disorganized, too inefficient, and too lacking in time to devote itself to the intricacies of public finance.[69]

But Hamilton's dominance and Congress' dependence on him for leadership only embittered his Jeffersonian Republican foes. Pennsylvania Republican Senator William Maclay, for example, commenting on the ease with which Hamilton could secure congressional assent to his proposals and those of his colleagues in the cabinet, complained that a "listlessness, or spirit of laziness pervaded the House of Representatives: "Anything which comes from a Secretary is adopted, almost without any examination."[70] In summary, Maclay said, "Nothing is done without him."[71] Georgia Republican Representative James Jackson, who sought to raise objections to a Hamilton-inspired appropriations bill, said:

According to the ideas of some gentlemen, the House had no right to add to the appropriations proposed by the Secretary. . . . According to this doctrine the whole business or legislation may as well be submitted to him, so in fact the House will not be the Representatives of their constituents, but of their Secretary.[72]

The bitterness of the Jeffersonian Republican came to a head on February 27, 1793, when Virginia Republican Representative William Giles, a longtime critic of the congressional practice of referring all financial matters to Hamilton, introduced the first of six resolutions demanding greater congressional scrutiny of the Treasury Department and charging Hamilton with violating appropriations laws. Hamilton was ultimately cleared of all charges brought by Giles. Yet he nonetheless had to endure almost two more years of abuse from the Republicans in Congress, who harassed him with incessant demands for more and more information, reports, and explanations. Hamilton finally concluded that growing opposition had made him too ineffective to be of further service. On December 1, 1794, he submitted his resignation. He left office on January 31, 1795.[73]

Hamilton's departure from Washington's cabinet ended his efforts to establish ministerialism as a means of organizing executive power in the government of the United States. But Washington himself still had more than two years of precedent-establishing service as president of the United States ahead of him.

CONCLUSION

The impact George Washington had on the evolution of the American presidency was definitive. That the president became both chief of state and chief executive—both dignified and efficient—was probably due more to the example he set than to any other factor, including the wording of Article II of the Constitution itself. Indeed, the Constitutional Convention might well have produced a different, weaker presidency had it not known that George Washington would be its first incumbent. The presidency might have become the three-member committee the convention considered, or it might have been hamstrung with an executive council. But it almost certainly would not have become the office of executive leadership that George Washington fashioned, if for no other reason than that the convention would not have supplied the office with the potential to become a position of leadership.

Thus, Washington shaped not only the evolution of the presidency but the evolution of the government of which it is a part and the country that government serves. Had the Constitutional Convention not been able to count on Washington's service, it might have created a government with a weaker executive branch and thus a government with nobody able to promote national unity.

But did Washington have to personally administer the executive branch of government? Could he not have allowed himself to be chief of state to Hamilton's de facto chief executive? Could a government based on Hamilton's ministerialism have been successful? Probably the best answers to these ultimately unanswerable questions are yes, no, and no.

It was noted earlier that Hamilton wanted to deprive the president of the power to dismiss department heads without the consent of the Senate. His goal was to strengthen the position of department heads at the expense of the president, allowing them to serve indefinite terms regardless of the president's wishes and thereby promote "stability in administration." But the arrangement Hamilton proposed would have seriously weakened the government itself. On the face of it, Hamilton's system would have eliminated the president as a source of executive leadership without substituting anyone else. Indeed, Hamilton's system would have resembled the organization of executive power under the Articles of Confederation, in which the executive department heads were elected by the Congress. The only difference is that under Hamilton's system they would be leading in the name of a chief of state, yet still not under his effective direction or that of anyone else.

Of course, Hamilton may well have expected that he himself, as Treasury

Secretary, could have emerged as the de facto prime minister and chief executive, even as the office of British prime minister was evolving from the Chancellorship of the Exchequer, Great Britain's functional equivalent to the Treasury Secretaryship.[74] How he discharged his duties under Washington seems to indicate as much. But even under Washington, Hamilton was unable to survive politically when so fiercely opposed by the Jeffersonian Republicans in Congress. Could he have done better without Washington?

Not only would Hamilton have failed to establish himself as prime minister, but the system itself might well have been doomed for at least two reasons, one structural and the other political.

The system Hamilton wanted could not have evolved into a modern parliamentary system because the Constitution explicitly prohibited department heads from serving in Congress. In theory, the Constitution could have been changed to allow senators or representatives to simultaneously serve in the cabinet, but such a change would have violated the principle of separation of powers, and hence would probably have attracted little support.

Moreover, Hamilton proposed to unite the cabinet with the Senate, not the House of Representatives, while in most modern parliamentary regimes, the prime minister and his or her ministers serve in the functional equivalent of our House of Representatives. But the Senate in the 1790s commanded far less prestige than it does today. It was smaller, elected indirectly by state legislatures, and more aristocratic and elitist than the larger, popularly elected, and therefore more prestigious House of Representatives.[75]

Thus, both Washington and Hamilton believed in a strong central government based on the effective organization of executive power. But Hamilton sought to create a system of government in which executive power would have been exercised by a group of appointed department heads with no official leader, united with an elitist institution in a newly democratic political system. Washington, however, wanted to create a system in which executive power would be exercised by a chief executive who would bring to his duties the prestige based on his role as chief of state as well. Because Hamilton's system was never really tried, it cannot be said definitively that it would have failed. Yet given the new nation's need for strong executive leadership, it was America's good fortune that Washington's approach prevailed.

NOTES

1. James Thomas Flexner, *Washington: The Indispensable Man* (New York: Signet, 1984), 219.

2. Leonard D. White, *The Federalists: A Study in Administrative History* (New York: Macmillan, 1956), 99.

3. Typical discussions of the distinction between the two roles can be found in Clinton Rossiter, *The American Presidency*, rev. ed. (New York: Mentor Books,

1960), 16–20; Richard M. Pious, *The Presidency* (Boston: Allyn and Bacon, 1996), 11–12.

4. Walter Bagehot, *The English Constitution*, with an introduction by the earl of Balfour (London: Oxford University Press, 1942), 4.

5. Ibid.

6. Ibid.

7. Ibid., 30–155.

8. Pious, *The Presidency*, 259–298; Louis W. Koenig, *The Chief Executive*, 6th ed. (Fort Worth: Harcourt Brace College, 1996), 187–191.

9. U.S. Constitution, art. II, sec. 1.

10. Ibid., sec. 2.

11. James Thomas Flexner. *George Washington and the New Nation (1783–1793)* (Boston: Little, Brown, 1969, 1970), 91.

12. Ibid., 101.

13. Clinton Rossiter, *1787: The Grand Convention* (New York: Macmillan, 1966), 45.

14. Hamilton included a provision for the appointment of state governors by the national government in his draft constitution, art. VIII, sec. 1, reprinted as Appendix F in Max Farrand, ed., *The Records of the Federal Convention of 1787*, rev. ed., vol. 3 (New Haven, CT: Yale University Press, 1937), 628. Hamilton does not precisely say who he thinks should have the power to appoint state governors, although given the extensive appointment powers he wanted to delegate to the president of the United States, it is reasonable to infer he intended the national president to have the power to appoint state governors. Hamilton's remarks, as paraphrased by James Madison, are in Farrand, 1:293.

15. White, *The Federalists*, 103.

16. Ibid.

17. Alexander Hamilton, James Madison, and John Jay, *The Federalist Papers*, with an introduction, table of contents, and index of ideas by Clinton Rossiter (New York: Mentor Books, 1961), 423.

18. Forrest McDonald, *Alexander Hamilton: A Biography* (New York: W. W. Norton, 1979), 125–126. Hamilton is also referred to as Washington's prime minister in Pious, *The Presidency*, 49–50.

19. McDonald, *Alexander Hamilton*, 84.

20. Mark N. Hagopian, *Regimes, Movements, and Ideologies: A Comparative Introduction to Political Science* (New York: Longman, 1978), 55–56.

21. White, *The Federalists*, 91.

22. Farrand, *Records*, 1:288.

23. Ibid., 292.

24. David Hutchison, *The Foundations of the Constitution*, with an introduction by Ferdinand Lundberg (Secaucus, NJ: University Books, 1975), 20–21.

25. Forrest McDonald, "A Mirror for Presidents," *Commentary* 62.6 (December 1976): 34–35; also, see Pious, *The Presidency*, 39–40.

26. The quotation is from Hamilton's draft constitution, art. V, sec. 10, in Farrand, *Records*, 3:625. Madison paraphrased his remarks in ibid., 1:292.

27. Hamilton, *Federalist Papers*, 422.

28. Ibid., 435–436.

29. The quotation is from Hamilton's draft constitution, art. IV, sec. 624, re-

printed in Farrand, *Records*, 4:624. Madison paraphrased Hamilton as saying, "Let the Executive also be for life," in ibid., 1:289.

30. Madison's paraphrasing of Hamilton, in Farrand, ibid., 1:290.

31. Ibid.

32. U.S. Constitution, art. II, sec. 1.

33. Hamilton, *Federalist Papers*, 436.

34. Ibid.

35. Ibid.

36. Ibid., 459.

37. Ibid.

38. White, *The Federalists*, 100.

39. Flexner, *George Washington and the New Nation*, 133.

40. Washington's preference for the first title was asserted in Max Farrand, *The Framing of the Constitution of the United States* (New Haven, CT: Yale University Press, 1913), 163. However, it should be noted that Farrand's statement is contradicted by Douglas Southall Freeman, *George Washington, Patriot and President*, vol. 6 in his biography of Washington (New York: Charles Scribner's Sons, 1954), 186. Freeman wrote that "Washington wished this discussion [of an appropriate title for the president] be dropped because he believed that exalted titles would arouse public resentment which opponents in the new government would seek to aggravate."

41. Washington's lifestyle is described in Flexner, *George Washington and the New Nation*, 192–209, and Freeman, *George Washington*, 226–243.

42. Freeman, *George Washington*, 252.

43. Flexner, *George Washington and the New Nation*, 418.

44. The incident is recounted in both ibid., 230–231, and Freeman, *George Washington*, 244–245. Both Flexner and Freeman report that Washington's stated purpose in making the trip was to acquire more knowledge and that Washington never said he wanted to act as a symbol of national unity, even if the promotion of national unity was one of his implicit goals. Forrest McDonald, in *The Presidency of George Washington* (New York: W. W. Norton, 1975), asserts, without mentioning this particular incident, that Washington was well aware of his importance as a symbol of national unity and wanted to exploit the hold he had over the hearts and minds of his fellow Americans to strengthen their allegiance to their new nation. See pages v, 25.

45. White, *The Federalists*, 21–22.

46. Ibid., 22.

47. Ibid., 23.

48. McDonald, *The Presidency of George Washington*, 39.

49. White, *The Federalists*, 25.

50. Ibid., 27.

51. Ibid., 102.

52. Ibid., 105.

53. Ibid., 104.

54. Ibid., 35.

55. Ibid., 118.

56. The organization of financial administration before the adoption of the Constitution is discussed in Merrill Jensen, *The New Nation: A History of the United States during the Confederation 1781–1789* (1950; reprint, Boston: Northeastern

University Press, 1981), 55–56, 366–374. Between 1781 and 1784, public financial management was the responsibility of financier Robert Morris, who replaced congressional committees and was subsequently replaced by a commission appointed by Congress.

57. 1 Stat. 65–67, in Ralph V. Harlow, *The History of Legislative Methods in the Period before 1825* (New Haven, CT: Yale University Press, 1917), 132.

58. Ibid., 130–133; White, *The Federalists*, 118–119.

59. The importance of controlling the flow of information is discussed in Charles Perrow, *Complex Organizations: A Critical Essay*, 2nd ed. (Glenview, IL: Scott, Foresman, 1979), 149–153. Perrow bases many of his ideas on James G. March and Herbert Simon, *Organizations* (New York: John Wiley & Sons, 1958), and Herbert A. Simon, *Administrative Behavior*, 2nd ed. (New York: Macmillan, 1957).

60. White, *The Federalists*, 495–496. White reports that by the end of his term, Washington had expanded his personal staff to three secretaries.

61. See ibid., 164–172, for a discussion of the role of the attorney general as Washington's part-time legal adviser. The date of the establishment of the Justice Department is reported in Robert Farmighetti, ed., *The World Almanac and Book of Facts 1995* (Mahwah, NJ: Funk & Wagnalls, 1994), 100.

62. The legally authorized positions in the State and War Departments are listed in Hamilton's first budget, printed in Harold C. Syrett and Jacob E. Cooke, eds., *The Papers of Alexander Hamilton*, vol. 5, June 1788–November 1789 (New York: Columbia University Press, 1962), 383–384, 389–390.

63. Ibid., 386–387.

64. The central position of the Treasury Department is discussed in White, *The Federalists*, 117.

65. Hamilton's circulars are printed in Syrett and Cooke's edition of *The Papers of Alexander Hamilton*. Circulars for his first year are in volumes 5 (June 1788–November 1789) and 6 (December 1789–August 1790). An analysis of Hamilton's Reports is in Jacob E. Cooke, ed., *The Reports of Alexander Hamilton* (New York: Harper & Row, 1964), vii–xxiii.

66. *History*, Harlow, 129–130, 211.

67. McDonald, *The Presidency of George Washington*, 64–65.

68. Ibid., 65.

69. Harlow, *History*, 148–149.

70. Ibid., 141.

71. Ibid.

72. Ibid.

73. Ibid., 152–154. The investigation is also discussed in White, *The Federalists*, 352–354, and the dates of Hamilton's letter of resignation and when it took effect are from McDonald, *Alexander Hamilton*, 303.

74. McDonald, *Alexander Hamilton*, 126.

75. Edward G. Carmines and Lawrence C. Dodd, "Bicameralism in Congress: The Changing Partnership," in Lawrence C. Dodd and Bruce I. Oppenheimer, eds., *Congress Reconsidered*, 3rd ed. (Washington, DC: Congressional Quarterly Press, 1985), 418–419.

Chapter 5

The Power of Making Treaties: Washington, Madison, and the Debate over the Jay Treaty

JOHN W. KUEHL

Following an exhausting congressional battle over implementing the Jay Treaty with Great Britain, George Washington invited James Madison to dine with him on May 19, 1796.[1] The two Virginians had been close political associates during the 1780s and early 1790s. Before the Constitutional Convention, Madison confided to Washington his hopes and objectives for the new government; the two worked together at the convention; and they collaborated closely in launching the new government.[2] Madison wrote the draft of Washington's First Inaugural Address, and during his first term, Washington frequently sought Madison's advice on political appointments and policies. Madison was Washington's first choice for Secretary of State when Thomas Jefferson resigned in 1793.[3]

By Washington's second term, however, the friendship between the two Virginians became strained as Madison assumed leadership of the congressional party opposed to the Federalist administration. In mid-October 1794 Washington pointedly expressed the hope that Madison would not get "entangled" in the Democratic–Republican societies.[4] Madison branded Washington's attack on those societies the worst mistake the president had ever made.[5] Because the Jay Treaty battles in 1795 and 1796 strained their friendship to the breaking point, it is tempting for historians of the early Republic to speculate about the topics of conversation that might have engaged the two on that evening in May. Some believe that Washington wanted Madison's input on his Farewell Address, the early version of which Madison wrote at Washington's request in 1792.[6] Others have argued, somewhat less convincingly, that because Washington gave the message to Hamilton for final revisions the day after the dinner with Madison, he and Madison did not discuss it.[7] In any event, by the dinner meeting, Washington was eagerly anticipating his departure from public office, and Madison had decided not to stand for re-election to Congress.[8] Relieved that Congress had finished its grueling deliberations on the treaty, both men had paid a heavy emotional and political price in the struggle through which they had passed.

Washington's and Madison's initial reaction to the treaty had been negative. Washington cautiously weighed the pros and cons of accepting it and finally endorsed it because he believed that war with England would result if the treaty was not ratified. Once Washington made up his mind, he courageously maintained his policy in the face of initial public disapproval and England's failure to stop seizing American vessels.[9] As a leader of the Federalists, Washington effectively used his prestige through the fall of 1795 and spring of 1796 to influence public opinion through his correspondence with other Federalists and through selective responses to the resolutions sent him by town meetings across the nation.

For Madison, who shared with Thomas Jefferson a loathing of England and had worked consistently in the House to impose economic sanctions on Great Britain, the treaty was horribly unfair. By giving England most favored nation status, it deprived the United States of the ability ever to use economic coercion against the former mother country. In Madison's judgment, the treaty provided nothing of advantage to America. Moreover, Madison did not believe that England would go to war with the United States, its best customer.[10]

Late in March 1796 the House of Representatives demanded that the president supply all of the papers related to the Jay negotiations with England. Following consultation with his cabinet and the chief justice, Washington summarily rejected the House demand. In an uncompromising response, he established a precedent for executive independence in making treaties through adroit practical, Constitutional, and historical arguments. On April 30 the president gained his objective of getting the House to vote funds to carry the treaty into effect. Nevertheless, he was wounded deeply by intense public criticism, which continued after his approval of the initially unpopular treaty. Always sensitive about fulfilling his duty, Washington was particularly stung by Madison's and other Republicans' charge that he ignored the "voice of the people."[11]

Madison's efforts to get the treaty rejected failed miserably, and he lost his leadership role among House Republicans as Edward Livingston and Albert Gallatin led the charge in demanding that Washington surrender the Jay papers. The great balance in republican government was disturbed by the preemptory and uncompromising way in which the House had demanded the Jay papers from the executive, but he was angered by Washington's absolute refusal to supply any of the papers requested by the House. Moreover, he worried about the way in which public support for the treaty after Washington signed it influenced Republican congressman to waffle in their opposition to the treaty, thereby destroying the party's majority in the House and giving the administration a major foreign policy victory. The Republican House majority against the treaty evaporated in the heat of Washington's prestige and an immensely successful Federalist petition campaign. Madison was ridiculed by the Federalists and criticized by fellow Republicans as he worked to oppose the Jay Treaty without directly challenging the executive's treaty-making powers.

This chapter examines the arguments advanced by Washington and Madison in the debate over the House of Representatives' call for the Jay Treaty papers in the spring of 1796, and it assesses the impact of the debate on their opinions regarding presidential independence in making treaties and establishing foreign policy.

I

Washington understood clearly the many criticisms leveled against the treaty.[12] He shared with critics an anxiety about France's response to the treaty, and he retained substantial doubts about England's compliance as that nation continued to seize American vessels after formal ratification. Once Washington endorsed the treaty in the summer of 1795, however, he used his influence and the considerable political skill that his years as president had refined to urge Federalists to make the administration case to the public. Hence, he encouraged Alexander Hamilton to defend the treaty in the press after the first "Camillus" letter appeared. The opponents of the treaty were, he claimed, ever "working, like bees, to distil their poison," while the friends of order and good government "depend[ed], often times *too much*, and *too long* upon the sense, and good dispositions of the people to work conviction."[13] Washington no doubt learned firsthand about local hostility to the treaty while he was in his home state immediately after approving the treaty in July 1795, and he acknowledged that even friends of the administration in Virginia were hostile to the treaty.[14] The terms of the treaty were being misrepresented,[15] Washington lamented, and he likened the government to "a ship between the rocks of Sylla and charibdas."[16]

By late August 1795 Washington was more optimistic that the tide of opposition was beginning to turn.[17] Refusing to answer many of the "insulting" public resolutions addressed to him by town meetings, Washington continued, nonetheless, to fret about answering the initial public outrage, and he skillfully used his responses to selected addresses in order to enhance public support for his position.[18] In these responses, he invariably contended that he was above party considerations because "party," according to Washington, made truth so

enveloped in mist, and false representation that it is difficult to know through what channel to seek it. This difficulty to one, who is of no party, and whose sole wish is to pursue, with undeviating steps a path which would lead this country to respectability, wealth and happiness is exceedingly to be lamented.[19]

As he assessed public opposition, Washington acknowledged that the citizens of the southern states were particularly hostile to the treaty, but fully 90 percent of the citizens would probably support the measure absent the "abominable misrepresentations" that dominated the meetings.[20] Washington admitted that he was being charged with "disregarding the voice of the people," but, he asserted, the true voice of the people had not been heard "unless the misrepresentations of party, or at best partial meetings can be called so."[21] He wished ardently that he could "give satisfaction" to his "constituents"; not to do so would "always give [him] . . . pain." He must, nonetheless, always follow measures "conducive to their interest and happiness." Once the treaty was better understood, he maintained, the public would understand his motives.[22]

In response to a favorable set of resolutions from the Maryland General Assembly, Washington wrote, "I have long since resolved (for the present time at least) to let my calumniators proceed, without taking notice of their invectives myself, or by any other with my participation or knowledge."[23] He did not respond directly to his critics, but he continued to write disparagingly about them to fellow Federalists, expecting that they would champion his cause with the public. "The dregs," said Washington, "will always remain and the slightest motion will stir them up."[24] The "torrent of abuse" heaped upon him by the "factious newspapers" that sought "to withdraw the confidence of my constituents" would not change his policies. "I have nothing to fear from invective," he boldly but unconvincingly asserted.[25]

Once the treaty was ratified, Washington insisted that the public meetings were improper.[26] Public gatherings should not continue to comment once the government had set foreign policy. For Washington, some "criterion more infallible than partial (if they are not party) meetings" had to be found "as the touch stone of public sentiment."[27]

By the end of October 1795 it was clear to the president that despite his skillful correspondence with constituents and Federalist lieutenants and despite his hopeful observations that public support for the treaty was growing, Madison and other Republican leaders in the House of Representatives were not willing to carry the treaty into effect. Convinced that a more direct approach might be necessary, the president floated the possibility of a direct address to the Congress. Washington wondered if he could address the legislature without appearing to give up the right of the president, with the advice and consent of the Senate, to make treaties.[28] Washington dropped the idea, however, and in his December annual message to Congress, he made virtually no mention of the treaty.[29]

On March 30, 1796, he responded to the March 24 demand of the House for the Jay papers. "The nature of foreign negotiations requires caution, and their success must often depend on secrecy," he said.[30] Even after negotiations were completed, disclosure of all relevant materials would be "impolitic" because it would make future negotiations very difficult. A major reason for vesting the power of making treaties in the president, Washington asserted, was the need to confine the function to a small number of individuals. "A dangerous precedent" would be set by admitting the House's right to all papers respecting confidential negotiations.[31] Important as the precedent, however, was Washington's keen awareness that the Republicans were seeking to gain political advantage by exposing the papers to public examination. Consequently, Washington told the legislators that there really was no need for them to see the papers short of their conducting impeachment hearings. He reminded the House that all of the papers had been turned over to the Senate in their treaty deliberations.

Washington was also interested in setting the historical record straight, and the second half of his message denying the papers assessed the intention of the Founders and advanced historical proof that the president, with the advice and consent of the Senate, was to make treaties that became the law of the land. He reminded the Republicans that he had been a member of the Constitutional Convention. Foreign nations depended on the procedure established in the Constitution. All previous treaties made had been understood by foreign signatories to be the work of the executive branch, and every previous House of Representatives had "acquiesced" in the president's independence in negotiating treaties. "Nay [Washington asserted], they have more than acquiesced; for till now without controverting the obligation of such treaties, they have made all the requisite provisions for carrying them into effect."[32] State ratifying conventions had also clearly understood that the president, with the advice and consent of two-thirds of the senators present, made treaties that were the law of the land. Moreover, the "amity and mutual concession" that made the Constitution possible had given power to the Senate so that the interests of the small states could be protected. Washington had himself deposited the journals of the Constitutional Convention in the State Department. At the convention, a proposal that treaties must be ratified by law in order to be binding was specifically rejected. Consequently, the House had no right to the papers, and the president would be remiss in his duties if he supplied them.[33]

II

James Madison faced a dilemma with regard to Washington's refusal to provide the papers on the Jay Treaty. When, in late February 1796, Livingston surprised him by calling for all of the Jay papers, Madison proposed to amend his fellow Republican's motion to request only the papers that Washington deemed proper to give to the House. Madison wanted to avoid a direct confrontation with the president not only because he hoped to avert a Constitutional impasse and believed in the essential treaty-making powers of the executive but also because he believed that Washington would supply some of the papers. When his motion failed to gain a majority, however, Madison determined that he must support fellow Republicans in order to hold together the antitreaty forces in the House and ultimately to destroy the treaty.[34] As he had so often in his career, the Republican leader understood the delicate balance of powers that the Constitution created. Like Washington, Madison had employed his remarkable political skills to shape public opinion. When Washington issued his Neutrality Proclamation in 1793, Madison spearheaded a campaign for the drafting of remonstrances from communities in Virginia. His efforts to "collect the sense of the people," as he put it,[35] had started what one historian has called the "War of the Resolutions," which initiated public comment on foreign policy.[36] Before Washington approved the Jay Treaty, Madison encouraged the public remonstrances against it. Late in August 1795 he prepared a petition for the Virginia General Assembly that explicitly made the charge that so upset Washington, namely that the president was ignoring the will of the people. Washington, he charged, had "virtually refused to view the representations of the people as a source of information worthy of his consideration." All appeals to the president were thus "absurd and nugatory," and other "constituted authorities" must be addressed.[37] By the spring of 1796, however, the "sense of the people" had turned against Madison and the Republicans as the unhappy party leader took the floor first to justify the House call for papers and then to criticize Washington for his refusal to comply with the House demand.

Madison faced a daunting task in trying to justify the House call for papers on Constitutional grounds. He preferred to avoid such a discussion altogether, but that was impossible because of the Federalists' repeated charge that the House call for the papers challenged a responsibility that the Constitution unequivocally assigned to the president. As he had since the Constitutional Convention, Madison sought "middle ground," that balance of power between branches of government that would preserve justice and liberty. Madison's worries about the inadequate energy of the central government at the Constitutional Convention had been replaced by fears of a potentially tyrannical executive and an unjust central government as Hamilton's fiscal program was debated in the early 1790s.[38] In the highly political debates over the call for the papers, Madison thoughtfully prepared arguments that failed convincingly to make his case and seemed to contradict Constitutional positions that he had earlier advanced. He argued that the original intent of the Framers could not be known and that state ratifying conventions, though not perfect, were a more accurate source for interpreting the meaning of the Constitution. In his two major speeches on the call for papers, Madison insisted that it was wrong to assume that any branch of government was given an absolute power. Consequently, under the Constitution, the president did not have unchecked control of treaty making, even though Madison acknowledged that the Constitution did make treaty making essentially an executive function. As a political leader, Madison tried to make arguments about the Constitution that would unify a Republican coalition that was dissolving in the face of mounting public support for Washington's policy, but his task was made even more difficult by his own misgivings about the uncompromising way in which other Republican leaders had handled their politically motivated demand.

In his first speech on March 10, Madison justified House action on the basis of its legitimate legislative function. The Constitution was the expression of the sovereign will of the people, who, said Madison, had distributed powers in their government. To be faithful to the people's will, each branch of government must try not to encroach on the authority of another branch, but each must "guard [its] own authority against encroachments." The power of the president with the consent of the Senate to make treaties must be balanced with the claims of the House of Representatives to exercise its legislative function. Any passages of the Constitution taken "literally and without limit" would produce clashes. To allow the president and Senate an unrestrained right to make treaties would make it possible, for example, for the president to furnish troops to a foreign nation, thereby usurping Congress' power to declare war. For Madison, the Congress would "have no will of its own" if it automatically carried all treaties into effect. As he consistently claimed, the government operated under "a Constitution of limitations and checks. The powers given up by the people for the purposes of government have been divided."[39]

Still hopeful that the president would comply with a call for information, Madison reiterated that the legislative branch must maintain "the most respectful delicacy toward the other constituted authority," but it must also firmly insist upon carrying out its legislative function. The request for information was a part of the legislative process.

Madison was shocked by the president's absolute refusal to supply any papers. On April 2 House Republicans caucused to determine what if any response the House should give to the president's summary rejection. Washington's response seriously undermined the antitreaty coalition. The more aggressive Republican leaders insisted that the House was constitutionally obliged to refuse funds for the treaty. Madison continued to believe that the call for information by the House was justified, but he did not go so far as to support the more extreme view, partly because he saw the Republican opposition eroding, and partly because he wished at all costs to avoiding expanding a Constitutional crisis.[40] The stormy Republican caucus did reach a consensus that the House had to respond to the president. William Blount of North Carolina offered two resolutions on the floor. The first reasserted the House's right to call for the papers, and the second asserted that the House was not required to give the executive reasons for demanding the papers.[41]

On April 6 Madison delivered one of the most difficult speeches of his congressional career.[42] Taunted by the Federalists for his refusal to confirm the Founding Fathers' intention to give the president a free hand in making treaties,[43] Madison began by acknowledging the serious nature of a Constitutional topic "where two of the constituted authorities interpreted differently the extent of their respective powers." In a government in which "every department feels responsibility to the public will," there were bound to be disputes. Where severe clashes over powers between branches of government developed, popular elections and amendments to the Constitution provided the only solutions,[44] but Madison clearly hoped to avoid frequent appeals to those remedies in the operations of government.

The role of the House in treaty making was, Madison admitted, "a great constitutional question," but he denied emphatically that the majority of the House meant to raise that Constitutional issue in calling for the papers. The Constitutional debate, Madison lamely contended, "could only have been brought into view thro' the inauthentic medium of the newspapers."[45] More convincing, though still strained, was Madison's claim that the House was not claiming a role in making treaties. Madison denied the claim of some of his Republican colleagues that treaties were given legitimacy only by House approval. Reiterating what he had said earlier, Madison argued that only when legislative subjects were related to treaties must the House get involved.

What angered him most about Washington's rejection of the House request was the president's presumption in dictating to the legislative body what it needed to carry out its responsibilities. The president could judge what material he would supply, but he had no right to dictate what the House needed, nor did he have the right to ask why the House wanted the materials that it requested. Each department must judge for itself what it needed. For the House to explain why it wanted the papers, said Madison, would be improper. In an impeachment matter, for example (Washington had raised that issue in his rejection of the House request), it would clearly be ludicrous for the House to explain why it was asking for information and might indeed lead to inflicting pain on an innocent president.[46]

Madison's justification for the call on the basis that only the House could say what it needed to carry out its legislative function was a difficult position for him in view of his concern for properly balancing the powers of the branches of government and his insistence that each branch must respect the essential functions of the others. He wished to confine the discussion to the immediate need of the House for information, and he did not make clear how strongly such autonomy of judgment could be applied to other Constitutional crises. Moreover, the argument about the House's right to determine its needs in carrying out its legislative function in no way proved that Washington ought to give the House what it wanted, however insufficient Madison deemed the president's reasons for refusing to comply.

Madison systematically challenged each of the assertions made in Washington's rejection of the House's demand, but his arguments became increasingly strained when he denied that the original intent of the Framers could be known and turned to the state ratifying conventions and the amendments proposed by them to elucidate the meaning of the "voice of the people" expressed in the Constitution.[47] Because some of the drafters of the Constitution had led protests against the treaty, the father of the Constitution argued, it was not possible accurately to recapture the 1787 convention's views. Never, said Madison, had "the sense of the convention . . . been required or admitted as material, in any constitutional question." He referred to his own unsuccessful raising of original intent in the crisis over the bank and to the failure to raise original intent when the Supreme Court was considering whether states can be sued.[48] Washington had accurately pointed to a statement in the journals of the convention that showed that the convention specifically rejected a proposal that no treaty would be binding that was not ratified by law. Madison then contradicted his contention about the impossibility of recapturing the original intent of the Framers by asserting that what the convention rejection meant was that some treaties would require "ratification" by law and that others would not. Besides, said Madison, ratification itself had a technical meaning "different from the agency claimed by the house on the subject of treaties."[49]

Acknowledging that there was no "perfect precision" possible in interpreting the Constitution, Madison sought unsuccessfully to show that state ratifying conventions' proposed amendments demonstrated the people's intent to limit the president's treaty-making powers. He acknowledged that even the state ratifying conventions were not sure sources of accuracy because of "internal evidences in abundance of chasms, and misconceptions of what was said."[50] Nonetheless, amendments proposed by the state ratifying conventions "were better authority and would be found on a general view to favour the sense of the constitution which had prevailed in the house." Many of the state conventions had been jealous to preserve legislative power and check the potential for a tyrannical executive. He discussed the failed amendments referred to by Washington that required a two-thirds vote of the Senate on any commercial treaty and a three-fourths concurrence of both Houses on cession of any territory. Madison pointed out that Virginia, North Carolina, and Maryland had called for the power of the legislature to be supreme with regard to laws. The states, said Madison, believed "that no power could supersede a law without the consent of the Representatives of the people in the Legislature." New York, New Hampshire, and Maryland wanted to require between two-thirds and three-quarters of the legislature to approve such things as standing armies, navigation laws, war, borrowing money, and extending the time of enlistment for soldiers. Madison wondered, how could state conventions

who shewed so much jealousy with respect to the powers of commerce, of the sword, and of the purse, as to require for the exercise of them, in some cases *two-thirds*, in other *three-fourths*, of both branches of the Legislature, . . . have understood that by the treaty clauses in the constitution they had given to the President and Senate, without any controul whatever from the House of Representatives, an absolute and unlimited power over all those great objects?[51]

Madison's argument was a painstaking effort to advance his understanding of the appropriate balance of powers in government. He could not, however, make clear how amendments that had been rejected in 1791 could possibly override the explicit language of the Constitution in giving the president treaty-making powers.[52] Moreover, his claim that individual state ratifying conventions could genuinely reflect the "voice of the people" was untenable.[53] By pointing to illustrations from several state conventions, he no doubt hoped that the collective voice of the people would be ascertained, but that claim sharply contradicted the nationalist positions that he had taken in *The Federalist* and his assiduous earlier efforts to avoid any appeal to localized interests in political and Constitutional arguments.[54]

Like Washington, James Madison had been "greatly shaken" by the experience of the treaty.[55]

In the final weeks of the debate, Madison was silent, "wrapt [as one colleague put it] in his mantle of doubts and problems." What had been a sizable majority in the House had disappeared as pressure from the supporters of the treaty mounted in the fall of 1795 and spring of 1796. John Adams wrote his wife in April 1796, "Mr. Madison looks worried to death. Pale, withered, haggard." Madison admitted to Jefferson, "The progress of this business throughout has to me been the most worrying & vexatious that I ever encountered."[56] Madison's "doubts and problems" came not only from his sense of loss when the House voted to carry the treaty into effect but also from his concern with how far public opinion expressed in town meeting resolutions had led to the undermining of a sound foreign policy.

The Jay Treaty fiasco had shown Madison that bankers and urban special interests molded public opinion to support the "ruinous bargain." The public had been duped by the bankers, British merchants, and insurance companies "beating down the prices of produce, & sounding the tocksin of foreign war, & domestic convulsions." The cause of the defeat also lay, Madison concluded, "in the unsteadiness, the follies, the perverseness, & the defections among our friends, more than in the strength or dexterity, or malice of our opponents." He intimated to Jefferson that his consolation lay in his resolve to retire. Gloomily, Madison concluded, "An appeal to the people on any pending measure, can never be more than an appeal to those in the neighborhood of the Govt. & to the Banks, the Merchts. & the dependents & expectants of the Govt. at a distance."[57] Ever the proponent of that balance in the domestic arena, that "middle ground" about which he had written Washington in 1787, Madison worried about Constitutional crises such as the one raised by the House demand for the papers, and although he decided to go along with Livingston's peremptory demand, he thought that it was an impulsive and uncompromising way to oppose the treaty. His argument in the famous April 6 speech before the House was a reflection of his detestation of the treaty, his need to support fellow Republicans, and the fact that he had serious reservations about Livingston's resolution demanding the papers from Washington. Although he had led the charge to "collect the sense of the people" in 1793, Madison, like Washington, was having second thoughts about the influence of public meetings in shaping foreign policy for the new government and pressuring congressmen to change their votes.

Washington's leadership, coupled with the good fortune of a prosperous economy, turned the tide of opinion to support of his foreign policy. Yet in his letter to Henry Knox in the fall of 1795, Washington insisted that some other means than the popular meetings must be found as "the touchstone of public sentiment." Despite his claim that he was not partisan, Washington worked to shape and influence that public opinion that he believed so difficult to measure, and he was willing to sacrifice consistent application of executive independence in the foreign policy arena when he believed that he could gain popular support for his policies. Thus, when the French foreign minister, Pierre Adet, sharply criticized the administration for failure to respond to French objections to the Jay Treaty, Washington sought political advice from Alexander Hamilton on how to reply publicly to Adet's "indecent references." If he failed to respond, Washington sagely told Hamilton, "the antidote will not keep pace with the poison." He didn't want a newspaper squabble. The French papers were, however, inexorably linked with English diplomatic material. He reminded Hamilton that he had rejected the House call for papers on the Jay Treaty "as a matter of right, and the compliance therewith would have established a dangerous precedent."[58] Nonetheless, by raising the precedent that he established, Washington showed that he was sensitive to the appearance of inconsistency in supplying to the House all of the materials on French negotiations when he had so recently denied the Jay materials.

Political savvy overcame his concern with consistency, and on January 17, 1797, he provided to the House and Senate a substantial collection of diplomatic papers dealing with Franco–American relations. "A government [said Washington] which required only a knowledge of the *truth* to justify its measures could not but be anxious to have this [material] fully and frankly displayed."[59] The executive could thus voluntarily supply materials to the House that advanced its foreign policy in the popular branch of government, and the president could make diplomatic material available to public scrutiny when it served his political interests.

III

Ironically, at the very time when Washington established precedent for executive independence in making treaties and charting foreign policy, he and Madison as party leaders actually encouraged active participation by the public in shaping foreign policy. Despite their grave misgivings that public opinion could be measured accurately because town meeting resolutions were, they contended, often an unrealiable barometer of public sentiment, Washington and Madison both elicited public comment on foreign affairs in advancing partisan objectives.

A second conclusion drawn by this chapter is that in the debate over the constitutionality of the House call for the Jay Treaty papers, both Madison and Washington came more fully to understand the significant role that political partisanship would play in shaping debates about the meaning of the Constitution. Despite repeated denials that he was the leader of a party, Washington asserted the Constitutional independence of the executive in treaty making in order to thwart the designs of his political opponents in the House. Madison was forced by partisan loyalty to advance Constitutional positions that were strained and at odds with what he had argued earlier. He was not happy with the call for the papers because he hoped to avoid making the debate over the call for papers a Constitutional issue. Unable to effect a compromise in the House, Madison strained to make arguments against Washington's precedent by denying that the original intent of the Framers could be known and by discarding nationalist positions that he had espoused earlier.

Important as was the precedent set by Washington in his refusal to acquiesce in the House call for the Jay papers, that precedent must be viewed as part of the more significant simultaneous growth of public participation in the making of foreign policies and the increased influence of party politics in debates about the meaning of the American Constitution. The struggle between George Washington and James Madison in 1796 marked a significant episode in the democratization of American foreign policy. Both men were gravely concerned about the way in which parties were seeking to involve the people in dictating policies of government, but both men contributed substantially to the processes of seeking immediate public support for their positions by "collect[ing] the sense of the people." It is tempting to suspect that their realization of that fact may have added a bit of gloom to their dinner together as they both looked forward to retirement.

NOTES

1. For details about the Jay Treaty, see Samuel Flagg Bemis, *Jay's Treaty: A Study in Commerce and Diplomacy* (New Haven, CT: Yale University Press, 1962), and Jerald A. Combs, *The Jay Treaty: Political Battleground of the Founding Fathers* (Berkeley: University of California Press, 1970).

2. See, for example, James Madison to George Washington, April 16, 1787, in William T. Hutchinson et al., eds., *The Papers of James Madison* (hereafter cited as *PJM*), 17 vols. (Chicago, Charlottesville, and London: University Press of Virginia, 1962–1991, 9:383; Ralph Ketcham, *James Madison: A Biography* (New York: Macmillan, 1971), pp. 232, 268–269, 349; John C. Fitzpatrick, ed., *Diaries of George Washington*, 4 vols. (Boston, 1925), 3:384, 456–457.

3. In the first years of the government, Madison acted "as minister without portfolio in Washington's administration, 'the bridge between the executive and the legislature,' adviser to the president on protocol, appointments, and executive deportment." Lance Banning, *The Sacred Fire of Liberty: James Madison and the Founding of the Federal Republic* (New York: Cornell University Press, 1995), pp. 273, 293, 344. See also *PJM*, 12:121.

4. See Washington to Edmund Randolph, October 16, 1794, in John C. Fitzpatrick, ed., *The Writings of George Washington* (hereafter cited as *PGW*), 39 vols. (Washington, DC: U.S. Government Printing Office, 1931–1944), 34:3.

5. James Madison to James Monroe, December 4, 1794, *PJM*, 15:407.

6. In their chapter titled "The Most Momentous Debate," John Carroll and Mary Ashworth insisted that Washington's purpose in inviting Madison "could have been none other than to discuss the valedictory." John Carroll and Mary Ashworth, *George Washington: First in Peace*, vol. 7 of Douglas Southall Freeman's biography (New York: Charles Scribner's Sons, 1957), p. 381 n.288.

7. The editors of the Madison papers make this claim. See *PJM*, 15:355, n.1.

8. James Madison to James Monroe, April 7, 1796, and James Madison to Thomas Jefferson, May 1, 1796, *PJM*, 16:303, 342–343. Pierce Butler to Thomas Sumter, June 18, 1796, Butler Letterbook, Historical Society of Pennsylvania, cited in *PJM*, 16:149. Significantly, the first indication of Madison's intention to retire came in his letter to Monroe the day after his major speech on the constitutionality of the House legislative role in treaty making (see later). James Thomas Flexner demonstrates Washington's eagerness for retirement. See his *George Washington: Anguish and Farewell* (Boston: Little, Brown, 1972), pp. 271–273. See also Stanley Elkins and Eric McKitrick, *The Age of Federalism* (New York: Oxford University Press, 1993), p. 490. Elkins and McKitrick have an excellent discussion of Washington's Farewell Address (pp. 489–528).

9. For a good discussion of Washington's deliberations about approving the treaty, see Flexner, *Anguish and Farewell*, pp. 213–253.

10. Madison spoke in the House and wrote extensively to his correspondents about his opposition to the treaty, even though he did not take up Jefferson's plea to write against Hamilton's *Defence* in the newspapers. See particularly his letter to an unidentified correspondent (perhaps Alexander J. Dallas or some other Republican leader), August 23, 1795, *PJM*, 16:56–58. Between August 23, 1795, and April 15,

1796, when he made his last speech against the treaty in the House, Madison was consistent in denouncing what was for him "a ruinous bargain." James Madison to Robert R. Livingston, August 10, 1795, *PJM*, 16:46–48.

11. Describing Washington's wounds, John Adams wrote, "The turpitude of the Jacobins touches him more nearly than he owns in words. All the studied efforts of the Federalists to counterbalance abuse by compliment don't answer the end." *Letters of John Adams Addressed to His Wife* (Boston, 1841), 2:206, cited in Flexner, *Anguish and Farewell*, p. 277. Washington revealed his anguish in his own words, cited later in the chapter.

12. See, for example, George Washington to Alexander Hamilton, July 29, 1795, *PGW*, 34:263.

13. Washington to Hamilton, July 29, 1795, *PGW*, 34:263–264.

14. Washington to Edmund Randolph, July 31, 1795, *PGW*, 34:266. See Norman K. Risjord, *Chesapeake Politics, 1781–1800* (New York: Columbia University Press, 1978), pp. 452–457 for discussion of Virginia's outrage with the treaty, primarily because it legitimated American debts to the British.

15. In the immediate aftermath of the most intense protests against the treaty during the summer of 1795, the Federalist press underscored Washington's convictions about the conspiracy against the treaty, which had been launched even before its terms were known. See, for example, "A Brief History of the Rise and Progress of the Recent Mobs and Riots," in the *Columbian Centinel*, September 2, 1795. The Federalist author contended that during the 12 months between Jay's sailing for England and the meeting of the Senate to discuss the treaty, the Jacobins had been working and plotting to reject any treaty whenever it appeared. How else could one explain, the author asked, "the whole line of Jacobins, from *New Hampshire* to *Georgia*, at the moment of its appearance, and before any of them scarcely had seen it?" Riot tactics were used, said the editor, to push through resolutions by the people, 90 percent of whom had never heard or read a word of the treaty.

16. Washington to Randolph, July 31, 1795, *PGW*, 34:266.

17. George Washington to James Ross, August 22, 1795, *PGW*, 34:281.

18. See Fitzpatrick, *PGW*, 34:254. The numerous angry addresses to Washington can be found in his papers and in the newspapers of the day. For a discussion of the protest resolutions see John W. Kuehl, "American Nationalism and the Popular Resolutions of the 1790s: A Quantitative Analysis," *Canadian Review of Studies in Nationalism* 2 (Fall 1974), pp. 70–90.

19. George Washington to Timothy Pickering, July 27, 1795, *PGW*, 34:251.

20. George Washington to Henry Knox, September 20, 1795, *PGW*, 34:310–311.

21. Washington to Pickering, September 27, 1795, *PGW*, 34:315.

22. George Washington to Joseph Pierce, Westmoreland County chairman, October 9, 1795, *PGW*, 34:333–334. See also his response to the citizens of Frederick County, Virginia, December 16, 1795, *PGW*, 34:395–396.

23. George Washington to Governor John Hawkins Stone, December 6, 1795, *PGW*, 34:385.

24. George Washington to John Jay, December 21, 1795, *PGW*, 34:397.

25. Ibid., p. 402.

26. "These meetings in opposition to the constituted authorities are as useless as

they are *at all times*, improper and dangerous." George Washington to John Adams, August 20, 1795, *PGW*, 34:280.

27. George Washington to Henry Knox, September 20, 1795, *PGW*, 34:310.

28. "If good would flow from the latter [an address], by a just and temperate communication of my ideas to the community at large, through this medium; guarded so as not to add fuel to passions prepared to blaze, and at the same time so expressed as not to excite the criticisms, or animadversions of European Powers, I would readily embrace it. But I would, decidedly, avoid every expression which could be construed a dereliction of the powers of the President with the advice and consent of the Senate to make Treaties: or into a shrinking from any act of mine relative to it. In a word, if a conciliatory plan can be assimilated with a firm, manly and dignified conduct in this business, it would be desirable: but the latter I will never yield." Washington to Hamilton, October 29, 1795, *PGW*, 34:350.

29. George Washington, *Eighth Annual Address*, in James D. Richardson, ed., *A Compilation of the Messages and Papers of the Presidents, 1789–1908*, 10 vols. (Washington, DC: Bureau of National Literature and Art, 1908), 1:199–204.

30. Richardson, *Compilation of Messages and Papers of the Presidents*, 1:194.

31. The month after he refused the House request, Washington wrote, "For no candid man in the least degree acquainted with the progress of this business, will believe for a moment that the *ostensible* dispute, was about papers, or that the British Treaty was a *good* one, or a *bad* one; but whether there *should be a Treaty at all* without the concurrence of the house of Representatives, which was striking at once, and boldly too, at the fundamental principles of the Constitution; and if it were established, would render the Treaty making Power not only a nullity, but such an absolute absurdity as to reflect disgrace on the framers of it: for will anyone suppose, that they who framed, or those who adopted the Instrument, ever intended to give the power to the President and Senate to make Treaties (and declaring that when made and ratified, they should be the Supreme law of the land) wd. in the same breath place it in the powers of the house of Representatives to fix their Veto on them?" George Washington to Edward Carrington, May 1, 1796, *PGW*, 35:32.

32. Richardson, *Compilation of Messages and Papers of the Presidents*, p. 195.

33. Ibid., p. 196. The day after rejecting the House request, Washington wrote the Senate nominating five commissioners to serve under the terms of the treaty.

34. Even before the March 1796 call for papers by the House, Edward Livingston characterized Madison as indecisive. Madison, said Livingston, had "a habit of considering the objections to his own plans so long and so frequently that they acquire a real weight & influence his conduct. . . . He never determines to act untill he is absolutely forced by the pressure of affairs & then regrets that he has neglected some better opportunity." (Edward Livingston to R. R. Livingston, December 24, 1795, cited in *PJM*, 16:248, n.5. The original is at Haverford College, Haverford, PA.)

35. See James Madison to Thomas Jefferson, August 27, September 2, 1793, and James Madison to Archibald Stewart, September 1, 1793, *PJM*, 15:75, 88, 93.

36. See Harry Ammon, *The Genet Mission* (New York: Norton, 1973), pp. 132–146.

37. Petition to the General Assembly of the Commonwealth of Virginia, October 12, 1795, *PJM*, 16:95. The Virginia assembly never passed Madison's resolution but instead proposed amendments to the Constitution. See the editorial note on Madison's petition in *PJM*, 16:62–69. Thomas Jefferson had earlier urged a reluctant

Madison to counter Hamilton's "Camillus" *Defence* of the treaty, just as he had urged him in 1793 to respond with the "Helvidius" essays to counter Hamilton's "Pacificus." Thomas Jefferson to James Madison, September 21, 1795, *PJM*, 16:89. See also Thomas J. Farnham, "The Virginia Amendments of 1795: An Episode in the Opposition to Jay's Treaty," *The Virginia Magazine of History and Biography* 75 (January 1967), pp. 75–88.

In his brilliant study of Madison, Lance Banning suggested that Madison and other Republicans "continually underestimated the extent to which Washington was coming to agree with their opponents and was personally responsible for strategies that would defeat their own best plans." Madison's sharp criticism of Washington's denunciation of the Democratic–Republican societies and his criticism of Washington in the Virginia petition of 1795 suggest the need to qualify that generalization. By 1796 Madison had no illusions about Washington's position on the treaty, however surprised he was by Washington's complete refusal to supply any papers to the House. Moreover, he clearly understood the implications of Washington's foreign policy.

Banning suggests the need for further study of the leadership of Washington and Madison in the Jay Treaty crisis. Banning, *The Sacred Fire of Liberty*, p. 532.

38. See, for example, John W. Kuehl, "Justice, Republican Energy, and the Search for Middle Ground: James Madison and the Assumption of State Debts," *The Virginia Magazine of History and Biography* 103 (July 1995), pp. 321–338.

39. Madison's March 10 speech, *PJM*, 16:255–263.

40. The editors of the Madison papers argued, convincingly in my judgment, that following the passage of Livingston's resolutions on March 24, the Jay Treaty debate itself unraveled for the Republican leadership. When Washington refused to supply any papers, their expectation that they could resolve to refuse to carry the treaty into effect because it "encroached on their Constitutional duties" was shattered. *PJM*, 16:270–271.

41. Irving Brant claimed that Madison drafted the Blount resolutions. See Brant, *James Madison: Father of the Constitution 1787–1800* (Indianapolis: Bobbs-Merrill, 1950), p. 436.

42. "Madison's speeches on Jay's Treaty rank among his most elaborate and agonized attempts to understand the spirit and provisions of the Constitution." Banning, *The Sacred Fire of Liberty*, p. 382. Jack Rakove provides excellent discussion of Madison's shifting Constitutional perspective and his increased awareness of the politicization of the Constitution. Rakove examines Madison's difficulty in coping with what he calls "originalism." Jack Rakove, *Original Meanings: Politics and Ideas in the Making of the Constitution* (New York: Knopf, 1996), pp. 355–365. See also Ketcham, *James Madison*, pp. 361–362.

43. See Rakove, *Original Meanings*, pp. 359–362.

44. *PJM*, 16:291.

45. This suggestion by Madison was not at all convincing and indicates his frustration as he sought to defuse the Constitutional issue and to hold together a divided Republican coalition. Alexander Hamilton, in his lengthy series defending the treaty, raised the Constitutional issue in No. 38 of *The Defence*, and Madison probably had the *New York Herald* paper and those who read Hamilton's essays in mind. The *New York Herald*, January 6, 1796. The Federalists in the House, however, consistently challenged the constitutionality of the House call for papers the moment Livingston raised the issue, and there were numerous appeals to the original intent of

the drafters at the Constitutional Convention. Federalists in Congress chided Madison for his unwillingness to affirm the Constitutional Framers' original intent in according the president treaty-making powers with the advice and consent of the Senate. William Vans Murray sarcastically likened Madison to the "Pythia in the temple" who ought to "explain the ambiguous language of the oracle." *Annals of Congress* 5:700–702. In their correspondence, congressional observers pointedly referred to the difficulty of Madison's position. Of course, they put a partisan spin on his predicament, but their observations accurately reflect Madison's discomfort in the discussion of original intent. Four days before Madison's speech, Jonathan Trumbull wrote, "The conduct of Mr. Madison has been insidious and uncandid in a high degree. . . . Although repeatedly called upon by Members to inform the House what was the understanding on this head in the Convention for framing the Constitution—and tho' known to be perfectly conversant and particularly active in all that passed in that body—yet he has been reserved and silent as the Grave—not an explanation could be drawn from him—this conduct will serve to plunge him in infamy—and ruin his hard earned and long-continued reputation." The ill Fisher Ames gloated that Madison was "irrevocably disgraced, . . . devoid of sincerity and fairness." Jonathan Trumbull to John Trumbull, April 2, 1796, Connecticut State Library, and Fisher Ames to George Minot, April 2, 1796, Seth Ames, ed., *Works of Fisher Ames with a Selection from His Speeches and Correspondence* (Boston: Little, Brown, 1854), 1:191.

46. Madison's April 6 speech, *PJM*, 16:293–294.

47. "Whatever veneration might be entertained for the body of men who formed our constitution [said Madison in the most often quoted section of his April 6 speech], the sense of that body could never be regarded as the oracular guide in the expounding the constitution. As the instrument came from them, it was nothing more than the draft of a plan, nothing but a dead letter, until life and validity were breathed into it, by the voice of the people, speaking through the several state conventions. If we were to look therefore, for the meaning of the instrument . . . we must look for it not in the general convention, which proposed it, but in the state conventions, which accepted and ratified the constitution." *PJM*, 16:296.

48. Ibid., pp. 294–295.

49. Ibid., p. 295.

50. Ibid., p. 296.

51. Ibid., p. 299.

52. See Rakove, *Original Meanings*, p. 363.

53. See James Madison to Robert R. Livingston, August 10, 1795, *PJM*, 16:48.

54. See Rakove, *Original Meanings*, p. 363. Madison had repeatedly tried to avoid discussion of state interests in the Jay Treaty debate. Scholars have pointed out that he never made his attacks on the Jay Treaty based on the interests of the state of Virginia. Hence, he was loath to raise the issue of the compensations for freed slaves in his writings.

55. Elkins and McKitrick, *The Age of Federalism*, p. 449.

56. Joshua Coit, April 22, 1796, *Annals of Congress*, 4 Congress, I Session, 1151. John Adams to Abigail Adams, April 28, 1796, cited in Elkins and McKitrick, *Age of Federalism*, pp. 449, 846, n.241.

57. James Madison to Thomas Jefferson, May 1, 1796, *PJM*, 16:342–343. Elkins and McKitrick in their marvelous *The Age of Federalism*, p. 841, n.241, suggested

that Madison lost his nerve. Richard Matthews argued that Madison was closer to Alexander Hamilton than he was to Thomas Jefferson in his suspicion of the role of the people in government. Richard K. Matthews, *If Men Were Angels: James Madison and the Heartless Empire of Reason* (Lawrence: University Press of Kansas, 1995). For a sharp critique of Matthews' thesis, see Ralph Ketcham's review in *William and Mary Quarterly* 52 (October 1995), pp. 697–702.

58. George Washington to Alexander Hamilton, November 2, 1796, *PGW*, 35: 253.

59. Richardson, *Compilation of Messages and Papers of the Presidents*, p. 211.

Chapter 6

The Father of Our Country as Court-Packer-in-Chief: George Washington and the Supreme Court

HENRY J. ABRAHAM AND BARBARA A. PERRY

It has long been accepted as an article of faith that the title of "Champion Supreme Court Packer" belongs to President Franklin D. Roosevelt (1933–1945), for he appointed 9 members of the august tribunal between 1937 and 1943. Yet it was not our only four-times-elected president but the very first president of the fledgling United States, George Washington, who holds that record. In a seven-year period (1789–1796), he nominated fully 14 individuals to the Court, of whom 11 actually served (one, Rutledge, on an ultimately unsuccessful recess basis as chief justice for four months). In order of their nomination by the chief executive, they were:

1. John Jay, as chief justice (1789)

2. John Rutledge, as associate justice (1789)

3. William Cushing, as associate justice (1789)

4. Robert H. Harrison, as associate justice (1789)—refused to serve after confirmation

5. James Wilson, as associate justice (1789)

6. John Blair, as associate justice (1789)

7. James Iredell, as associate justice (1789)

8. Thomas Johnson, as associate justice (1791)

9. William Paterson, as associate justice (1793)—nomination withdrawn but resubmitted later

10. William Paterson (again), as associate justice (1793)

11. John Rutledge, now as chief justice (1795)

12. William Cushing, now as chief justice (1796)—refused to serve after confirmation

13. Samuel Chase, as associate justice (1796)

14. Oliver Ellsworth, as chief justice (1796)

Of those 14, William Cushing had the distinction of having been confirmed by the Senate twice (September 1789 and January 1796), yet on the latter occasion—to Chief Justice—he declined to serve. Robert Henry Harrison, confirmed in September 1789, also declined to serve (in favor of assuming the post of chancellor of the University of Maryland). William Paterson's initial nomination (1793) was not acted upon by the Senate and was withdrawn at Washington's request (February), but he resubmitted it just a week later, and Paterson was confirmed that March. John Rutledge, initially confirmed as an associate justice in 1789—a post from which he resigned to assume the chief justiceship of his home state of South Carolina in 1791—was subsequently (1795) nominated as chief justice of the United States but was rejected by the Senate 10:14 several months after his nomination. However, he actually served in the center chair on a recess basis for four months while the Senate pondered his fate. Rutledge was succeeded as chief justice by Oliver Ellsworth, President Washington's 14th and final nomination in March 1796.

In choosing his candidate, Washington, probably more than any other of our presidents, established and resolutely clung religiously to a septet of criteria for Supreme Court candidacy: (1) support and advocacy of the Constitution; (2) distinguished service in the Revolution; (3) active participation in the political life of state or nation; (4) prior judicial experience on lower tribunals; (5) either a "favorable reputation with his fellows" or personal ties with Washington himself; (6) geographic suitability; (7) love of our country. Of these criteria, evidently the most important to him was advocacy of the principles of the Constitution—the more outspoken the better. Perhaps more than many of his contemporaries he recognized the potential strength and influence of the judicial branch, keenly sensing the role it would be called on to play in spelling out Constitutional basics and penumbras. In letters of commission to his initial six nominees to the Supreme Court in September and October 1789, he wrote: "The Judicial System is the chief Pillar upon which our national Government must rest."[1] That pillar needed strong men—proponents of the federalist philosophy of government. Seven of those the president sent to the bench had been participants in the Constitutional Convention of 1787. He knew most, if not all, of his appointees intimately. Indeed, with the exception of Abraham Lincoln, who *personally* selected his five Supreme Court nominees, without input from any advisers, Washington was more directly involved in identifying and choosing his nominees than any other president to date.

John Jay of New York, the youngest of eight children—lawyer, the

Empire State's first chief justice, diplomat (the negotiator of the Treaty of Paris), soldier, political leader—at 44 years of age was Washington's first appointment and his choice for chief justice of the Supreme Court of the United States, the first and to date youngest to head the nation's highest tribunal. (According to some historians,[2] the president had also seriously considered Patrick Henry and even offered him the post, but Henry declined—he preferred to remain in active politics.) All but unique among the Founding Fathers, Jay claimed a line of ancestry of entirely non-British stock—his forebearers were French Huguenot refugees to England. Jay, a supreme diplomat, whom Washington had known since the first Continental Congress and with whom he had worked closely and corresponded for well over two decades, had not been in Philadelphia during the summer of 1787. Yet he had contributed to *The Federalist Papers*, had been influential in Hamilton's cliff-hanger struggle to secure New York's ratification of the Constitution, and, while president of the Continental Congress in 1778–1779, had staunchly defended the general's military conduct and authority when George Washington was under heavy political attack. The president's choice was a true-blue loyalist, both as a product and as an architect of the initial phases of the American Revolution.

Another among the first president's original choices, however, had been a key figure at the convention, John Rutledge of South Carolina—a former governor and colonial and state legislator of that state and a judge of its chancery court. As chairman of the Committee on Detail, which composed the first draft of the Constitution, he was regarded as one of the central personalities behind the creation of a *United* States of America. In fact, Washington referred to Rutledge rather extravagantly and quite *in*correctly as the individual who "wrote the Constitution."[3] Washington had seriously considered appointing Rutledge as the first chief justice—which is what Rutledge and his supporters had really craved—but opted for Jay because he wanted to honor the key state of New York, whose ratification of the Constitution had proved so decisive. Rutledge, age 50, was nominated and confirmed in 1789 as associate justice, but he stepped down from the bench in 1791, before the Court actually heard any cases, to assume the chief justiceship of South Carolina, a post he regarded as being more challenging and more significant. When Jay resigned as chief justice of the United States in 1795 to become governor of New York, Washington again chose Rutledge, this time for the center chair, yet the Senate now rejected the nomination because of Rutledge's pronounced opposition to the Jay Treaty. Rutledge did, however, actively serve in the post of chief justice on a recess appointment, presiding over the August 1795 term of the Court, during which he participated in just two decisions[4]: one, *Talbot v. Jansen*, in which he concurred with the unanimous Court and the other, as one of the majority, in *United States v. Peters*. (Until John Marshall became chief justice in 1891, the justices rendered their opinions *seriatim*.) Both cases involved the legality of ship seizures by French privateers. Yet the Hamilton-led Senate defeated him by a 10:14 vote on December 15, 1795—the only justice on record among the 15 who functioned in such a recess capacity who was not eventually confirmed. There had been persistent rumors regarding his mental stability—he suffered from deep depressions. Despondent, he attempted suicide unsuccessfully after the defeat.

Born in Scotland, Pennsylvania's James Wilson, a signer of the Declaration of Independence, was also a key member of the convention. One of the outstanding lawyer-scholars of his time, he would become the fledging Republic's first law professor (University of Pennsylvania) and was one of the few Founding Fathers to propound "a general theory of government and law."[5] Wilson was greatly instrumental in strengthening the role of the judicial branch and was widely regarded as the father of Article III, the judicial article, of the Constitution. He had fought successfully for a judiciary independent of both the states and the national legislative and executive branches. He had argued in favor of the establishment of lower ("inferior") federal courts, advocated judicial appointment by the president, and fortuitously convinced his fellow delegates that judicial independence would be impaired if the president—at the request of Congress—were able to remove justices from the bench (a proposal that a good many future presidents would have loved to have had available!).

A nationalist and an advocate of direct democracy and minority rights, Wilson argued for the direct election of representatives, senators, and executives; yet he also supported such countermajoritarian checks as judicial review. At the ratifying convention of his home state, Wilson was among those most influential in obtaining its consent to the U.S. Constitution, and he was the architect of Pennsylvania's Constitution of 1790. He not only proposed his own nomination to President Washington in writing but expressed a preference for the chief justiceship. Yet it was Jay, of course, who was named chief justice, and the president, who was initially torn between Wilson and the latter's fellow Pennsylvanian Chief Justice Thomas McKean, chose the 47-year-old Wilson as an associate justice—the first of the new Court's members to be sworn in, even two weeks before Jay took the oath of office as chief justice. Wilson's selection would prove to be a fortunate decision, indeed, for McKean later became a rabid states' rights advocate who rejected the power of judicial review by the federal courts and by the U.S. Supreme Court in particular.

Lawyer and staunch Federalist John Blair of Williamsburg, Virginia, was an aristocratic, wealthy, influential planter, legislator, and jurist. At 57 he became the second-oldest member of the first Supreme Court. Blair had also been a participant at the convention, although he had figured much less prominently than Wilson. An amiable, consensus-prone Tidewater Virginian, Blair had shown himself an excellent team player when, subordinating his own strong personal preferences, he had cast his lot with Washington and Madison to carry the Virginia delegation and the convention for the establishment of the electoral college, just as the convention seemed hopelessly deadlocked over the method of selecting presidents. Ultimately, Blair, Washington, and Madison were the only members of the Old Dominion delegation to vote for the Constitution in its entirety.

William Cushing, chief justice of the Supreme Judicial Court of Massachusetts, completed the group of five chosen for the Court in 1789. At 57 plus (a few months older than Blair), he was the oldest appointee. Although he had not attended the Constitutional Convention, he had been active in the cause of the Constitution, having initially persuaded Massachusetts to send delegates to Philadelphia. In 1788 he had served as vice president of his state's ratifying convention, emerging as its most dominating single figure, playing a leading role in securing ratification, just as he had in abolishing slavery in his home state. While sitting as an associate justice of the Supreme Court, he became Washington's second choice (after John Rutledge had been rejected) for chief justice to succeed Jay in 1795. The Senate confirmed him; but Cushing, who was now 64 years old, pleaded advanced age and ill health—he was also disinclined to take on what he viewed as the chief justice's "additional burdens." Thus, the strong supporter of judicial review rejected the post and opted for continued service as associate justice until death 14 years later.

The last of the original six justices of the first Supreme Court was James Iredell, former attorney general of North Carolina, nominated and confirmed in February 1790, five months later than the initial group of five justices, all of whom had been confirmed on September 26, 1789. He was the youngest member of that Court at 38. Although he had not been a convention participant, he had been an influential proponent of ratification, and he served as floor leader for the Federalist forces at the North Carolina ratification convention. Very likely it was because of the massive public educational campaign by the sophisticated, intellectual lawyer that the state approved the Constitution. Actually, Iredell was Washington's second choice for the position: he had first nominated, and the Senate confirmed, his close personal friend and former private military secretary during the Revolutionary War, Robert Hanson Harrison. But Harrison was chosen chancellor of Maryland just a few days after his confirmation to the Supreme Court, which he had initially reluctantly accepted yet then almost immediately declined, accurately citing ill health. Nonetheless, he decided to accept the state post—notwithstanding Washington and Hamilton's warmly urgent pleas to decline it. Iredell, however, would prove to be a source of considerable satisfaction to Washington during his service on the high bench—so much so that the president seriously considered the native Englishman's promotion to chief justice when Cushing stepped aside.

Washington's pattern of seeking men with convention participation or support continued with his remaining four successful appointments. In late

1791 he chose his friend Thomas Johnson of Maryland, 59, a brigadier general in charge of his state's troops and a former governor as well as chief judge of that state at the time of his appointment (having earlier declined Washington's offer to become the first federal district judge for Maryland). There was no doubt as to Johnson's adherence to Federalist principles. He had been a delegate to the Constitutional Convention and had faithfully supported the finished document. Extremely reluctant to accept appointment to the Supreme Court because of his strong aversion to the rigors of circuit riding, Johnson saw his fears realized when he began to serve, and he resigned in January 1793, citing deteriorating health after only 14 months in office—but unquestionably chiefly because of the trauma of circuit-riding obligations.

Johnson's replacement was William Paterson, the 48-year-old chancellor of New Jersey and former state attorney general as well as U.S. senator. A strong Federalist "with such consistency as possible to a small-state man,"[6] Paterson had been one of the foremost leaders of the Constitutional Convention, offering the small-state, or New Jersey, plan for equal representation of all states in the national legislature. One of his most significant services to the new Union was his work—second only to Oliver Ellsworth's—on behalf of the Judiciary Act of 1789, which implies the judicial review that was so vital to Washington's visualization of a strong federal judicial system. The first nine sections of the seminal statute, establishing federal district and circuit courts, were in Paterson's handwriting. His nomination was initially withdrawn by Washington because the former's term in the U.S. Senate had still four days to run, but he was readily confirmed on resubmittal.

A signer of the Declaration of Independence and a hero of the Revolution, Chief Justice Samuel Chase of Maryland, 55, was the president's initial choice to fill the vacancy caused by the Senate's rejection of John Rutledge as chief justice in December 1795, yet wisely he refrained from designating the acid-tongued, outspoken Chase. Instead, he named him to the associate's seat vacated by Blair in January 1796, which had not yet been filled. Washington had been widely cautioned about the brilliant but cantankerous Chase's character and temperament, but the president knew him well and eventually decided that his service to the causes of independence warranted his appointment. Chase had opposed the adoption of the Constitution on grounds that were rather nebulous, and he had voted against its adoption at the Maryland ratifying convention. Subsequently, he had seen the light, recognized the merits of the Constitution, and become a zealous, vocal backer of the Union.

Once on the high bench, however, Chase immediately began to make a specialty of denouncing democracy and condemning the principles of the Republican Party and rendered himself thoroughly obnoxious to the party. In 1796 he predicted that under Jefferson "our republican institution will sink into a mobocracy, the worst of all possible governments"[7]; and he charged Jefferson, both before and after his election as president, with "seditious attacks on the principles of the Constitution." For these attacks the House of Representatives impeached Chase on grounds of eight articles of "high crimes and misdemeanors" by a vote of 72:32 in March 1804. Fortunately for the cause of judicial independence and the principles of separation of powers, when the Senate voted on the charges brought by the House on March 1, 1805, enough Republicans joined the Federalists to acquit the colorful figure 19:15 on the most grievous charge, six of the other seven receiving not even a simple majority, let alone the needed two-thirds to convict him.[8] It was just as well that Washington did not live to see the controversies that surrounded his but mildly contrite appointee—he would have been chagrined and embarrassed.

In 1796, one year before the end of his second term, Washington made his last appointment: Oliver Ellsworth of Connecticut, one of that state's first two U.S. senators, 51, and a devout Calvinist who studied theology for a year but then switched to law. A staunch Federalist, state jurist, federal legislator, diplomat, and the principal author of the so vital Judiciary Act of 1789, Ellsworth was nominated to be chief justice. Like the other Washington appointees, Ellsworth, a lawyer and College of New Jersey (Princeton) graduate, with a long career of public service at hand, was an influential spokesman in behalf of the Union and had been a delegate to the Philadelphia convention, after serving for six years as a delegate from Connecticut to the Continental Congress. He had also been particularly effective in bringing about Connecticut's ratification of the Constitution in 1788. During the Philadelphia debates he emerged as an early and articulate exponent of the Supreme Court's inherent power of judicial review, which he, like Washington, saw as an essential Constitutional check on potential legislative excess. Yet Ellsworth remained at the helm for only a brief time. Notwithstanding grave inherent questions of the propriety and constitutionality of assigning nonjudicial functions to a sitting jurist, President John Adams had appointed him envoy to France in 1799. While still in France late in 1800, Ellsworth resigned because of ill health (although he recovered and would live until 1807)—thus setting the stage for the appointment of John Marshall by the lame-duck Adams.

In addition to insisting on strong Federalist credentials, Washington searched for men who had rendered service during the Revolution and, if possible, men who had been active in the affairs of their home states and communities. Seven of his successful appointees had been delegates to the Constitutional Convention, the exceptions being John Jay, William Cushing, and James Iredell. But Jay, in addition to having written the New York Constitution of 1777, had been a member of the Second Continental Congress and had been appointed "chief foreign relations officer" of the Confederation. Cushing had been chief justice of Massachusetts during the difficult and crucial period of 1777–1789; and Iredell had served North Carolina as attorney general, as a member of the Council of State, and as a superior court judge. Six of the president's choices—John Jay, Oliver Ellsworth, Samuel Chase, William Paterson, Thomas Johnson, and John Rutledge—had been members of the Continental Congress at various times. Samuel Chase, William Paterson, and James Wilson were signers of the Declaration of Independence. To the president's particular delight, several of the 10 had experienced active involvement in the field during the Revolutionary War struggles. For example, Paterson had served as an officer in a company of Minutemen, and Cushing, indomitably energetic, had ridden circuit and held court in Massachusetts during the entire revolutionary era. The president was perhaps proudest of all of Thomas Johnson: in 1777, when General Washington was literally struggling to keep his army on its feet, Governor Johnson of Maryland had recruited a force of 1,800 men and personally led them to Washington's camp. Indeed, for three successive terms as governor, Johnson displayed an uncanny ability to supply food, arms, supplies, and men to the embattled Continental Army. (But he would be a very unhappy Supreme Court justice.)

Washington sought still other attributes in his candidates—among them previous judicial experience—and with the exception of Wilson and Paterson all came to the Court with such a background. In fact, his eight other appointees had 63 years of collective judicial experience. Four had served on the Supreme Court of their respective states (Jay, Ellsworth, Chase, and Cushing); the remaining four had been jurists on other high state courts: Iredell on the Superior Court of North Carolina; John Rutledge on the South Carolina Court of Chancery; Johnson as chief judge of the General Court of Maryland; and Blair on both the General Court and the High Court of Chancery of Virginia. As for Paterson and Wilson, the mitigating circumstances were clearly acceptable: Paterson was a coauthor of the federal Judiciary Act of 1789 and, while governor of New Jersey, codified its laws and updated the rules of practice and procedure in its courts. Wilson, one of the country's most widely acclaimed legal scholars and a superb practitioner at the bar, had emerged as an expert on the judiciary in the Constitutional Convention.

Geography must also be noted as one of the elements that strongly influenced Washington's appointments. He regarded it as extremely important in the light of his constant endeavor to be president of *all* the states of the fledgling nation and repeatedly stated his desire to see each section "represented" on the Supreme Court. On several occasions Washington rewarded a strategic state. For example, in commenting on Iredell's appointment, the president frankly stated that "he is a State [North Carolina] of some importance in the Union that has given no character to a federal office."[9] Perhaps the decisive consideration in his appointment of Jay rather than John Rutledge as the first chief justice was that Jay hailed from

New York, a critical state that had so narrowly and recently ratified the Constitution. Rutledge, Wilson, and Jay had been Washington's three finalists for the post. The president eliminated Wilson because of what he regarded as a lack of appropriate administrative and political experience, leaving the New Yorker and the South Carolinian as contenders. Because Washington himself, Secretary of State Thomas Jefferson, and Attorney General Edmund Jennings Randolph were all Virginians, Washington determined that yet another top federal office occupied by a southerner would be unwise. Hence, Rutledge had to settle for an associate justiceship, from which he resigned 17 months later.

Unlike many of his successors, especially those of the twentieth century, Washington, notwithstanding his septet-catalog of required qualifications, did not resort to the narrow confines of what today would be labeled nominee "litmus tests," such as—to point to a few contemporarily popular ones—position on abortion, affirmative action, and privacy, all of which played such a crucial role in the notorious confirmation battles of Robert H. Bork and Clarence Thomas.[10] The first president's criteria were characterized by a far more fundamental, more encompassing, more broadly gauged sweep, emphasizing such seminal commitments as, among others, love of country, service in the Revolution, active participation in the life of state or nation. Determined to do all in his power to create a strong, indeed a powerful, third branch of the government, he endeavored to staff it with indubitably qualified, patriotic, service-oriented, professionally experienced public servants devoted to the essentials of a successful governmental process.

But what of the verdicts rendered by lawyers, political scientists, and historians of the performance of Washington's appointees? As the senior author reports in his works on the issue,[11] their evaluations were hardly enthusiastic. None of the 11 who served have been ranked as "great," and none as "near great." Nine—Jay, Rutledge, Cushing, Wilson, Blair, Iredell, Paterson, Chase, and Ellsworth—have received an "average" rating, Rutledge being given that score for both of his brief stints on the high tribunal. One, Thomas Johnson, was regarded as "below average," and none as a "failure"— although one reviewer, the late Bernard Schwartz, categorized Samuel Chase as 8th among his roster of "the worst" 10 justices.[12] It is a fair question, however, to ask whether the low rankings of Washington's justices may not be at least partly due to a general unfamiliarity by the mid- and late-twentieth-century raters with those early jurists.[13]

Washington died too soon—just two years after he left the presidency— to see the full on-the-bench record of his Federalist Supreme Court appointees, but he would have been well pleased with their performances. Practically no anti-Federalist decisions were rendered by them or their Federalist successors; and none of them wrote what could be called an anti-Federalist dissenting opinion. It was a pity that the first president could not witness the momentous decisions of the Court under the firm guidance of its fourth, and generally regarded as greatest, chief justice, the towering John Marshall, who by his opinions and decisions recorded during 34 years in the center chair did so much to bring to fruition Washington's dreams for a strong Republic.

NOTES

1. Fred L. Israel, "John Blair," in Leon Friedman and Fred L. Israel, eds., *The Justices of the United States Supreme Court, 1789–1969* (New York: Chelsea House, 1969), 1:111.

2. For example, Warren M. Billings, *The Bill of Rights and Virginia* (Madison, WI: Madison House, 1991), p. 22.

3. Richard Barry, *Mr. Rutledge of South Carolina* (New York: Duell, Sloan, & Pearce, 1942), p. 353.

4. 3 Dallas 133 (1795) and 3 Dallas 121 (1795), respectively.

5. As quoted by Marvin Meyerson and Dilys Pegler Winegrad, "Justice James Wilson," *Pennsylvania Gazette*, April 1978, p. 28.

6. Gertrude S. Wood, *William Paterson of New Jersey, 1745–1806* (Fair Lawn, NJ: Fair Lawn Press, 1933), p. 101.

7. As quoted in Samuel Eliot Morison, Henry Steele Commager, and William E. Leuchtenburg, *The Growth of the American Republic*, 6th ed. (New York: Oxford University Press, 1969), 1:346.

8. For authoritative commentaries and interpretations of Chase's travail, see William H. Rehnquist, *Grand Inquests: The Historic Impeachments of Justice Samuel Chase and President Andrew Johnson* (New York: Morrow, 1992); Richard Tillich, "The Chase Impeachment," *American Journal of Legal History* 4 (1960), 49.

9. Israel, "James Iredell," in Friedman and Israel, *Justices*, 1:128, n.1.

10. See Henry J. Abraham, *Justices and Presidents: A Political History of Appointments to the Supreme Court*, 3rd ed. (New York: Oxford University Press, 1992) and his *Justices, Presidents, and Senators: A History of the United States Supreme Court Appointments from Washington to Clinton* (Lanham, MD: Rowman & Littlefield, 1999).

11. Abraham, *Justices and Presidents*. See textual materials, *passim* and Appendix A.

12. See his *A Book of Legal Lists: The Best and the Worst in American Law* (New York: Oxford University Press, 1997). His other nine were Moore, Whittaker, Vinson, McReynolds, Peckham, Barbour, Butler, Minton, and Salmon P. Chase.

13. For an excellent study of the most notable members of the pre-Marshall Court see Scott Douglas Gerber, ed., *Seriatim: The Supreme Court before John Marshall* (New York: New York University Press, 1998).

thought it necessary and proper to do so. He was both firm about protecting his own prerogatives and respectful of the legitimate role of Congress at the same time. He left a legacy on the doctrine of executive privilege that is a model for other presidents to follow—even in the modern era.

Not all presidents have been so successful at finding the right balance between the often competing needs of secrecy and democratic accountability. But all have been well served by the precedent that Washington established for the exercise of executive privilege.

NOTES

1. See most prominently Raoul Berger, *Executive Privilege: A Constitutional Myth* (Cambridge, MA: Harvard University Press, 1974).

2. George Washington, letter to James Madison, May 5, 1789, quoted in John Fitzpatrick, ed., *The Writings of George Washington*, 39 vols. (Washington, DC: U.S. Government Printing Office, 1931–1944), 30:311.

3. "Queries on a Line of Conduct," May 10, 1789, quoted in Fitzpatrick, *The Writings of George Washington*, 30:321.

4. The Eisenhower administration first coined the phrase "executive privilege."

5. *3 Annals of Congress* (1792), p. 493.

6. Paul Ford. *The Writings of Thomas Jefferson*, vol. 1 (New York: Putnam, 1892), pp. 189–190.

7. Berger, *Executive Privilege*, p. 167.

8. Abraham Sofaer, "Executive Privilege: An Historical Note," *Columbia Law Review* 74 (1975), p. 1319.

9. Ibid.

10. Ibid.

11. Ibid., p. 1320.

12. Ibid., p. 1321; Abraham Sofaer, "Executive Power and Control over Information: The Practice under the Framers," *Duke Law Journal* 1977 (March 1977), p. 8.

13. Quoted in Forrest McDonald, *The American Presidency: An Intellectual History* (Lawrence: University Press of Kansas, 1994), p. 242.

14. James Richardson, *A Compilation of the Messages and Papers of the Presidents* (New York: Bureau of National Literature, 1897), vol. 1, pp. 186–187.

15. *5 Annals of Congress* (1796), pp. 771, 782–783.

16. Ibid., p. 773.

17. Ibid., p. 438.

18. Quoted in Gary Schmitt, "Executive Privilege," in Joseph Bessette and Jeffrey Tulis, eds., *The Presidency in the Constitutional Order* (Baton Rouge: Louisiana State University Press, 1981), p. 188n.

19. Ibid., p. 187n.

20. See Mark J. Rozell, *Executive Privilege: The Dilemma of Secrecy and Democratic Accountability* (Baltimore: Johns Hopkins University Press, 1994); Mark J. Rozell, "In Nixon's Shadow: Executive Privilege and the Modern Presidents," *Minnesota Law Review* (May 1999): 1069–1126.

21. "Ruff's Argument for Executive Privilege," unsealed May 27, 1998

(www.washingtonpost.com/wp-srv/politics/special/clinton/stories/ruff052898.
htm); "White House Motion Seeking Privilege," unsealed May 27, 1998 (www.
washingtonpost.com/wp-srv/politics/special/clinton/stories/whitehouse052898.htm).

22. *In re Sealed Case*, U.S. Court of Appeals of the District of Columbia, June
17, 1997 (ftp://www.11.Georgetown.edu/pub/Fed-Ct/Circuit/dc/doc/96-
3124a.txt).

23. "Judge Johnson's Order on Executive Privilege," issued May 26, 1998
(www.washingtonpost.com/wp-srv/politics/special/clinton/stories/order052898.
htm).

24. Although at this point the Clinton White House conveyed that the issue of
executive privilege had thus been settled, additional claims of privilege followed. See
*Communication from Kenneth W. Starr, Independent Counsel, Transmitting a Re-
ferral to the United States House of Representatives in Conformity with the Require-
ments of Title 28, United States Code, 595(c)*, H.R. Doc. No. 105–310, pt. XI.C.,
n.494 (September 11, 1998).

25. See especially Berger, *Executive Privilege*.

26. The most important modern Supreme Court case on this subject is, of course,
U.S. v. Nixon, 418 U.S. 683 (1974).

Part III

Washington and the Press

Chapter 7

George Washington and the Origins of Executive Privilege

MARK J. ROZELL

In April 1998 the independent counsel Kenneth Starr gave a nationally televised speech on executive privilege. At that time Starr was embroiled in a legal battle with the Clinton White House over multiple claims of executive privilege to prevent the Office of the Independent Counsel from securing the grand jury testimony of key presidential advisers. Starr insisted that he needed the testimony of these advisers in order to properly conduct his investigation into allegations that the president may have committed perjury or tried to cover up illegal White House actions during a scandal. The Clinton White House insisted that the doctrine of executive privilege protected key advisers from having to testify about matters germane to the official duties of the president.

In his speech Starr did not directly address the details of his legal battle with the Clinton White House. Rather, he focused on the issue of the proper breadth of this constitutional power, which grants the president and key advisers the right to withhold information from those with compulsory power—usually Congress, but also the courts or, more specifically in this case, an independent counsel—when it is in the public interest to do so. Unlike some legal scholars,[1] Starr did not dispute the legitimacy of executive privilege. He acknowledged that executive privilege exists, but with substantial limits. Like other constitutional powers, he correctly pointed out, executive privilege must be balanced against other governmental needs.

To substantiate his argument that executive privilege must be a limited power and subject to the public interest standard, Starr invoked the actions of the nation's first president, George Washington, as the model for understanding the proper use of this presidential power. Washington recognized that presidential secrecy sometimes is a necessity and that the power to compel testimony or White House correspondence is not absolute. During the nation's first controversy between the Congress and the president over access to White House information, Washington determined that the president has a right to withhold information, but only when the public interest is at stake.

In other secrecy disputes during his presidency, Washington similarly applied the public interest standard as the basis for deciding to withhold information. Washington both stood his ground in protecting the prerogatives of his office while at the same time he showed proper deference to Congress' power of investigation. By citing Washington's example, Starr by implication was criticizing the Clinton White House for failing to follow the model of the nation's first president when it came to asserting executive privilege.

Certainly, it is a common and sometimes effective rhetorical device for contemporaries involved in a political or legal battle to invoke the image of a revered former president as substantiation for the correctness of their own views. To suggest that one's actions are compatible with what, for example, Washington, Jefferson, or Lincoln would have done under the same circumstances is an attempt to lend such actions credibility.

In this latest battle over executive privilege, Starr picked the right former president as a standard model. What makes Washington's presidency of particular real importance to the executive privilege controversy—as with debates over other presidential powers as well—is the fact that, as the nation's first president, he was well aware that his actions would establish standards for future administrations. Consequently, he was very conscious of the need to act in accordance with the true principles of the constitutional founding.

Indeed, Washington had written to James Madison, "As the first of everything, *in our situation will serve to establish a precedent*, it is devoutly wished on my part that these precedents be fixed on true principles."[2] In May 1789 Washington wrote, "Many things which appear of little importance in themselves and at the beginning, may have great and durable consequences from their having been established at the commencement of a new general government."[3]

In what follows, I describe and analyze the exercise of executive privilege in the Washington administration. Washington's actions—indeed, fixed on firm constitutional principles—established the legitimacy of this presidential power for future administrations. His exercise of executive privilege has importance to the contemporary exercise of this power and therefore can appropriately be regarded as a model for modern presidents. I apply Washington's standards for the use of executive privilege to the latest controversial exercise of that power by the Clinton administration in what became known as the Monica Lewinsky investigation.

WASHINGTON AND EXECUTIVE PRIVILEGE

The phrase "executive privilege" actually did not exist at the time of the Washington presidency.[4] Nonetheless, on several occasions Washington contemplated or exercised what we today call executive privilege. Washington's actions established important precedents for the exercise of this constitutional power by his successors.

The first such action concerned a congressional request to investigate information relating to the failure of a November 1791 military expedition by General Arthur St. Clair against Native American Indians. The military expedition had cost hundreds of lives as well as the total loss of supplies. The event was an enormous embarrassment to the Washington administration.

The House of Representatives established an investigative committee on March 27, 1792, "to call for such persons, papers and records, as may be necessary to assist their inquiries."[5] The investigating committee requested from the president testimony and documents regarding St. Clair's expedition.

Washington convened his cabinet to determine how to respond to this first-ever request for presidential materials by a congressional committee. The president wanted to discuss whether any harm would result from public disclosure of the information and, most pertinently, whether he could rightfully refuse to submit documents to Congress. Along with Hamilton, Knox, and Edmund Randolph, Thomas Jefferson attended the April 2, 1792, cabinet meeting, and he later recalled the group's determination.

We had all considered, and were of one mind, first, that the House was an inquest, and therefore might institute inquiries. Second, that it might call for papers generally. Third, that the Executive ought to communicate such papers as the public good would permit, and ought to refuse those, the disclosure of which would injure the public: consequently were to exercise a discretion. Fourth, that neither the committees nor House has a right to call on the Head of a Department, who and whose papers were under the President alone; but that the committee should instruct their chairman to move the House to address the President.[6]

Washington eventually determined that public disclosure of the information would not harm the national interest and that such disclosure was necessary to vindicate General St. Clair. Although Washington chose to negotiate with Congress over the investigating committee's request and ultimately to turn over relevant documents to Congress, his administration had taken an affirmative position on the right of the executive branch to withhold information. Furthermore, in agreeing to cooperate with Congress, Washington established as a condition that legislators review in closed session any information that, if publicly disclosed, would bring harm to the national interest. The historian Raoul Berger correctly concluded that the

St. Clair incident "teaches that Washington would not claim privilege to hide a shameful failure within his administration, a lesson that has been lost on several presidential administrations."[7]

On January 17, 1794, the U.S. Senate advanced a motion directing Secretary of State Edmund Randolph "to lay before the Senate the correspondence which have been had between the Minister of the United States at the Republic of France, [Morris] and said Republic, and between said Minister and the Office of Secretary of State."[8] The Senate later amended the motion to address the president instead of Minister Morris. Significantly, the amended version also "requested" rather than "directed" that such information be forwarded to Congress.[9]

Believing that disclosure of the correspondence would be inappropriate, Washington sought the advice of his cabinet as to how to handle the Senate's request. On January 28, 1794, three of Washington's cabinet members expressed their opinions.

General Knox is of the opinion, that no part of the correspondence should be sent to the Senate. Colonel Hamilton, that the correct mode of proceeding is to do what General Knox advises; but the principle is safe, by excepting such parts as the president may choose to withhold. Mr. Randolph, that all correspondence proper, from its nature, to be communicated to the Senate, should be sent; but that what the president thinks is improper, should not be sent.[10]

Attorney General William Bradford wrote separately that "it is the duty of the Executive to withhold such parts of the said correspondence as in the judgment of the Executive shall be deemed unsafe and improper to be disclosed." On February 16, 1794, Washington responded as follows to the Senate's request:

After an examination of [the correspondence], I directed copies and translations to be made; except in those particulars, in my judgment, for public considerations, ought not to be communicated. These copies and translations are now transmitted to the Senate; but the nature of them manifest the propriety of their being received as confidential.[11]

Washington allowed the Senate to examine some parts of the correspondence, subject to his approval. He believed that information damaging to the "public interest" could constitutionally be withheld from the Congress. The Senate never challenged the president's authority to withhold the information.[12]

In 1796 John Jay had completed U.S. negotiations with Great Britain over issues unsettled from the American Revolution. Because many considered the settlement unfavorable to the United States, Congress took a keen interest in the negotiations. Not only did the Senate debate ratification of the Jay Treaty, but the House set out to conduct its own investigation. The House passed a resolution requesting from Washington information concerning his instructions to the United States minister to Britain regarding the treaty negotiations, "excepting such of the said papers as any existing negotiation may render improper to be disclosed."[13] That resolution raised the issue of the House's proper role in the treaty-making process. Washington refused to comply with the House request and explained:

The nature of foreign negotiations requires caution, and their success must often depend on secrecy; and even when brought to a conclusion a full disclosure of all the measures, demands, or eventual concessions which may have been proposed or contemplated would be extremely impolitic; for this might have a pernicious influence on future negotiations, or produce immediate inconveniences, perhaps danger and mischief, in relation to other powers. The necessity of such caution and secrecy was one cogent reason for vesting the power of making treaties in the President, with the advice and consent of the Senate, the principle on which that body was formed confining it to a small number of members. To admit, then, a right in the House of Representatives to demand and to have as a matter of course all the papers respecting a negotiation with a foreign power would be to establish a dangerous precedent. . . . [T]he boundaries fixed by the Constitution between the different departments should be preserved, a just regard to the Constitution and to the duty of my office . . . forbids a compliance with your request.[14]

The House of Representatives debated Washington's refusal to disclose the documents. After a lengthy debate, the House took no substantive action other than passing two nonbinding resolutions—one asserting that Congress need not stipulate any reason for requesting information from the executive; the other proclaiming that the House has a legitimate role in considering the expediency with which a treaty is being implemented.[15]

During that debate, our chief constitutional architect, then Representative James Madison, proclaimed on the House floor

that the Executive had a right, under a due responsibility, also, to withhold information, when of a nature that did not permit a disclosure of it at the time. . . . If the Executive conceived that, in relation to his own department, papers could not be safely communicated, he might, on that ground, refuse them, because he was the competent though responsible judge within his own department.[16]

In response to a proposed resolution requesting information from the president, Madison introduced to the House language to except such information "so much as, in [the president's] judgment, it may not be consistent with the interest of the United States, at this time, to disclose."[17] The House ultimately voted to appropriate funding for the treaty without reviewing the disputed materials.

Washington never included the Senate in the negotiation stage of the Jay

Treaty. During the ratification stage, the Senate voted to keep the treaty secret, as Hamilton wrote, "because they thought it [the secrecy] the affair of the president to do as he thought fit."[18] The Senate minority opposed to ratification listed seven objections to the treaty. None cited Washington's decision not to seek Senate advice.[19]

WASHINGTON'S EXECUTIVE PRIVILEGE LEGACY

There are important common threads to these early exercises of executive privilege. First, presidents do not possess an unlimited right to withhold information. Rather, Congress has the right of inquiry and may request the production of materials and testimony. Second, the president's constitutional authority to withhold information must necessarily be limited to matters of national importance (e.g., diplomatic negotiations, national security) or to protecting the privacy of internal deliberations when it is in the public interest to do so (or perhaps when disclosure may result in public embarrassment for no public gain). Third, the legislative power of inquiry, though substantial, is not absolute.

These common threads established the framework for the proper exercise of executive privilege by presidents. Over time, executive privilege came to mean that presidents may withhold information regarding weighty matters of national importance: for example, national security and internal White House deliberations over official governmental matters.

To be sure, as the Nixon and Clinton years so clearly reveal, not all presidents have acted properly in exercising this constitutional power. Nonetheless, few today reject the right of presidents on occasion to withhold information. Washington established irrefutable precedents for the exercise of executive privilege by his successors. Some used this power quite elaborately—none more so than President Dwight D. Eisenhower, who asserted executive privilege at least 40 times. Others have claimed executive privilege sparingly; for example, there were four executive privilege controversies during Ronald Reagan's two terms, and in each case the president backed away from his initial refusals to provide information to Congress.[20]

Because of the misuse of that power by President Richard Nixon—he unsuccessfully tried to use executive privilege as a shield to cover up presidential wrongdoing—executive privilege developed an unfortunately negative connotation. With the exception of Bill Clinton, presidents since the Watergate scandal have been reluctant to assert executive privilege for fear of being characterized as engaged in Nixonian efforts to conceal and deceive.

The Clinton presidency has brought about a reinvigoration of the debate over executive privilege. Unlike his immediate predecessors, Clinton has not been shy about asserting executive privilege. He has claimed that power on numerous occasions—none so controversial as his failed effort to use executive privilege in the Monica Lewinsky investigation.

stood that presidential secrecy must be formally exercised by the president himself, not by White House staff on behalf of the president's interest. The proper standard today, as in Washington's time, is that the president must personally and openly invoke executive privilege.

Once Judge Johnson ruled against Clinton, the White House dropped its flawed claim of executive privilege.[24] In a face-saving gesture, the White House counsel Charles Ruff declared victory after the defeat because Judge Johnson, in ruling against the president, had nonetheless upheld the legitimacy of the principle of executive privilege. Ruff maintained that the Clinton White House's real motivation in asserting executive privilege was to preserve this presidential power for Clinton's successors.

The doctrine of executive privilege certainly did not need this kind of help. That doctrine already stood as a legitimate presidential power, although one clearly tainted in the public mind by the Watergate episode. Reestablishing the good reputation of executive privilege required a much more compelling circumstance for its exercise than a personal scandal—a military action, for example.

The ultimately unfortunate outcome of Clinton's flawed claim of executive privilege—as with the Watergate episode—was to give that presidential power a bad name. Critics of executive privilege are quick to argue that this doctrine in itself is constitutionally flawed because it enables the president to undermine the functions of the legislative and judicial branches—specifically, by stopping Congress from exercising its power of investigation and prohibiting the courts from securing evidence.[25]

Properly exercised, executive privilege is necessary to the proper conduct of the presidency. It is now a long-standing constitutional principle that presidents are entitled to candid advice from their aides and that the chief executive has formidable national security responsibilities that may necessitate secrecy.[26]

As with all governmental powers, executive privilege may be used by presidents for good or ill purposes, and there is no absolute guarantee that every president will act prudently and properly in exercising this, or any other, power. Our constitutional system is predicted on the notion that individuals of character will ascend to the nation's highest office and will act in accordance with the rule of law. That system also anticipates that there must be proper checks against the potential abuse of power by presidents and other public officials.

President Washington, well aware that his actions in office would establish enduring precedents for the exercise of presidential powers, was very cautious about the use of secrecy. Along with his advisers he examined the Constitutional basis for secrecy and concluded that it was an appropriate presidential power, but only when exercised for the public benefit. Washington went to considerable effort to accomodate the needs of Congress during investigations, and he deferred to the legislative branch where he

How did Clinton's exercise of executive privilege in the Lewinsky investigation measure up to the traditional standards for applying that doctrine? There was obviously no national security justification to withholding information about presidential and staff discussions over how to handle that episode, although Clinton's White House counsel tried to make the argument that by harming "the president's ability to 'influence' the public," the investigation undermined his ability to lead foreign policy and protect the national interest.[21] Judged against the standards established by Washington, this argument does not withstand scrutiny. The St. Clair incident, for example, was a huge embarrassment to the Washington administration that clearly harmed the president's public reputation. Yet the president believed that it was more important to be forthcoming and accept any public rebuke for a policy mistake than to conceal information to protect his reputation. Washington did not equate his personal political interests or his public reputation with the national interest.

The Clinton White House claim of executive privilege ultimately hinged on the argument that the president had the right to protect the privacy of internal deliberations. In 1997 the U.S. Court of Appeals for the District of Columbia ruled that presidents, indeed, are entitled to candid, confidential advice and that executive privilege therefore extends to presidential advisers because they must be able to deliberate and discuss policy options without fear of public disclosure. Without that protection, the candor and quality of presidential advice would suffer.[22]

The Clinton White House maintained that this court decision justified any claims of executive privilege on behalf of discussions between the president and his aides, between and among aides, and even between the First Lady and an aide. Yet the key issue is whether the White House discussions had anything to do with official governmental business as opposed to being merely deliberations over how to handle political strategy during a scandal. The federal judge, Norma Holloway Johnson, ruled against the president's claim of privilege and determined that the constitutional balancing test weighed in favor of Independent Counsel Kenneth Starr's need for access to information that was crucial to a criminal investigation.[23]

For the White House position instead to have prevailed, Clinton needed to make a compelling argument that the public interest would have somehow suffered from the release of information about discussions over the Lewinsky investigation. Once again, this was the ultimate standard that President Washington had established for claims of executive privilege—protecting the public interest.

Not only had Clinton failed to make a case for executive privilege based on the public interest standard, but for months he even refused to answer basic questions as to whether he had formally invoked the privilege. When President Washington either considered withholding information or actually did so, he never concealed his own role in making the decision. He under-

Chapter 8

George Washington and the Press

CAROL SUE HUMPHREY

> Retire immediately; let no flatterer persuade you to rest one hour longer
> at the helm of state. You are utterly incapable to steer the political ship
> into the harbour of safety. If you have any love for your country, leave
> its affairs to the wisdom of your fellow citizens; do not flatter yourself
> with the idea that you know their interests better than other men; there
> are thousands amongst them who equal you in capacity, and who excel
> you in knowledge.

Such was the advice given by a newspaper writer to the president of the
United States. Though it sounds as if it might be a recommendation given
to several twentieth-century officeholders, it is actually the comments that
"Scipio" directed to George Washington in 1795.[1] The tension between
the press and public officials that seems so obvious and almost overwhelming
today actually began almost as soon as the United States came into existence
and has continued ever since. Even the "Father of His Country," George
Washington, faced a variety of media criticisms while holding the nation's
highest office.

Throughout his adult life, George Washington had interactions with the
press. As a Virginia planter, he used local newspapers to advertise for horses
and jackasses for sale or for use as stud animals. As Commander in Chief of
the Continental Army during the American Revolution, he feared the media
gave too much military information to the British, but he still encouraged
the use of newspapers in order to boost American morale. As president, he
perceived the importance of the press in keeping the people informed, but
he also became increasingly upset over media attacks aimed at him person-

ally. After leaving public office in 1797, he continued to read newspapers in an effort to remain knowledgeable about national and international events.

Although always interested in the media, George Washington seldom participated in the press directly. He occasionally advertised for runaway slaves, but his primary use of newspapers occurred because of various advertisements for stud animals that he owned. For example, beginning in the mid-1780s, he promoted the breeding of Royal Gift, a jackass presented to him by the king of Spain following the victory over Great Britain in 1783.[2]

During the American Revolution, Washington continually perceived the usefulness of newspapers as sources of information and as encouragers of morale. He feared the negative impact of the press, particularly when newspapers published materials that hurt the American military effort. In 1777 he complained to the president of the Continental Congress about the unthinking actions of the patriot printers:

It is much to be wished, that our Printers were more discreet in many of their Publications. We see almost in every Paper, Proclamations or Accounts transmitted by the Enemy, of an injurious nature. If some hint or caution could be given them on the Subject, it might be of material Service.[3]

Washington tried to control reports about the activities of the Continental Army in order to deny information to the enemy while, at the same time, working to gain copies of Loyalist papers (particularly from New York City) in hopes of finding out details about the movements of the British forces.

Washington encouraged people to save rags for making paper so that newspapers would continue to be published, thus providing reports about the war to their readers. His greatest support for the newspapers, however, came about because of the media's role as a wartime morale booster. The most famous example of this type of encouragement came when General Washington assembled the troops to publicly hear a reading of the first of Thomas Paine's Crisis essays, published in the *Pennsylvania Packet* in December 1776.[4] In 1777 he requested that a printing press be provided for the army in order to provide the tools necessary to keep the people properly informed:

A Small travelling Press to follow head Quarters would be productive of many eminent advantages. It would enable us to give speedy and exact information of any Military transactions that take place with proper comments upon them; and thereby frustrate the pernicious tendency of falsehood and misrepresentation, which, in my opinion of whatever complexion they may be, are in the main, detrimental to our Cause. If the People had a Channel of Intelligence, that from its usual authenticity they could look up to with confidence, they might often be preserved from that dispondency, which they are apt to fall into from the exaggerated pictures our Enemies and their emissaries among us commonly draw of any misfortunes we meet with; and from that diffidence of truths favorable to us, which they must naturally feel from the frequent deception they are exposed to, by the extravagant colourings our friends often give to our Successes.[5]

As has generally proven true for military commanders throughout the history of the United States, George Washington faced little criticism from the newspapers during the Revolution. Only once (in 1779) did a printer dare to produce something critical of Washington's leadership. William Goddard, printer of the *Maryland Journal*, published an article by General Charles Lee following Lee's forced resignation from the Continental Army after the Battle of Monmouth. Lee questioned Washington's military judgment and leadership ability.[6] A mob, led by several army officers, visited Goddard following the publication and nearly lynched him. He printed a retraction[7] but denied that action once public opinion had died down.

Loyalist printers in areas controlled by the British faced no such threats and opposition. They continually attacked Washington, accusing him of all sorts of crimes and atrocities. For example, James Rivington used the pages of his *Royal Gazette* to accuse Washington of complicity in murder (the execution of Major John Andre as a spy).[8] However, such accusations had little direct impact on Washington, and his treatment by the patriot press continued to be favorable throughout the war.

Following the end of the war, Washington returned to private life. He continued to subscribe to a number of newspapers in order to gather information about national and world events. However, he did not always find them satisfactory. He frequently requested news from his correspondents, particularly those from overseas. In 1786 Washington thanked the Marquis de Lafayette for information he had sent him about events in Europe, declaring that "newspaper accounts are too sterile, vague and contradictory, on which to form any opinion, or to claim even the smallest attention."[9]

Washington's next public service occurred in 1787, when he served as the president of the Constitutional Convention in Philadelphia. Following the publication of the Constitution, newspapers throughout the United States discussed the proposed new government. Washington took no direct part in the media debate over the Constitution in 1787–1788, but his name was used frequently in the press by the Federalists, the supporters of the Constitution. Washington's role as president of the Constitutional Convention provided some authority to the actions of that group and helped convince many people to vote for the Constitution. Washington depended on the newspapers to keep up with the actions of the various state ratifying conventions, and he became very frustrated when they failed to report on these activities:

While we are waiting the result with the greatest anxiety, our Printers are not so fortunate as to obtain any papers from the Eastward. Mine which have generally been more regular, have, however, frequently been interrupted for some time past.[10]

Washington's concern over the availability of information about the Constitutional debates grew out of a new Post Office policy forbidding printers
to exchange newspapers through the mails. Washington believed this alteration constituted a big mistake. He bemoaned this change at length in a
letter to John Jay, the Secretary of Foreign Affairs:

It is extremely to be lamented, that a new arrangement in the Post Office, unfavorable
to the circulation of intelligence, should have taken place at the instant when the
momentous question of a general Government was to come before the People. I
have seen no good apology, not even in Mr. Hazard's[11] publication, for deviating
from the old custom, of permitting Printers to exchange their Papers by the Mail.
That practice was a great public convenience and gratification. If the privilege was
not from convention an original right, it had from prescription strong pretensions
for continuance, especially at so interesting a period. The interruption in that mode
of conveyance, has not only given great concern to the friends of the Constitution,
who wished the Public to be possessed of every thing, that might be printed on both
sides of the question; but it has afforded its enemies very plausible pretexts for dealing
out their scandals, and exciting jealousies by inducing a belief that the suppression
of intelligence, at that critical juncture, was a wicked trick of policy, contrived by an
Aristocratic Junto. Now, if the Post Master General (with whose character I am
unacquainted and therefore would not be understood to form an unfavorable opinion
of his motives) has any candid Advisers who conceive that he merits the public employment they ought to counsel him to wipe away the aspersion he has incautiously
brought upon a good cause; if he is unworthy of the office he holds, it would be
well that the ground of a complaint, apparently so general, should be inquired into,
and, if [well] founded, redressed through the medium of a better appointment.[12]

Postmaster General Hazard failed to solve this concern before Washington
became president in 1789. As a result, Washington tried to take care of the
problem himself by replacing Hazard as Postmaster General with someone
whom he believed would be more amenable to allowing newspapers to travel
easily through the mails.

The members of Congress, however, did not totally agree with President
Washington on this issue, and they placed a tax on newspapers delivered by
the Postal Service as a means to raise money for the support of the federal
government. Washington continually spoke out in opposition to this tax,
using his annual messages to Congress to request that it change this policy.
As he prepared his First Inaugural Address in 1789, Washington originally
planned to declare that he "need not say how satisfactory it would be, to
gratify the useful curiosity of our citizens by the conveyance of News Papers
and periodical Publications in the public vehicles without expense."[13] In
1792 he addressed the issue directly in his annual message to Congress:

It is represented that some provisions in the law which establishes the post-office
operate, in experiment, against the transmission of newspapers to distant parts of the

country. Should this, upon due inquiry, be found to be the fact, a full conviction of the importance of facilitating the circulation of political intelligence and information will, I doubt not, lead to the application of a remedy.[14]

Again, in 1793 he asked Congress to reconsider the duty:

But here I cannot forbear to recommend a repeal of the tax on the transportation of the public prints. There is no resource so firm for the Government of the United States as the affections of the people, guided by an enlightened policy; and to this primary good nothing can conduce more than a faithful representation of public proceedings, diffused without restraint, throughout the United States.[15]

As president during the early years of the new nation, Washington perceived the press as an essential mechanism for keeping good citizens informed and involved and, thus, to keep the government of the young country functioning properly. His attempts to free the press from taxation that interfered with circulation reflected his belief that newspapers provided a communications network that was important for the survival and growth of the young nation.

Washington's belief in the important role of the media in a republic continued throughout his public career because he thought great benefits came from the existence of a free press. However, the rise of political parties in the 1790s produced partisan newspapers that impugned the opposition in strong, derogatory language. Both the Hamiltonian Federalists and the Jeffersonian Republicans established weekly gazettes with the primary purpose of supporting their political agenda and castigating the efforts of the other party. John Fenno's *Gazette of the United States* and Phillip Freneau's *National Gazette* led the way in the development of party journals, which dominated newspaper publishing from the 1790s until the 1830s. Washington mourned that the press missed its calling by engaging in such practices:

It is to be lamented that the Editors of the different Gazettes in the Union, do not more generally, and more correctly (instead of stuffing their papers with scurrility, and nonsensical declamation, which few would read if they were apprised of the contents) publish the debates in Congress on all great national questions, and this with no uncommon pains, everyone of them might do. The principles upon which the difference of opinion arises, as well as the decisions would then come fully before the public, and afford the best data for its judgment.[16]

Furthermore, Washington believed that such inflammatory statements and derogatory attacks hurt the international reputation of the United States. He expressed this fear in a 1792 letter to Gouverneur Morris:

From the complexion of some of our News-papers Foreigners would be led to believe that inveterate political dissensions existed among us, and that we are on the very verge of disunion; but the fact is otherwise; the great body of the people now feel the advantages of the General Government, and would not, I am persuaded, do any thing that should destroy it.

Still, Washington went on to state that the positive aspects of the press outweighed the negatives:

but these kind of representations is an evil which must be placed in opposition to the infinite benefits resulting from a free Press; and I am sure you need not be told that in this Country a personal difference in political sentiments is often made to take the garb of general discussions.[17]

Even Washington himself, the great hero of the Revolution, did not escape newspaper attacks. His first term in office proved a quiet one as far as press criticism was concerned. However, Washington's determination to run for re-election in 1792 opened the door for some newspaper attacks because opposition editors used this decision to increasingly describe Washington as a politician rather than a statesman. Shortly after the election, "Mirabeau" bemoaned the "ceremonial distance between the officers of the government and the people" and warned against the formal celebration of the birthdays of public officials (a practice that had begun in the case of Washington's birthday during the Revolution).[18] In early February, "A Farmer" warned "that it is dangerous in the extreme to set up any man as an idol . . . witness Cromwell's grip in the name of republicanism."[19] The first direct criticisms of Washington came following the public celebrations of his birthday in 1793. Philip Freneau's *National Gazette* criticized these rituals, declaring that "even Cincinnatus received no adulation of this kind. . . . Surely the office [the president] enjoys is a sufficient testimony of the people's favor, without worshipping him likewise."[20] In a later issue, Freneau criticized the American people for engaging in "the absurdities of levees, and every species of royal pomp and parade" and for attributing the success of the Revolution entirely to Washington's efforts: "The glory and achievement of the late Revolution have been entirely imputed to him, and were he Virtue's self the strains of panegyric could not have been louder in order to complete the shame and disgrace of republican dogmas."[21] Later that same year, Thomas Greenleaf's *New-York Journal* abused Washington for having "aristocratical blood" in his veins and having spent all of his youth "gambling, reveling, horseracing, and horse whipping." Furthermore, Washington's iron will "did not and could not brook restraint," and he was a "most horrid swearer and blasphemer."[22] The charges of aristocracy and monarchy continued for the rest of Washington's presidency. In 1795 one author declared:

We have given him [Washington] the powers and prerogatives of a King. He holds levees like a King, receives congratulations on his birthday like a King, receives ambassadors like a King, makes treaties like a King, answers petitions like a King, employs his old enemies like a King, shuts himself up like a King, shuts up other people like a King, takes advice of his counsellors or follows his own opinion like a King . . . swallows adulation like a King and vomits offensive truths in your face.[23]

Washington refused to respond publicly to these verbal assaults, but he considered them dangerous because of their potential impact on the future of the country:

That there are in this, as well as in all other Countries, discontented characters, I well know; as also that these characters are actuated by very different views: Some good, from an opinion that the measures of the General Government are impure: some bad, and (if I might be allowed to use so harsh an expression) diabolical; inasmuch as they are not only meant to impede the measures of that Government generally, but more especially (as a great mean towards the accomplishment of it) to destroy the confidence, which it is necessary for the people to place (until they have unequivocal proof of demerit) in their public servants; for in this light I consider myself, whilst I am an occupant of office; and, if they were to go further and call me their slave, (during this period) I would not dispute the point.—But in what will this abuse terminate? The result, as it respects myself, I care not; for I have a consolation within, that no earthly efforts can deprive me of, and that is, that neither ambitious nor interested motives have influenced my conduct. The arrows of malevolence, therefore, however barbed and well pointed, never can reach the most vulnerable part of me; though, whilst I am *up* as a *mark*, they will be continually aimed. The publications in Freneau's and Bache's papers are outrages on common decency; and they progress in that style, in proportion as their pieces are treated with contempt, and are passed by in silence, by those at whom they are aimed. The tendency of them, however, is too obvious to be mistaken by men of cool and dispassionate minds, and, in my opinion, ought to alarm them; because it is difficult to prescribe bounds to the effect.[24]

Although Washington refused to respond to newspaper attacks publicly, his comments in letters and in conversations recorded by friends and colleagues indicated that he suffered greatly in private for what was said about him in print. Thomas Jefferson commented in his diary on several occasions about Washington's reactions to press criticisms. Generally, Washington expressed sorrow at the attacks, but occasionally he lost his temper over something printed in a newspaper. Jefferson recorded one such event in his notes for a cabinet meeting in August 1793:

The President was much inflamed, got into one of those passions when he cannot command himself. Ran on much on the personal abuse which had been bestowed on him. Defied any man on earth to produce one single act of his since he had been in the government which was not done on the purest motives. That he had never repented but once the having slipped the moment of resigning his office, and that was every moment since. That *by god* he had rather be in his grave than in his present situation. That he had rather be on his farm than be made *emperor of the world*, and yet that they were charging him with wanting to be a king. That that "rascal Freneau" sent him 3 of his papers every day, as if he thought he would become the distributor of his papers, that he could see in this nothing but an impudent design to insult him. He ended in this high tone.[25]

Although very upset with the media in 1793, the worst was yet to come for Washington and his administration. The greatest newspaper attacks came in the aftermath of the Jay Treaty with Great Britain in 1795. Washington had originally been castigated, following the appointment of John Jay to go to England, for attempting to avoid impeachment proceedings by sending the Chief Justice (Jay) out of the country.[26] Problems related to the treaty itself resulted from the publication of its contents in the *Aurora* after two senators leaked it to the editor, Benjamin Franklin Bache. The news leak infuriated Washington because he had hoped to present the treaty to the American public only after its approval by the Senate. However, faced with spreading rumors in the press, he ordered the entire treaty published in order to avoid as much false information as possible.

Once the treaty's provisions became public knowledge, the newspapers centered their attacks on the president. One writer in Boston's *Independent Chronicle* declared that Washington was not as wise as he had been portrayed and that the British treaty showed this very clearly.[27] "Pittachus" attacked Washington for his distance from the people, accusing him of maintaining "the seclusion of a monk and the supercillious distance of a tyrant."[28] He also attacked the president for seeking power and glory during the Revolution and accused the American people of having "spoiled their President as a too indulgent parent spoils a child."[29] "Belisarius" urged Americans not to place Washington on a pedestal, declaring that he was a "frail mortal whose passions and weaknesses are like those of other men."[30] In probably the worst attack to that time, "Valerius" accused Washington of "dark schemes of ambition" and "political degeneracy" and branded him a "usurper." Furthermore, Washington's successes as commander of the Continental Army during the Revolution resulted from luck and accident rather than any leadership talent that the president possessed. Finally, Washington had been elected because of the "insipid uniformity of a mind which had been happy in proportion to the contracted sphere of its operations." The American people, knowing that "nature had played the miser when she gave you birth" and that "education had not been lavish in her favours," elected a less-intelligent leader in order to reduce the dangers of tyranny from personal ambitions.[31]

The most damaging assaults began in late 1795 when a writer in Bache's *Aurora*, using the pseudonym of "A Calm Observer," declared that President Washington had overdrawn his annual expense appropriation of $25,000. Washington's government could not ignore such a specific charge.

Oliver Wolcott, Secretary of the Treasury, responded quickly, declaring that his office advanced money to the president's secretary for personal expenses whenever needed. Such disbursements might have exceeded the quarterly division of the money allotted, but Washington could not be held responsible for this event. Rather, according to Wolcott, the blame should be laid either on the Department of the Treasury, which disbursed the money, or on Congress, which approved the spending of the money. Bache dutifully printed Wolcott's letter on October 26 and followed it on the next day with another missive from "A Calm Observer," which labeled Wolcott's piece as "a complete acknowledgment of guilt." The essayist called for an investigation to see if Washington had ever received more than $25,000 in a year or $100,000 in four years, asserting that the president should be impeached for violating the law if such was found to be true. On October 28 "One of the People" presented specific evidence indicating that the president had overspent his allotment on several occasions and that he was currently heavily overdrawn.[32]

Clearly, Wolcott's comments did not assuage Bache or the other Republican opposition editors. Because the charges were technically true, the Federalists in general and Washington's vocal supporters in particular could not really provide a satisfactory answer to the press attack. The Republican newspapers continued to castigate the president in print and accused him of using the American people for his own personal gain. The *Independent Chronicle* declared that "the veil is taken off the eyes of the people in this particular" so that they could now see Washington for the untrustworthy politician that some Republicans had said he was all along.[33] After the election of 1796, when Washington had chosen not to run again, and John Adams had been selected, one of Bache's correspondents summed up the feelings of those who had attacked the president in the press:

If ever a nation was debauched by a man, the American nation has been debauched by WASHINGTON. If ever a nation was deceived by a man, the American nation has been deceived by WASHINGTON. Let his conduct then be an example to future ages. Let it serve to be a warning that no man may be an idol, and that a people may confide in themselves rather than in an individual. Let the history of the federal government instruct mankind, that the masque of patriotism may be worn to conceal the foulest designs against the liberties of a people.[34]

The Federalists attempted to defend Washington but could only attack the attackers. They declared that the Republican editors were "prompted more by ill nature than by any love for the good of the people."[35] Bache in particular received caustic criticism for his calumnies against President Washington:

The Cerberus of Democracy, Bache, barks more furiously than ever and snaps so much that its fangs will lose their power of wounding . . . unless it make a speedy exit by madness. . . . The President is the continual mark of his abuse, to which no bound is set.[36]

Washington himself perceived Bache to be at the center of the criticism aimed against him. He declared in a letter to Jeremiah Wadsworth that "this man [Bache] has celebrity in a certain way, for His calumnies are to be exceeded only by his Impudence, and both stand unrivalled."[37]

Personal attacks such as those contained in the *Aurora* proved particularly upsetting to Washington. In the debate over the Jay Treaty, Washington could not understand how he could be accused "of being the enemy of one nation, and subject to the influence of another" when he was only trying to avoid a military conflict. Furthermore, he could not believe "that every act of my administration would be tortured and the grossest and most insidious misrepresentations of them made (by giving one side *only* of a subject—)." Washington concluded that the papers referred to him "in such exaggerated and indecent terms as could scarcely be applied to a Nero, to a notorious defaulter, or even to a common pick pocket."[38] For Washington, such attacks were incomprehensible and served no useful purpose in the public arena. They were as "indecent as they [were] void of truth and fairness,"[39] and their impact was uncertain:

That Mr. Bache will continue his attacks on the Government, there can be no doubt, but that they will make no Impression on the public mind is not so certain, for drops of Water will Impress (in time) the hardest Marble.[40]

Washington feared the results of a press with no restraints:

I shall be happy in the mean time to see a cessation of the abuses of public Officers, and of those attacks upon almost every measure of government with which some of the Gazettes are so strongly impregnated; and which cannot fail, if persevered in with the malignancy they now teem, of rending the Union asunder. The Seeds of discontent, distrust, and irritations which are so plentifully sown, can scarcely fail to produce this effect and to Mar that prospect of happiness which perhaps never beamed with more effulgence upon any people under the Sun; and this too at a time when all Europe are gazing with admiration at the brightness of our prospects. And for what is all this? Among other things, to afford Nuts for our transatlantic, what shall I call them? Foes! In a word if the government and the Officers of it are to be the constant theme for Newspaper abuse, and this too without condescending to investigate the motives or the facts, it will be impossible, I conceive, for any man living to manage the helm, or to keep the machine together.[41]

Washington finally escaped the public eye in 1797 by not running for re-election in 1796. He decided to retire because "he could not believe or conceive himself anywise necessary to the successful administration of the Government." Furthermore, his continuation in office did not seem designed to foster tranquility, and thus "his return to private life was consistent with every public consideration."[42] He announced his decision to leave public office in September 1796, when he issued his Farewell Address, published in the *American Daily Advertiser.*[43] Even as Washington planned his retirement, he could not ignore or forget the important role that he believed the press played in a democracy, and he used it to inform the people of his thoughts and plans for the future.

Still, Washington's unhappiness over how the newspapers had treated him while he served as president had not disappeared. His original draft for his final public comments to the American people included an attack on the press for its behavior:

As some of the gazettes of the United States have teemed with all the invective that disappointment, ignorance of facts, and malicious falsehoods could invent, to misrepresent my politics and affections—to wound my reputation and feelings—and to weaken, if not entirely destroy, the confidence you have been pleased to repose in me; it might be expected at the parting scene of my public life that I should take some notice of such virulent abuse. But, as heretofore, I shall pass them over in utter silence.[44]

Although these comments never appeared in a public form, they reflect the hurt and anger that Washington felt toward those who had attacked his character in the press. Those who assaulted him did not cease their attacks. Bache tried to get in one final jab by stating that the "perfidious" Washington chose not to run for re-election for a third term not from "a want of ambition or lust of power" but because he knew that he could not win.[45]

Following his return to Mount Vernon, Washington continued to subscribe to several newspapers in an attempt to keep up with events in the world outside the boundaries of his plantation. However, they did not always publish what he hoped to find. Editorializing often covered up whatever news was presented and made reaching conclusions about events almost impossible. He declared to Oliver Wolcott that

there is so little dependence on Newspaper publications, which take whatever complexion the Editors please to give them, that persons at a distance, and who have no other means of information, are oftentimes at a loss to form an opinion on the most important occurrences.[46]

Washington's reputation recovered from the press attacks against his presidency following his death in 1799, but his struggles with, and his concerns about, the media during his public career reflected the ongoing tension between government officials and the press that has been a part of American politics ever since.

NOTES

1. Philadelphia *Aurora*, September 20, 1795.

2. Various letters beginning in 1785 refer to this gift and Washington's various breeding experiments. See, for example, John C. Fitzpatrick, ed., *The Writings of George Washington*, 39 vols. (Washington, DC: U.S. Government Printing Office, 1931–1944, 27:446, 447; 28:74, 147, 160, 161, 208, 244, 296–302, 309, 331, 359, 360–362, 373, 385, 399, 409, 423, 426, 454, 459, 471, 478, 479, 528; 30: 127; 31:217, 312; 32:377, 401; 33:205, 273–275, 278, 279, 283, 284, 295, 297, 336; 34:112, 498, 508; 37:104.

3. May 5, 1777 in Fitzpatrick, *Writings*, 8:17.

4. Eric Foner, *Tom Paine and Revolutionary America* (New York: Oxford University Press, 1976), p. 139.

5. George Washington to Philip Livingston, Elbridge Gerry, and George Clymer, July 19, 1777, in Fitzpatrick, *Writings*, 8:443–444.

6. Baltimore, *Maryland Journal*, July 6, 1779.

7. *Maryland Journal*, July 14, 1779.

8. New York *Royal Gazette*, November 15, 1780.

9. May 10, 1786, in Fitzpatrick, *Writings*, 28:421.

10. July 18, 1788, in Fitzpatrick, *Writings*, 30:16.

11. Ebenezer Hazard was the Postmaster General under the Articles of Confederation government.

12. July 18, 1788, in Fitzpatrick, *Writings*, 30:16–17.

13. This statement appeared in a draft of a message that Washington did not deliver. Fitzpatrick, *Writings*, 30:305.

14. Fourth Annual Message, November 6, 1792, in Fitzpatrick, *Writings*, 32:210.

15. Fifth Annual Message, December 3, 1793, in Fitzpatrick, *Writings*, 33:169.

16. George Washington to David Stuart. March 28, 1790, in Fitzpatrick, *Writings*, 31:30.

17. October 20, 1792, in Fitzpatrick, *Writings*, 32:189–190.

18. Philadelphia *National Gazette*, December 12, 1792.

19. *National Gazette*, February 2, 1793.

20. *National Gazette*, February 27, 1793.

21. *National Gazette*, March 2, 1793.

22. *New-York Journal*, December 7, 1793.

23. *New York Argus*, December 26, 1795.

24. George Washington to Governor Henry Lee, July 21, 1793, in Fitzpatrick, *Writings*, 33:23–24.

25. "Notes of Cabinet Meeting on Edmond Charles Genet," *The Papers of Thomas Jefferson*, edited by John Catanzariti, vol. 26 (Princeton, NJ: Princeton University Press, 1995), pp. 602–603.

26. *Gazette of the United States*, June 2, 1794.

27. Boston *Independent Chronicle*, September 7, 1795.

28. *Aurora*, August 22, September 27, 1795.

29. *Independent Chronicle*, October 15, 1795. Reprinted from the *Aurora*.

30. *Aurora*, September 15, 1795.

31. *Aurora*, September 9, 25, October 21, 1795.

32. *Aurora*, October 23, 1795, through October 28, 1795.

33. *Independent Chronicle*, November 30, 1795.

34. *Aurora*, December 23, 1796.

35. Newfield, later Bridgeport (Connecticut) *American Telegraphe*, November 18, 1795.

36. Rachel Bradford to Samuel Bayard, November 26, 1795, in Jane J. Boudinot, ed., *The Life, Public Services, Addresses, and Letters of Elias Boudinot* (Boston: Houghton Mifflin, 1896), pp. 113–114.

37. March 6, 1797, in Fitzpatrick, *Writings*, 35:421.

38. George Washington to Thomas Jefferson, July 6, 1796, in Fitzpatrick, *Writings*, 35:120.

39. George Washington to Timothy Pickering, the Secretary of State, July 18, 1796, in Fitzpatrick, *Writings*, 35:144.

40. George Washington to Oliver Wolcott, the Secretary of the Treasury, July 6, 1796, in Fitzpatrick, *Writings*, 35:126.

41. George Washington to Edmund Randolph, the Attorney General, August 26, 1792, in Fitzpatrick, *Writings*, 32:136–137.

42. Washington originally made these statements to James Madison in 1792, when he first expressed his desire to leave the office of president. Madison, along with others such as Thomas Jefferson and Alexander Hamilton, convinced him to run for another term. However, by 1796, Washington was fully convinced that it was time for him to retire. "Memorandum on President's Retirement," *The Papers of James Madison*, edited by Robert A. Rutland et al., vol. 14 (Charlottesville: University Press of Virginia, 1983), p. 301.

43. Philadelphia *American Daily Advertiser*, September 19, 1796.

44. Fitzpatrick, *Writings*, 35:59.

45. *Aurora*, December 21, 1796.

46. May 15, 1797, in Fitzpatrick, *Writings*, 35:447.

Chapter 9

Beginning a Legend: George Washington in the Boston Newspapers, 1754–1758

FRANK E. DUNKLE

In 1775, when the Continental Congress needed a Commander in Chief for its army, the delegates appointed George Washington, apparently with confidence in his military experience from the previous war. Indisputably, the single greatest reason the Congress choose Washington the Virginian in 1775 was to wed the interests of the southern colonies to the fight in the North. New England congressmen worried that southern colonies might leave Massachusetts to work out its own problems with the British government. They astutely perceived that giving command of the makeshift army encamped around Boston to any man from Virginia, the most populous southern colony, would win support for the conflict among southerners. Yet, as Don Higginbotham has noted, no southerner would have been acceptable unless he were perceived as having adequate qualifications.[1] Evidence indicates that New Englanders had a favorable attitude toward Washington's abilities, based at least partially on the image of him that Boston's newspapers had created 20 years previously.

In nominating him for the post, John Adams said Washington was "well known to all of us, a gentleman whose skill and experience as an officer . . . would command the approbation of all America."[2] Historians might justly suspect that as a politician Adams was merely lauding Washington to win support for his nominee. However, a private letter to his wife reveals that Adams the private citizen held a genuinely high regard for the Virginian's military experience and ability.[3] Eliphalet Dyer and Robert Treat Paine were delegates to Congress who also wrote favorable estimations of the general's reputation for military accomplishment.[4] In a letter to his wife, Silas Deane not only commented on Washington's impressive soldierly appearance but also reminded her of how the Virginian had made his reputation. "He . . .

was in the first action in 1753 & 1754 on the Ohio & in 1755 was with Braddock, & was the means of saving the remains of that unfortunate army."[5] This information about Washington had become widely known in New England through the only mass medium of the time: the newspapers.

If one asks why, when congressmen wanted a southerner to lead the Revolutionary army, they chose Washington over others with more military experience and training, one answer is that the favorable image of him that had appeared in Boston newspapers made a lasting impression. Twenty years after the event, New Englanders remembered the young Virginian who had leaped to national prominence because of his involvement in a contention between France and Britain over control of the Ohio River valley, a contention that sparked the French and Indian War. In reports of the earliest fighting of that conflict, Washington's name appeared often and almost always favorably in the columns of Boston's newspapers.[6] This occurred despite the fact that he was victorious in only one small skirmish and subsequently suffered two significant defeats. Washington's reputation survived and even surpassed that of men who attained greater success on the battlefield—such as New York's William Johnson—because Boston publishers strove to promote New England support for the French and Indian War, explaining away defeats and extolling the virtues of British and American soldiers. This, incidentally, also helped make a certain Virginia militia officer one of the most famous soldiers in North America, as much by coincidence as because of any merit he had yet displayed.[7]

Boston had four weekly newspapers in 1754, reduced to three in 1755. They were the *Boston Newsletter*, published and printed by John Draper; the *Boston Gazette or Weekly Journal* by Samuel Kneeland; the *Boston Evening Post* by Thomas Fleet; and the *Boston Postboy*, published by Boston's postmaster Ellis Husk. This paper ceased publication in December 1754.[8] In April 1755 Benjamin Edes and John Gill in partnership took over the *Gazette*, expanding the size of the paper, and began using a new typeface. It soon became one of the best newspapers in the country, and the printer's tendency to include in it opinionated political essays also made it one of the most controversial.[9] These printers or men who had been apprenticed to them were still publishing Boston's newspapers during the Stamp Act Crisis and the Revolution, during which time they actively used propaganda to influence their countrymen.[10] It is perhaps not a coincidence that Edes and Gill, who became radical Revolutionaries in the 1770s, provided the most favorable presentation of Washington in the 1750s. In the mid-1750s the print runs of Boston newspapers averaged around only 600 each, but this is not an accurate measurement of their effectiveness in reaching and influencing a large audience.[11] Carl Bridenbaugh noted, "Boston papers enjoyed a large number of readers for the times, and their circulation extended all over New England and the colonies to the southward."[12] James Franklin, who began Boston's third paper in 1721, claimed that his *New England*

Courant had a very large circulation because each copy was borrowed and read by several people. Papers were relatively expensive at that time, so they were passed around, and most people preferred reading a slightly used one to buying their own.[13] The few New England farmers who could not read listened to others read the news aloud in a neighbor's home or in the local tavern.[14] Indeed, taverns and coffeehouses probably provided the bulk of readership for newspapers. In addition to the price of their beverages, these public houses typically charged patrons a penny to cover the cost of maintaining lights and newspapers.[15] In small villages one justification for frequenting a tavern was that it often had the only newspaper in town. These rare sheets saw much hard usage in such places where most men read or listened to others read them and then discussed current political issues.[16] Thus, one can conclude that when Boston newspapers presented a favorable image of Washington in the 1750s, a significant portion of New England's population could be influenced by it.

Readers of Boston papers first learned of imminent conflict between Britain and France and were introduced to the future hero in early 1754. That winter the papers reprinted a series of speeches by Virginia governor Robert Dinwiddie to the House of Burgesses telling of French troops advancing in a "hostile manner" "to invade" western territory claimed by the Old Dominion.[17] Dinwiddie revealed that in late 1753 he had sent a young Major George Washington as an ambassador into the wilderness to meet the French and respectfully ask them to leave British territory. Soon after, another of Governor Dinwiddie's fiery warnings to the Burgesses includes a brief account of the dramatic story of that brave militia officer's journey.[18] Thus, the first times Washington's name appeared in print in New England, he was cast in the role of a hero.[19]

Washington kept a journal during his journey, and the tale of his mission was so exciting and made such a strong case against French aggression and duplicity that Dinwiddie speedily had it printed as a pamphlet. The *Boston Gazette* ran it serially over six issues, giving many New England readers the opportunity to follow the two-and-one-half-month adventure of Washington's dangerous winter journey through a snowy wilderness. The journal described in his own words how the young major held Indian conferences in the deep forest to win allies before meeting the enemy commander face-to-face within a French fort near Lake Erie. There they engaged in a subtle contest to win support from local Indians while debating whose empire could justly claim the rich Ohio valley. During the grueling trip home through the frozen forest, hidden snipers shot at Washington and a companion. They hastily built a raft for a river crossing, but it overturned, plunging them into icy waters far from any shelter. Saved from death by his superb physical strength, Washington continued the journey. Through several sleepless nights he rode back toward Williamsburg, where he finally conferred with the governor, reporting French refusal to leave the disputed territory.[20] This completed Washington's dangerous mission, but his service and the Boston papers' account of it were really only the beginning of Washington's longer public journey.

By the time the Virginia legislature—and Boston's newspaper readers—learned the results of Washington's meeting with the French commander, Dinwiddie was ready to report that he already had commissioned a small group of frontiersmen to occupy and fortify the forks of the Ohio River (modern Pittsburgh).[21] Boston newspapers thereafter carried many stories telling how the southern colonies were raising men and money to defend their frontier. They also reported that Washington, now a lieutenant colonel, was leading the advance force of 200 men who were to cut a road through the forest and garrison the new fort. A much larger force, led by Colonel Joshua Frye, would follow when it had assembled.[22] But the next big news in the papers about the expedition was of a quick, victorious battle—and Washington again appeared a hero.

That May Indian scouts had warned the lieutenant colonel that a group of approximately 40 French soldiers was secretly advancing toward him. Washington immediately led a small force of his own on an overnight march to make a surprise attack against the enemy at dawn. His party killed 10 Frenchmen and took the rest prisoner. That July an early account of the skirmish appeared in several Boston papers. It was grossly inaccurate but clearly portrayed the French as cowards and Washington as a hero. It said that as the Virginians approached, the French fired the first shots. Eight of them then fell in the Americans' return volley, and the rest "took to their heels." Being cut off by the small group of English-allied Indians who had accompanied Washington, the French cowardly ran back to the Virginians, begging for quarter. Although the Half King, an Iroquois sachem who accompanied the Virginians, claimed that these same Frenchmen had boiled and eaten his father, Washington demonstrated civility in sparing their lives and protecting his prisoners from the avenging Indians.[23]

In all, the Boston papers printed at least four different versions of the fight. The most accurate finally came out in late July. It seems that the attack made good copy and perhaps helped sell newspapers as well as popularize the growing conflict.[24] Apparently, Boston's printers would have published as many accounts of the story as they could obtain. One thing all of them had in common was that in them the Virginia militia officer appeared as a daring and brave commander. The name Washington became a regular feature in the Boston press and was associated with success. Washington gained further prestige when he rose to the rank of full colonel in the Virginia militia at the age of 22 because Colonel Frye unfortunately died from a fall from his horse.[25]

Washington's success would prove to be short-lived, though. A more powerful force of French and Indians soon marched against him. He made a valiant stand at the tiny, hastily built Fort Necessity (some 40 miles south-east of the Ohio forks) but had to surrender after a daylong battle. The story was widely retold in the press in a variety of versions. One that was printed early and often claimed that the heavily outnumbered Virginia commander had arranged honorable surrender terms, but the French then acted dishonorably in allowing their Indians to ravage the British camp, plundering supplies and killing wounded Virginia soldiers.[26]

A goal of modern propagandists is to conceal or justify an enemy victory so the home audience will not lose heart. One well-used method of doing this is to claim the enemy had launched a surprise attack, with superior numbers.[27] This is how Washington's defeat appeared in the Boston papers. His loss of Fort Necessity was explained as a surprise attack by a larger force. This was not particularly difficult to believe because it was partially true— the French did have at least twice the number of the Virginia troops. Of course, the same stories that intended to save the honor and reputation of America's fighting ability incidentally also helped save the honor and reputation of George Washington.

Full accounts of the battle said that Washington had only 300 men, many of them sick, fighting 900 French and Indians. One story estimated the enemy at more than 1,500! Washington's official report said, "The French having been reinforced . . . were in full march with 900 men to attack us. Upon this, as our numbers were so unequal (our force not exceeding 300), we prepared for our defence in the best manner we could."[28] In truth, the French and Indians numbered only about 650, but this was still about twice as many men as Washington commanded, and the French surely wanted him to believe their numbers were even higher.[29] The varied reports all agreed that the attack came with little warning and that the French and Indians ignobly refused to fight the standard open field battle offered by the Virginians, as Washington's report told.

We immediately called all our men to their arms and drew up in order before our trenches. They advanced in a very irregular manner . . . they had no intention of attacking us in the open field. We continued this unequal fight, with an enemy sheltered behind the trees, ourselves without shelter, in trenches full of water, in a settled rain, and the enemy galling us on all sides incessantly from the woods.[30]

Later in the year an apologist claimed that Virginia soldier's bravery and zealousness had been partially responsible for the setback. Only 300 or 400 men bravely but rashly went forward against a foe triple their number when they should have been receiving reinforcements and larger guns from other colonies.[31] Thus, the writer not only explained the loss but also put much of the responsibility on other colonies by implying that they should have been as diligent in the king's service as Virginia.

Reports of the battle also took care to note other extraordinary disadvantages Washington and his men faced to explain how they could have been defeated in spite of British American martial superiority. Bad weather and a shortage of supplies caused the defeat rather than poor leadership or lack of courage. One writer explained that "our men had been eight days without bread, and instead of a large convoy, which we expected, there arrived only a few bags of flour . . . and a little bacon for the support of 300 men!" He later added that "by the continued rains, and water in the trenches, most of our arms were out of order, and we had only two screws in the whole regiment to clean them."[32]

In September Boston newspaper readers had the opportunity to read a letter by an officer of the Virginia regiment specifically defending Washington's reputation. He claimed that some were criticizing the young colonel without knowing what really happened "and thereby seem to reflect dishonor on Col. Washington, who is a brave and worthy young gentleman." The writer detailed many difficult and unavoidable circumstances that led to Washington's surrender. A large part of the blame was placed on a British regular army captain who had hindered the operation as much as the weather, inadequate supplies, and ill-trained, exhausted men. The letter concluded:

Let any one of those brave gentlemen who fight so many successful campaigns over a bottle imagine himself at the head of 300 men, whose lives in a great measure he is answerable for, laboring under all the disadvantages above mentioned, and environed with four times his number of an active enemy, and would not he be glad to accept of worse terms than Colonel Washington did?[33]

The evidence indicates that the Virginia colonel's reputation survived the black mark of defeat, at least partially because newspaper writers sought to explain away the defeat and maintain enthusiasm for the war itself. The same excuses that could absolve Americans in general of charges of military incompetence also relieved Washington of the responsibility for defeat.

In Europe diplomats would long argue about Washington's actions and their results. The capitulation agreement ending the engagement at Fort Necessity stated in French that Washington had assassinated official envoys of France when he made his surprise attack on the French party. Washington did sign this statement but claimed that his translator, a Dutchman named Jacob Van Braam, had incorrectly translated the document, saying only that Washington was responsible for killing French officers, not assassinating them. He maintained that his offensive action had been a just move to thwart French espionage.[34] Those concerned with imperial relations debated the intention and meaning of Washington's rash actions, and many of them deprecated the foolhardiness of fighting at Fort Necessity, but such discussions did not appear in the Anglo-American press. To most British colonials it was enough that the Virginia colonel had acted bravely in the face of a larger number of enemy troops, unselfishly striving to serve his king and country. In James Thomas Flexner's words, "[W]hatever the situation in the greater world, Washington had become a hero to his neighbors."[35]

In 1754 Washington had become famous throughout America. From that point forward he never lost his good reputation, and for the next two years, his name seemed to hold particular attraction for the Boston press. Despite the greater influence of policymakers in the East, in 1754 Washington was at the center of the action, and he became somewhat of an icon during this opening stage of the war. His name appeared in the Boston newspapers in 1754 as many times—48—as all other military officers combined. Naturally, most references to Washington were in the spring and summer in reports of his exploits in the West. Yet, his named appeared in print throughout the rest of the year as well.

In 1755 the Virginian received much less attention from Boston's newspapers, and his fame might have faded except for the bravery he and fellow colonial soldiers would display that summer in one of the war's most famous battles—Braddock's defeat. In January 1755 the *Boston Newsletter* repeated a rumor that Washington would serve as an officer in one of the two New England regiments to be formed.[36] The rumor proved to be unfounded, but fortunately for Washington's reputation the Boston papers did not inform readers that during that winter he faced a reduction in rank to captain when Dinwiddie reorganized the Virginia forces. Nor did the New England press report how with hurt pride Washington had resigned his commission and refused to serve in a winter campaign Maryland Governor Horatio Sharpe proposed to lead over the Alleghenies.[37] That campaign never developed, and Washington would soon leave his brief retirement to join the one that did set out in the spring of 1755.

Major General Edward Braddock led two regiments of the British army to Virginia that spring and, after considerable difficulty obtaining supplies and transport, began a march to the Ohio valley to dislodge the French. Braddock greatly desired the services of the military officer most familiar with the route and landscape, and he convinced Washington to serve on his personal staff. They avoided the troublesome issue of rank by allowing the Virginian to serve as a volunteer without rank or pay; Braddock promised to exert his influence to help Washington obtain a royal commission once the campaign was concluded.[38] Although the Boston papers printed a few sparse reports of the army's slow progress westward, the former Virginia colonel's name was absent from the papers until news of a disaster appeared in August. That disaster was a complete rout of the army only a few miles from the contested Ohio forks. An attacking force of French and Indians surprised Braddock's army, which consisted mostly of regular British troops with only a few provincial auxiliaries. Not used to forest fighting and terrified at the prospect of being tortured by French-allied Indians if captured, the regulars fell into irreversible confusion. Many officers and men died, and the general was mortally wounded.[39] Washington was on the scene as one of Braddock's aides-de-camp and thus once again in a position that captured the attention of Anglo-American newspapers.

News of the defeat left the press little to say that was positive or encouraging, but the young Virginia officer provided one bright spot. He acted bravely during and after the battle—in stark contrast to the performance of the British army as a whole—and Boston's papers did not miss the chance to report his valor. The first account of the incident described the scene of confusion in which officers tried vainly to rally their men. While riding with Braddock amid the battle, "Mr. Washington had two horses shot under him and his clothes shot thro' in several places, behaving the whole time with the greatest courage and resolution."[40] Another Boston paper, briefly mentioning a report the Virginian had made on the conflict, remarked that "dependence may be placed upon what Col. Washington writes . . . this officer behaved with great bravery, and brought off the general after he was wounded."[41] He had indeed provided what little order the army had in its initial retreat because all the high-ranking officers present and every other member of Braddock's staff had become casualties. Washington's actions in and after the battle undoubtedly were commendable, but chance circumstances had uniquely placed him in a position to win recognition for them and to share what little honor could be found in such a disaster.

Thus, though once again directly involved in a major military defeat, Washington's reputation—at least the image portrayed in Boston's newspapers—remained good. In fact, as writers cast around for scapegoats to blame for the debacle, the American colonial troops who were present rose in reputation. Almost every account of the defeat castigated the British enlisted men for cowardice and disorder while praising their officers for brave attempts to restore order to the army.[42] Of course, one must remember that most of these reports were, in fact, written by officers, who would certainly have wanted to defend their own reputations. Even before the year was out, some were publicly putting most of the blame on Braddock himself, who, being dead, was not able to defend himself and thus made an excellent scapegoat.[43] However, almost all writers praised the colonial troops for maintaining their cool and taking brave action. The *Boston Evening Post* reprinted a story from the *London Magazine* saying that, "the American Militia behaved with extraordinary bravery."[44] It claimed that the colonial soldiers covered the regulars' confused retreat and saved them from complete destruction.[45] Another account said that, "the Virginia officers and troops behaved like men and died like soldiers."[46] Washington, who had already been lauded for his part in the fight, could only benefit the more from these comments because he was the most prominent of the colonial troops and was soon to be Virginia's highest-ranking soldier.

Even with the open fighting that had occurred between French and British armies in the summer of 1755, the two empires would delay officially declaring war for another year. During that period Washington received much less attention from the Boston press, but when his name did appear, it was always in light of his reputation as a brave and skillful commander. In September 1755 Bostonians read that Virginia was adding 1,000 men to its military forces defending the western frontier, and Colonel George Washington would lead those men.[47] The colonel was only 23 years old at the time he became Virginia's top military officer, a position he would hold until fighting in that part of the continent ceased late in 1758.

In November Boston newspapers reported yet another example of Washington's dedication to defending his homeland. Stories told how 150 hostile Indians had staged a raid on the frontier while the colonel was absent. He was on his way to Williamsburg for a conference with the governor and would have been justified in continuing there. Instead, he immediately returned to the frontier, organized his troops, and led the pursuit.[48] The papers never reported whether or not he succeeded in the chase, but at a time when two American armies advancing on Crown Point in northern New York had stalled well short of their objective, Washington's quick, decisive action could hardly fail to win the admiration of those who read of it.

The Boston newspapers' treatment of Major General William Johnson provides a contrasting example of how the press could denigrate, rather than promote, a military leader's reputation. Not long after the discouraging news of Braddock's defeat, with all the justification accompanying it, word arrived of a victory won by a colonial army near Lake George in New York. Although the forces led by Johnson had simply repelled a botched enemy attack, Americans hailed it as a tremendous victory that avenged the defeat near Ohio.[49]

News of the battle first appeared in the Boston papers during the third week of September, and almost immediately they printed Johnson's official report. It was a fairly straightforward narrative.[50] Other writers, however, emphasized anything that made the American victory seem outstanding. Estimates of the enemy force ranged from 1,800 to well over 3,000, of which Johnson's army was said to have killed or wounded more than 1,000—and, of course, they were the best troops France had.[51] Some reports and exaggerations of the battle went out of their way to praise Johnson, but most emphasized the military skill and ardor of the New England men who fought under him.[52]

While Johnson had the potential to develop a greater reputation in the Boston press than Washington, he never did so, although his capture of Fort Niagara in 1759 would finally raise him to an equal level. Probably the biggest reason Boston printers so slighted Johnson was a rivalry between New England and New York.[53] Toward the end of 1755, the *Boston Gazette*, published by Benjamin Edes and John Gill, began a series of critical essays wondering quite pointedly why Johnson had moved so slowly in his march north and had stopped far short of capturing the French fort at Crown

Point. They also denounced government actions honoring Johnson as a hero.[54]

Readers of Boston's newspapers learned in early 1756 that Johnson was being rewarded by Parliament for his services with £5,000 and later that the king had created him a baronet.[55] This seemed too much for Edes and Gill, for that winter they printed several biting, often sarcastic essays in the *Gazette* challenging Johnson's accomplishments and merits as a hero. One said that

as the conduct of the general and others concerned with him is now on the point of inquiry, it might be well enough to have reserved the laurel until the true reasons be known why the monsieur were not more severely chastized . . . and why c—n p—t still remains in their possession?[56]

Another essay said that as the New York government planned to honor Johnson for his services, an inquiry should be made into what those services were, so that New England could also honor him if any evidence showed him deserving. The author claimed that "it may not be impertinent to declare *negatively* what these services were not. Tis certain, it was service to the cause he was engaged in," meaning he had not captured Crown Point.[57] Throughout that winter, Edes and Gill printed a number of such essays denouncing Johnson, some subtle and some brazenly contemptuous, until finally, Massachusetts Governor William Shirley acted to curb their vehemence.[58]

George Washington, on the other hand, in 1756 still appeared in the Boston press as a positive symbol of the conflict with France. Commanding Virginia's military forces, he would not participate in any more pitched battles during the war, but by merely traveling to Boston to confer with Governor Shirley, Washington received considerable attention from the Boston press. In a manner usually reserved for governors, newspapers there reprinted reports from Philadelphia and New York papers detailing the Virginia colonel's progress while riding to and from the north.[59] While he was in Boston, Edes and Gill—who were so derisive of Johnson, who had won a significant victory—said of the soldier who had experienced so much defeat, "Last Friday came to this town from Virginia the Hon. Col. Washington, a gentleman who has deservedly a high reputation for military skill, integrity, and valor; tho' success has not always attended his undertakings."[60] This seems to reflect the general attitude of New Englanders toward Washington. He was by this time, as James Thomas Flexner notes, "celebrated throughout the colonies and known in England and France."[61]

Although little of military significance occurred that year in Virginia, once Washington returned there, the distant Boston newspapers took occasion to inform readers of his movements in overseeing that colony's armed forces. A scattering of stories described him bravely pursuing Indian raiders and arranging the defense of Virginia.[62] Thus, in 1756 his name seems to have still retained an attraction for the Boston press that caused it to report on his actions relatively often and always in a favorable light.

In the following years, as major military events in the northern theater of operations drew attention there, Boston's newspapers paid less and less attention to minor events in Virginia and to Washington. His name appeared in print only a few more times during the war, most of them because of his service in the 1758 campaign, which finally did capture the forks of the Ohio without a fight.[63] Even as Virginia's senior officer, Washington gained little prominence in that operation because his troops formed only one part of a large army led by British Brigadier General John Forbes. Moreover, the provincial colonel did not get along particularly well with his commander and never fully exerted himself in Forbes' service.[64] With the war in his part of the continent ended, Washington retired from the military in January 1759 to begin a new marriage and a term in the House of Burgesses.[65] Boston's newspapers carried no mention at all of these momentous events, though two years earlier they had reported any available news of the Virginian's actions. Readers now concerned themselves instead with Britain's continuing conquest of North America.

During this time Boston papers had to recognize the now Sir William Johnson for his role in leading the capture of Fort Niagara on July 24, 1759. While Washington had already retired from military service, Johnson's name appeared in more than 30 stories in Boston papers that summer. Perhaps it is stretching a point to note that only two of these reports say anything positive about the person of Johnson. Better to acknowledge that whereas once held in derision by some Boston printers, Johnson seemed to have finally won their respect. This did not, however, detract from the favorable image the press had built a few years previously for Washington. In fact, after Canada had been conquered in 1760, the *Boston Evening Post* and the *Boston Gazette* both printed a chronology of major events of the war that seems to indicate the comparative lasting impression of these two heroes. Whereas Johnson's victories of 1755 and 1759 are only tersely noted without adjectives, Washington is remembered for performing a "remarkable service" in 1753.[66]

Washington's moment of fame in the 1750s was relatively brief but would have significant results 20 years later. A study of Boston newspapers shows that in the events that led Great Britain and France to declare war on each other in 1756, a young George Washington not only played an important role but in New England also gained fame and respect for his ability to lead troops. This is not to imply that his favorable reputation was entirely undeserved. He did acquit himself well, for the most part, but just as important from the perspective of 1775 was the fact that thousands of people in British America had been able to read about his exploits in their newspapers. The press brought Washington admiration and respect from many who otherwise may never have heard of him. How likely is it that John Adams and the other delegates to the second Continental Congress would have chosen this particular Virginia planter to lead America in its fight for independence if they and their neighbors had not read exciting and complimentary stories about him in the previous war? It is impossible to know for sure; however, it is evident that they did read those stories and remembered them years later. Washington's actions in the 1750s were heroic, but the press made him a public hero.

NOTES

1. Don Higginbotham, *The War of American Independence: Military Attitudes, Policies, and Practice, 1763–1789* (New York: Macmillan, 1971), 84–85. The attitude of delegates to the Continental Congress concerning a southern general is revealed in Lyman H. Butterfield, ed., *The Adams Papers: Diary and Autobiography of John Adams*, 4 vols. (Cambridge, 1971), 3:321–324.

2. Charles Francis Adams, ed., *The Works of John Adams*, 10 vols. (Boston: Haskell, 1850–1856), 2:417.

3. John Adams to Abigail Adams, May 29, 1775, in Lyman H. Butterfield, ed., *The Adams Family Correspondence*, 3 vols. (Cambridge, MA: Harvard University Press, 1963), 1:207, 215.

4. Edmund Cody Burnett, *Letters of Members of the Continental Congress*, 8 vols. (Washington, DC: Carnegie Institute of Washington, 1921–1936), 1:49, 499.

5. Ibid., 1:61–62.

6. The *Boston Newsletter* (hereafter abbreviated *BNL*), the *Boston Gazette or Weekly Journal* (hereafter abbreviated *BGZ*), the *Boston Evening News* (hereafter abbreviated *BEP*), and the *Boston Postboy* (hereafter abbreviated *BPB*—this paper ceased publication in December 1754) are all reproduced on microprint card or film for the American Antiquarian Society by Readex Inc., 1974. In this chapter, newspaper stories are cited from the newspaper in which the author encountered them, though many appear identically in two or more of Boston's papers.

7. The demonstration of propaganda technique in Boston's press during the beginning of the French and Indian War is the subject of this author's current research, although demonstrating publishers' deliberate use of propaganda is incidental to the thesis of this chapter. Hundreds of studies on propaganda theory exist. Some of interest include Edward L. Bernays, *Crystallizing Public Opinion* (New York: Liverwright, 1923); James W. Carey, *Communication as Culture: Essays on Media and Society* (Boston: Unwin Hyman, 1989); Philip Davidson, *Propaganda and the American Revolution, 1763–1783* (Chapel Hill: University of North Carolina Press, 1941); Harold Dwight Lasswell, *Propaganda Technique in World War I* (New York: P. Smith, 1938); Sal Randozzo, *Mythmaking on Madison Avenue: How Advertisers Apply the Power of Myth and Symbolism to Create Leadership Brands* (Chicago: Probus, 1993); Arthur M. Schlesinger, *Prelude to Independence: The Newspaper War on Britain, 1764–1776* (New York: Alfred A. Knopf, 1957); Oliver Thomson, *Mass Persuasion in History: An Historical Analysis of the Development of Propaganda Technique* (Edinburgh: Paul Harris, 1977).

8. Isaiah Thomas, *The History of Printing in America, with a Biography of Print-

ers, 2 vols., 2nd ed. (New York: Burt Franklin, 1874), 1:84–176; Clarence Brigham, *History and Bibliography of American Newspapers, 1690–1820*, 2 vols. (Worcester: American Antiquarian Society, 1947), 1:335.

9. Thomas, *Printing in America*, 2:54; Benjamin Franklin V, *Boston Printers, Publishers and Booksellers, 1640–1800* (Boston: G. K. Hall, 1980), 324; *BGZ*, April 7, 1755.

10. See Schlesinger, *Prelude to Independence*, and Davidson, *Propaganda and the American Revolution*.

11. Thomas, *Printing in America*, 2:187.

12. Carl Bridenbaugh, *Cities in the Wilderness: The First Century of Urban Life in America, 1625–1742* (New York: Ronald Press, 1938), 452–453.

13. Sydney Kobre, *The Development of the Colonial Newspaper* (Gloucester, MA: P. Smith, 1960), 36; Richard Burket Kielbowicz, *News in the Mail: The Press, Post Office, and Public Information, 1700–1860s* (Westport, CT: Greenwood Press, 1989), 20.

14. Richard D. Brown, *Knowledge Is Power: The Diffusion of Information in Early America, 1700–1865* (Englewood Cliffs, NJ: Prentice-Hall, 1984), 147.

15. Alice Morse Earle, *Stagecoach and Tavern Days* (New York: Macmillan, 1911), 48.

16. Ibid., 91–92; Carl Bridenbaugh, "The New England Town: A Way of Life," *Proceedings of the American Antiquarian Society* 56 (1946), 38.

17. *BNL*, January 3, 1754; *BGZ*, March 19, 1754. Dinwiddie's formal title was lieutenant governor, but as the Virginia's governorship was at that time a sinecure held by William Keppel, earl of Albemarle, Dinwiddie effectively exercised the full authority of the governorship.

18. *BNL*, March 8, 1754.

19. *BNL*, March 28, 1754.

20. *BGZ*, April 16, 23, 30, 1754, May 7, 14, 21, 1754.

21. *BNL*, March 7, 28, 1754; *BGZ*, March 26, 1754.

22. *BNL*, March 28, April 5, 18, 1754; *BPB*, March 4, April 22, 1754; *BGZ*, April 16, 1754; *BEP*, April 22, 1754.

23. *BEP*, July 1, 1754; *BGZ*, July 2, 1754; *BNL*, July 4, 1754.

24. *BGZ*, June 25, July 23, 1754; *BNL*, June 20, 27, July 25, 1754; *BEP*, July 22, 1754.

25. *BNL*, July 4, 1754.

26. *BNL*, August 1, 1754; *BPB*, August 5, 1754.

27. Dwight H. Lasswell, *Propaganda in WWI*, 105–106; "Fearful Domestication: Future-War Stories and the Organization of Content," *Mosaic* 23 (Summer 1990), 4; Nancy Brcak and John R. Pavia, "Racism in Japanese and U.S. Wartime Propaganda," *Historian* 56 (Summer 1994), 671.

28. *BNL*, August 1, 1754; *BGZ*, August 5, 1754.

30. *BNL*, August 1, 8, 1754; BGZ, August 5, 13, 1754.

31. *BPB*, December 2, 1754.

32. *BPL*, September 5, 1754.

33. *BNL*, September 5, 1754.

34. James Thomas Flexner, *George Washington: The Forge of Experience, 1732–1775* (Boston: Little, Brown, 1965), 91, 104–105, 118; Marcel Trudel, "The Ju-

monville Affair," trans. and abridged by Donald H. Kent, *Pennsylvania History* 21 (October 1954), 15, 23–31.

35. Flexner, *Forge of Experience*, 108.

36. *BNL*, January 9, 1755.

37. Flexner, *Forge of Experience*, 112–114.

38. Paul Kopperman, *Braddock on the Monongahela* (Pittsburgh: University of Pittsburgh Press, 1977), 42–44; Flexner, *Forge of Experience*, 121–122.

39. All accounts of the French and Indian War discuss Braddock's defeat; notable among them are Lawrence Henry Gipson, *The British Empire before the American Revolution*, 14 vols. (New York: Alfred A. Knopf, 1949) and Douglas Edward Leach, *Arms for Empire: A Military History of the British Colonies in North America, 1607–1763* (New York: Macmillan, 1973). Specific discussions of Braddock's defeat may be found in Kopperman, *Braddock at the Monongahela*; O'Meara, *Guns at the Forks*, and Hugh Cleland, *George Washington in the Ohio Valley* (Pittsburgh: University of Pittsburgh Press, 1955).

40. *BNL*, August 14, 1755.

41. *BGZ*, August 25, 1755.

42. *BNL*, August 14, 21, 1755; *BGZ*, August 11, 25, September 1, 29, 1755.

43. Stanley Pargellis, "Braddock's Defeat," *American Historical Review* 41 (1936), 253–269; Kopperman, *Braddock at the Monongahela*, 93–94.

44. *BEP*, December 15, 1755.

45. *BEP*, December 1, 1755.

46. *BNL*, September 4, 1755. This quote actually originated with Washington himself in a July 18, 1755 letter to Dinwiddie reporting on the battle, but the *BNL* report does not attribute it to him or to any other author; John C. Fitzpatrick, ed., *The Writings of George Washington*, 39 vols. (Washington, DC: U.S. Government Printing Office, 1931–1944), 1:149.

47. *BGZ*, September 29, 1755.

48. *BGZ*, November 10, 1755; *BNL*, November 13, 1755.

49. Descriptions of the battle at Lake George can be found in histories of the French and Indian War, such as Gipson's *The British Empire before the American Revolution* and Leach's *Arms for Empire*, as well as treatments of Johnson, such as Milton W. Hamilton, *Sir William Johnson: Colonial American, 1715–1763* (Port Washington, NY: Kennikat Press, 1976).

50. *BNL*, September 18, 1755; *BEP*, September 22, 1755.

51. *BNL*, September 18, 1755; *BEP*, September 20, October 6, 1755; *BGZ*, September 22, 29, 1755.

52. *BNL*, October 9, 1755; *BGZ*, September 15, 22, 29, October 6, 13, 1755.

53. James Thomas Flexner, *Lord of the Mohawks: A Biography of Sir William Johnson* (Boston: Little, Brown, 1959), 126–127.

54. *BGZ*, October 13, 27, November 10, 1755.

55. *BNL*, February 5, 1756; *BGZ*, June 21, 1756.

56. *BGZ*, January 19, 1756.

57. *BGZ*, January 26, 1756.

58. *BGZ*, January 19, February 2, 9, 23, March 11, 15, 1756.

59. *BGZ*, February 23, March 22, April 26, 1756; *BEP*, February 23, 1756.

60. *BGZ*, March 1, 1756.

61. Flexner, *Forge of Experience*, 145.

62. *BGZ*, May 31, July 12, October 25, 1756; *BNL*, August 12, September 2, October 21, 1756; *BEP*, June 7, July 5, 1756.

63. *BGZ*, March 21, 1757, July 10, October 2, December 11, 15, 1758; *BNL*, March 24, 1757, October 5, December 14, 1758; *BEP*, June 27, 1757, December 15, 1760.

64. O'Meara, *Guns at the Forks*, 193.

65. Flexner, *Forge of Experience*, 223, 227.

66. *BEP*, December 15, 1760; *BGZ*, December 15, 1760.

Chapter 10

George Washington: The Origins of Presidential–Press Relations

GRAHAM G. DODDS

The first person to do anything is necessarily afforded a unique opportunity to establish precedents. No matter how remarkable subsequent people are, their actions are inevitably judged in relation to those of the first. This is especially so if the position in question is the new office of the presidency in 1788 and if its initial holder is the national hero George Washington. From the outset of his presidency, Washington appeared to be very much aware of his unique ability to establish important precedents:

Few who are not philosophical spectators . . . can realize the difficult and delicate part which a man in my situation has to act. . . . In our progress towards political happiness my station is new; and, if I may use the expression, I walk on untrodden ground. There is scarcely any part of my conduct which may not hereafter be drawn into precedent.[1]

Washington established numerous precedents during his presidency, ranging from Constitutional matters and the nature of the new federal government, to the conduct of foreign affairs and economic policy. He is less well recognized for the important role that he played in establishing precedents for relations between the press and the presidency. Washington was the first to experience things that are now commonplace, such as a shift from positive to negative press and the strategic use of government leaks to the press. Washington sought to establish precedents in executive–press relations, such as presidential distance from critical journalism and respect for a free press, both of which scarcely survived through his own tenure as president.

FROM GOD TO GOAT: WASHINGTON'S HONEYMOON

Perhaps Washington's most striking precedent with regard to the press was the first "honeymoon" period. Like his successors, Washington's press began as laudatory and deteriorated over time. No president has experienced the sort of extraordinarily favorable press that Washington enjoyed during his early years in office. As far as the press was concerned, Washington could do no wrong. Even before Washington became president, he was widely praised during the Revolutionary War and the 1787 Constitutional Convention:

Several publications stated that Washington's presence alone provided reason for hope and confidence in the meeting's results. The original report of his plans to attend the meeting made one contributor to the *Pennsylvania Evening Herald* happy because "this great patriot will never think his duty performed, while any thing remains undone." A writer in the *Pennsylvania Packet* assumed that "a Washington surely will never stoop to tarnish the lustre of his former actions, by having an agency in anything capable of reflecting dishonor on himself or his countrymen." The *Pennsylvania Gazette* [on August 22, 1787] summed up the feelings of almost everyone in its congratulatory message to Washington for his success as leader of the convention:

"How great . . . must be the satisfaction of our worthy Commander in Chief, to be called upon a second time, by the suffrages of three millions of people, to save his sinking country—In 1775, we behold him at the head of the armies of America, arresting the progress of British tyranny.—In the year 1787, we behold him at the head of a chosen band of patriots and heroes, arresting the progress of American anarchy, and taking the lead in laying a deep foundation for preserving that liberty by a good government, which he had acquired for his country by his sword. Illustrious and highly favored instrument of the blessings of Heaven to America—live—live for ever!"[2]

The press praise for Washington increased when he became president. According to Humphrey:

George Washington . . . became a national hero almost overnight. Describing him as the "American fabius" and the "American Cincinnatus," the newspapers portrayed Washington as the ultimate citizen-soldier who did not use his military achievements to gain political power. By the mid-1780s public celebrations of his birthday occurred throughout the country, an event dutifully reported by the newspapers. By the time the states adopted the Constitution, many saw Washington as one of the greatest human beings ever to live, one clearly destined to be the first president of the new nation.[3]

During most of Washington's first term, the little press criticism then extant was generally aimed at his subordinates. For example, some newspapers criticized Secretary of War Henry Knox for the disastrous St. Clair

Indian defeat and Secretary Alexander Hamilton for aggrandizement in the Treasury Department.[4] When press criticism did touch on Washington, it was relatively mild and was directed at custom rather than the individual.[5]

Rarely did a newspaper editor dare to take on the commander-in-chief outright, and then only at risk of extreme public opprobrium. One who did, William Goddard of the *Maryland Journal* in Baltimore, had second thoughts. Goddard printed an article by Charles Lee, upon Lee's forced resignation from the army after the Battle of Monmouth, which questioned Washington's judgement. As a result, Goddard was visited by a mob, and narrowly missed being lynched. Goddard had to print a retraction which, however, he editorially disavowed when public reaction subsided.[6]

Scholars disagree as to the precise date when sharper and more widespread press criticism of Washington began, but most cite dates between 1791 and 1793.[7]

The following sarcasm, from Philip Freneau's *National Gazette* of March 2, 1793, was typical of the first barrages: "The monarchical farce [of celebrations of Washington's birthday] was as usual kept. . . . The President has been pictured as spotless and infallible, as having no likes or dislikes. The glory and achievement of the late Revolution have been entirely imputed to him, and were he Virtue's self the strains of panegyric could not have been louder."[8]

As the House of Representatives considered Hamilton's proposal that U.S. coins be stamped with Washington's image, Freneau asked, "Shall Washington, my favorite child, be ranked 'mongst the haughty kings?"[9] The criticisms of Washington soon increased in shrillness and in number. The press criticized him as monarchical, pusillanimous, treacherous, inefficient, and brutal and called him a despot, tool of faction, Anglophile, embezzler, traitor, murderer, and a spoiled child.[10]

He was charged with being "infamously niggardly" in private dealings; it was said that "gambling, reveling, horseracing and horsewhipping" had been the essentials of his education, that he was "a most horrid swearer and blasphemer," even that he had taken British bribes when he commanded American troops. His subordinates fared no better, being denounced variously as rascals, liars, jackals, drunks, demagogues, atheists, and fops.[11]

One paper charged that Washington's reputation was due to "the seclusion of a monk and the supercilious distance of a tyrant," that his military reputation was owing to luck, that he was appointed to command in the Revolution because such a lackluster character would provoke no antagonism from members of Congress, and that he was made president because of the "insipid uniformity of a mind which had been happy in proportion to the contracted sphere of its operations."[12] Thomas Paine charged: "You

slept away your time in the field" until "the finances of the country were
completely exhausted, and you have but little share in the glory of the final
event," and "the world will be puzzled to decide whether you are an apos-
tate or an imposter; whether you have abandoned good principles or
whether you have any."[13] Pollard writes that press criticism of Washington
even extended to personal matters.[14]

After several years of virtual adulation in the press, sharp criticism of
Washington was the norm by the early 1790s. The president still enjoyed
favorable press from some quarters, but the uniformity with which the press
had at first praised him was no more, and his detractors in the press seemed
louder than his defenders. "Once the President had stated that he could
never hear the voice of the people without veneration and love, but his view
had changed now that that voice was critical."[15]

THE RISE OF THE PARTISAN PRESS

The change from Washington's highly positive to largely negative press
was undoubtedly the result of several factors, but the primary force was the
rise of the partisan press. Scholars generally trace the origins of the partisan
press to April 15, 1789, when John Fenno's *Gazette of the United States*
began publication in New York. The government selected Fenno's paper to
publish the laws of the new country, and it soon became an ardent supporter
of Washington and the Federalists. Hamilton wrote for the paper under
pseudonyms and relied on it to guide the opinions of the public.[16]

As the split in Washington's cabinet developed between Hamilton and
Jefferson, Jefferson sought a Republican alternative to Fenno's paper. As
Secretary of State, he asked Philip Freneau to begin such a paper and offered
to subsidize him with a clerkship. Freneau demurred at first but eventually
accepted the sinecure and began publishing the semiweekly *National Gazette* on October 31, 1791.[17] The paper soon became a harsh critic of Washington, and other presses followed its example. John Hancock and Samuel
Adams circulated the *National Gazette* in Massachusetts, and other anti-
Federalist editors throughout the nation reprinted its aggressive articles and
mimicked its editorial edge.[18]

Freneau lost his job in 1793, when Jefferson left Washington's cabinet,
and his paper soon folded. However, Benjamin Franklin Bache's *Philadelphia General Advertiser*, later called the *Aurora*, soon replaced Freneau's
paper as the leading voice of Republican sentiment.[19] Bache's paper had
been founded in 1790 by the American Philosophical Society, "a hotbed of
radicalism and opposition to federalism," and it became even more partisan
and vicious than Freneau's paper.[20]

Together, the Republican press "made Washington the object of as con-
certed a campaign of vilification as has ever been known in American political life."[21] Indeed, the press became an important instrument in the

Federalist–Republican debates.[22] For this reason, the 1790s saw the rise of heated press partisanship, the nature of which would shock modern sensibilities.[23] Historians often refer to this time as the "Dark Ages of Journalism."

Not all of Washington's successors had to deal with the partisan press, but many did. The partisan press grew in harshness, number, and political power from its origins in the Washington administration, through the presidencies of Adams and Jefferson. It abated somewhat in the second decade of the nineteenth century but came back stronger than ever in the elections of 1824 and 1828. The partisan press waned throughout much of the rest of the nineteenth century, and the independent popular press eventually supplanted it, although the yellow journalists and muckrakers who hounded later presidents echoed its vigor and venom.

CURRENT EVENTS

The increase in criticism of Washington was largely due to the partisan press, especially Freneau and Bache, but current events also played a role.[24] Domestically, Hamilton's fiscal system in 1790–1791, the disastrous St. Clair incident of 1791, and the Whiskey Rebellion in 1794 prompted widespread criticism of Washington.[25] However, foreign affairs seem to have been especially important in generating opposition to Washington and his policies. In fact, Washington witnessed the first instances of the domestic press influencing the nation's foreign policy.

One of the most important issues in the young country's international relations was the conflict between Britain and France. Republicans like Jefferson favored revolutionary France and advocated adherence to a 1778 alliance with King Louis XVI, but the Federalists were less sympathetic to the Revolution and instead advocated neutrality. The Federalists won, and Washington issued his Neutrality Proclamation on April 22, 1793.[26] This infuriated Republicans. "Hesitatingly at first, then with increasing vigor, attacks were made upon Washington himself and his motives in issuing the pronouncement."[27] Freneau was particularly critical of Washington for not supporting France and "charged that Washington was duped by a pro-British, monarchal-aristocratic faction. Freneau even went so far as to suggest the need for a Republican revolution."[28]

The Republican press soon found another means of criticizing Washington's policy of neutrality, as it rushed to support the French envoy Genet. Genet violated Washington's Neutrality Proclamation by "continuing to outfit captured British ships as French privateers in American ports."[29] Genet enjoyed considerable popular support, and Bache's paper became a mouthpiece for him.[30] Bache defended Genet and criticized Washington for "his de facto nullification of the Franco-American treaty [of 1778] contrary to the wishes of the American people and their elected representatives."[31]

Emboldened by the Republican papers, Genet appealed to Congress and directly to the people.[32]

GOVERNMENT LEAKS IN THE PRESS

Washington was the first president to have to contend with significant government leaks to the press. In 1795 someone leaked to Bache a summary of the treaty that Chief Justice John Jay had secretly signed with Britain the previous year. Bache received the summary shortly after the treaty's Senate approval but before Washington had signed it and before it had been officially published. The treaty's secrecy and the fact that it contained no provision to protect U.S. seamen from British imprisonment made it highly controversial. Bache's publication of the summary on June 29 prompted Senator Stevens T. Mason of Virginia to give him a copy of the treaty.[33] However, when Bache secured a full copy of the treaty, he then published an enormous number of copies and sold it as a pamphlet on July 1.[34]

In Boston, New York, and Philadelphia, there were many meetings and protests about the treaty. In Philadelphia "it was reported that Jay could walk from one end of the country to the other in the dead of night, finding his way with the light from the dummies of himself burning in effigy."[35]

Federalist editors, horrified that the contents of the treaty had been leaked to the opposition, sought to shore up public support for the administration. Benjamin Russell denounced the Republicans for seeking to embarrass President Washington, while Noah Webster, Alexander Hamilton, and Rufus King wrote a series of essays supporting the treaty. Webster, as "Curtius," wrote twelve essays defending the treaty, while Hamilton and King wrote a more famous series of thirty-eight supportive essays under the pseudonym of "Camillus."[36]

However, Bache's printing of the treaty, his attack on it, and the widespread protest that it spawned could not be undone by the Federalist press. Bache succeeded in arousing so much opposition to the treaty that Washington hesitated to sign it.[37] When Washington eventually signed it nevertheless, the Republican press responded even more bitterly and loudly. By November numerous authors were calling for Washington's impeachment.[38]

The *Aurora* asserted that Washington "had violated the Constitution and made a treaty with a nation abhorred by our people; that he answered the respectful remonstrances of Boston and New York as if he were the omnipotent director of a seraglio, and had thundered contempt upon the people with as much confidence as if he had sat upon the throne of Industan."[39]

WASHINGTON'S USE OF THE PRESS

Even before the rise of the partisan press and the furor over the Neutrality Proclamation and the Jay Treaty, Washington knew the press was important for political success. Before becoming president, he had sanctioned the *Federalist Papers* because he believed the press could play an important role in deciding the fate of the proposed Constitution.[40] Moreover, Washington knew that his public image was important. According to one scholar, Washington established the concept and practice of "politically creating and acting in accordance with a 'public image.' "[41] Washington was very concerned about his reputation and with receiving a favorable judgment by posterity.[42] He knew that his image and reputation would be mediated through newspapers. His awareness of these points is evidenced in the way he started his presidency, as Washington purposely took a long time to travel from his home in Virginia to the capital in New York to begin his term as president, "lest unseemly haste suggest that he was improperly eager for the office."[43] Washington knew that public support was crucial for his own political success and that of the new country, and he sought to use the press to secure both.[44]

As president, Washington read the newspapers carefully both because he wanted to keep in touch with popular opinion in general and because he wanted to keep in touch with his own portrayal in the press.[45] Washington's use or manipulation of the media to further his public image is also evidenced by his leaking a copy of his Farewell Address to a friendly Philadelphia printer.[46]

WASHINGTON'S RESPONSE (OR LACK THEREOF) TO PRESS CRITICISM

Despite his interest in and knowledge of the press, Washington seemed genuinely surprised by press criticisms. Washington's surprise is itself surprising, given his previous experience with newspapers. For example, Washington was certainly familiar with the harsh colonial press. He had vented anger at newspaper portrayals of his troops as frequently inebriated and unruly.[47] After the Revolution, Washington expressed disdain for newspaper coverage of his life.[48] Furthermore, shortly after his inauguration, Washington wrote to Edward Rutledge,

I greatly fear that my Countrymen will expect too much from me. I fear, if the issue of public measures should not correspond with their sanguine expectations, they will turn extravagant (and I may say undue) praises which they are heaping upon me at this moment, into equally extravagant (though I will fondly hope unmerited) censures.[49]

Nevertheless, Washington seems to have been unprepared for the barrage of criticism that the opposition press directed at him. In a letter to the governor of Virginia, Washington claimed that the attacks did not hurt him personally:

But in what will this abuse terminate? The result, as it respects myself, I care not; for I have a consolation within, that no earthly ambitions nor interested motives have influenced my conduct. The arrows of malevolence, therefore, however barbed and well pointed, never can reach the most vulnerable part of me; though, whilst I am up as a mark, they will be continually aimed.[50]

The preceding statement notwithstanding, Washington was, in fact, personally angered by attacks in the press. Indeed, Jefferson claimed that because of the unrelenting criticisms of the press, Washington suffered "more than any person I have ever met with," and many a time he interrupted cabinet meetings to indulge in tirades against the opposition press or in fits of self-pity.[51]

In June 1793 Washington complained that "the publications in Freneau's and Bache's papers are outrages on common decency" and that they described him "in such terms as could scarcely be applied to a Nero, to a notorious defaulter, or even to a common pick pocket."[52] Washington alternately dismissed press criticisms as indiscriminate attacks made for political advantage or as the product of sincere, but misguided, concerns with centralized power.[53] According to Jefferson, negative press was a major factor in Washington's not seeking a third term.[54] By the end of his second term, "the level of public discourse had degenerated so abysmally as to make continued public service unacceptable to him."[55]

Despite his clear anger toward the press, Washington did not respond in kind. He did not himself engage in newspaper polemics or otherwise publicly acknowledge or respond to the attacks. Even when the vehement criticisms of the Jay Treaty circulated, Washington did not respond publicly, although "inwardly he seethed."[56] Given Washington's clear concern about his portrayal in the press, it is perhaps surprising that he did not forcefully respond to or attempt to counter criticism. After all, he had done so previously. For example, Washington himself penned the news dispatch for the *Freeman's Journal* of Philadelphia describing the last and greatest victory of the war, the Battle of Yorktown.[57]

Nevertheless, as president, Washington had virtually no direct involvement with the partisan press. This was because he deemed active politicking in the press as beneath the dignity of the presidential office. In this regard, Washington's behavior is very much in keeping with what Stephen Skowronek has called the "Patrician" style of leadership.[58] Washington sought to preside, rather than actively to lead or to direct, and thus to remain above the fray of factions.[59] He saw the presidency as a nonpartisan office and felt that the president should lead by dint of his superior character, not by partisan means. Engaging in press politics was simply at odds with these ideals.

Even if inaction was politically unwise, Washington was unwilling to compromise his conception of the presidency by engaging in press politics.[60]

Washington came close to a public response on at least one occasion. In a draft of his Farewell Address that he submitted to Hamilton, Washington noted the abuse he had suffered in the press while in office:

as some of the Gazettes . . . have teemed with all the Invective that disappointment, ignorance of facts, and malicious falsehood could invent, to misrepresent my politics and affections; to wound my reputation and feelings; and to weaken, if not entirely destroy the confidence you had placed to repose in me; it might be expected at the parting scene of my public life that I should take some notice of such virulent abuse. But, as heretofore, I shall pass over in utter silence never having myself, nor by any other with my participation or knowledge, written or published a Scrap in answer to any of them.[61]

However, Washington omitted these remarks from the final form of the address. The statement would have constituted a public response to press criticism only by explicitly noting his practice of not responding, but Washington evidently felt that even that was too public.

The only real exception occurred on his last day in office, and it was limited at that. In 1796 Bache published seven letters wrongly attributed to Washington that the British had originally written in 1777 as propaganda. Washington responded to their publication in a limited, official way on his last day in office by writing a letter to his Secretary of State disavowing authorship of the letters. The secretary then passed along Washington's letter to several papers, which later published it.[62]

Because of his policy of not publicly responding to press criticism, Washington's responses were necessarily limited and private. Beyond complaining about the press in his correspondence and in front of his cabinet, Washington did try to weaken one of their sources, namely, Freneau's paper. Hamilton had accused Jefferson of being the patron of the *National Gazette*, which he certainly was, and, prodded by Hamilton, Washington questioned Jefferson about his role in Freneau's paper.[63] For his part, Freneau publicly denied Hamilton's charge that he had made a deal with Jefferson to establish the *National Gazette*.[64] Jefferson's response was to declare that "he had never written anything for the *National Gazette* except trivial pieces and that he had furnished Freneau only with some Leyden (Holland) papers [e.g., the *Leyden Gazette*], at that time, the best newssheets in Europe."[65]

Washington then questioned Jefferson as to why Freneau was in Philadelphia, and Jefferson responded that he brought Freneau to the capital only as a translating clerk.[66] Jefferson told Washington, "I cannot recollect . . . whether it was at that time, or afterwards, that I was told that he had thought of setting up a newspaper." Besides, Jefferson pointed out, he could control Freneau's activities as his clerk but not his activities as the editor of the *National Gazette*.[67] One scholar aptly characterizes this response to Washington's questions about his relationship with Freneau as "evasive and disingenuous."[68] Later, when Washington called Freneau a "rascal" in front of his cabinet, he again asked Jefferson to dismiss him. Jefferson again refused, claiming that Freneau "had saved the nation when it was 'fast galloping towards monarchy.' "[69]

Perhaps the main way in which Washington responded to press criticism was through his underlings, especially Hamilton.[70] The extent to which Washington wanted his policy of no public response to press criticism to apply to his cabinet members is not altogether clear. He may have wanted them to follow his example of public disinterestedness, but he may also have felt comfortable exempting them from a restraint applicable mainly to the chief executive. One scholar suggests that Washington was disappointed that his feuding cabinet members did not live up to his aim of impartiality.[71] However, Washington's awareness of the importance of the press and the following statement suggest he held the latter view:

The foes of [his] government, he lamented, were "always working, like bees, to distill their poison," while the supporters of the government neglected organizing the public and depended "too much, and too long upon the sense, and good dispositions of the people."[72]

FREE PRESS

One response to press criticism that Washington appears never to have considered seriously is suppression. This is because beyond his concern for the impact of the press on his own political fortunes, Washington believed that the press was essential for the political success of the young democracy. Washington believed that an informed public is crucial to a well-functioning democracy, especially a new one, and therefore that a free press was also crucial.[73]

So convinced was Washington of the value of the press that during the Revolutionary War he issued a plea to patriot women asking that they save all available material for conversion into paper for printing.[74] Later, Washington helped papers by establishing favorable postal rates. In December 1793, in his Fifth Annual Address, Washington advised Congress of the duty of papers:

There is no resource so firm for the Government of the United States, as the affections of the people guided by an enlightened policy; and to this primary good, nothing can produce more, than a faithful representation of public proceedings, diffused, without restraint, throughout the United States.[75]

Washington also lamented that the papers did not publish congressional debates more fully and accurately.[76]

As early as 1792 Washington voiced concern that

if the government and Officers of it are to be the constant theme for News-Paper abuse, and this too without condescending to investigate the motives or the facts, it will be impossible, I conceive, for any man living to manage the helm, or to keep the machine together.[77]

Thus, in Washington's view, critical journalism hindered the chief executive's ability to lead. Washington even believed that the antigovernment ranting of Freneau's *National Gazette* could destroy the union.[78] Still, Washington did not try to suppress the press.

Other political figures of the day did not share this enthusiasm for the free press. For example, Hamilton threatened to investigate the bothersome *Aurora* for treason, the Speaker of the House barred Bache from the House floor, Federalist merchants boycotted the paper, and Bache was even physically attacked.[79] After Washington, John Adams signed into law the Alien and Sedition Acts 1798, which essentially criminalized newspaper criticism of the president. Washington and Hamilton both opposed the Alien and Sedition Acts.

CONCLUSION: WASHINGTON AND THE EVOLUTION OF THE PRESS–PRESIDENCY RELATIONSHIP

The most striking of Washington's attempts at establishing precedents in president–press relations is surely his stance of noninvolvement with politically critical press. This precedent also was short-lived, as it did not last much past his administration. Washington was the first and only president elected without the help of newspapers.[80] Each of his successors had to respond in some fashion to critical press in order to survive politically. No other president ignored the press, although many disapproved: John Adams, Jefferson, John Quincy Adams, Tyler, and Pierce all expressed distaste for politicking in the partisan press. Today, Washington's insistence on not publicly responding to attacks in the press undoubtedly strikes some as quaint and others as admirable, but the changing nature of the presidency made it virtually impossible for his successors to adopt his position.

Even though Washington essentially made possible and then later defined the office of the presidency, not all precedents established during his administration would last. Some of Washington's precedents with regard to the press were matters of happenstance and likely would have occurred regardless of the individual in office. However, other precedents were very much the products of Washington himself, whether intentionally or not. He was the first president to experience laudatory press followed by sharply critical press, the partisan press, pressure from the domestic press concerning foreign policy, and government leaks to the press. His intended precedent of the president's not becoming involved with politicking in the press did not last, and not all of his successors shared his commitment to a free press. Nevertheless, Washington's experiences with the press very much color our present press–president relations.

Indeed, several characteristics of the modern free press emerged in his administrations: the freedom to criticize an incumbent president harshly without suffering retribution; the ability to obtain information about governmental activities through a variety of sources, including leaks from authorities; and the efforts of a president to manage the press. Ultimately, what is very striking about the experiences of Washington with the press is just how familiar they seem to us today. Some modern media scholars are quick to conclude that the late twentieth-century press–presidency relationship has deteriorated to the point of mutual distrust, overexposure of the personal aspects of presidents' lives, presidential obsession with managing the news and preventing leaks, and even presidential claims of journalists' harming the national interest. Yet all of these elements had their origins in the presidency of George Washington.

NOTES

1. John C. Fitzpatrick, ed., *The Writings of George Washington*, 39 vols. (Washington, DC: U.S. Government Printing Office, 1931–1944), 30:496.

2. Carol Sue Humphrey, *The Press of the Young Republic, 1783–1833* (Westport, CT: Greenwood Press, 1994), p. 8.

3. Ibid., p. 17.

4. Harry M. Ward, "George Washington and the Media," *Media History Digest* (1987), p. 23.

5. Donald Stewart, *The Opposition Press of the Federalist Period* (Albany: State University of New York Press, 1969), pp. 160, 520.

6. Ward, "George Washington and the Media," p. 24.

7. For example, in his *American Politics in the Early Republic*, James Sharp says personal criticism of Washington began to surface in 1792 (New Haven, CT: Yale University Press, 1993), p. 54, while Stewart sets the date at 1793 (Stewart, *Opposition Press*, p. 520).

8. Forrest McDonald, *The Presidency of George Washington* (Lawrence: University of Kansas Press, 1974), p. 132. (Future references to this work will be made as "GW" in order to distinguish it from McDonald's other works cited here.)

9. *National Gazette*, March 29, 1792. Quoted in Sidney Kobre, *Development of American Journalism* (New York: Wm. C. Brown, 1969), p. 128.

10. Stewart, *Opposition Press*, pp. 488, 519; William David Sloan and James G. Stovall, eds., *The Media in America: A History* (Worthington, OH: Publishing Horizons, 1989), p. 64; Ward, "George Washington," p. 27; Richard L. Rubin, *Press, Party, and Presidency* (New York: W. W. Norton, 1981), p. 47.

11. Forrest McDonald, *The American Presidency: An Intellectual History* (Lawrence: University of Kansas Press, 1994), p. 243.

12. Ward, "George Washington," p. 27.

13. Ibid.

14. James E. Pollard, *The Presidents and the Press* (New York: Macmillan, 1947), p. 20.

15. Stewart, *Opposition Press*, p. 523.

16. McDonald, GW, p. 91.

17. Ibid., p. 93.

18. Kobre, *Development*, pp. 128–129; Donald Stewart, "Jefferson Journalism: Newspaper Propaganda and the Development of the Democratic-Republican Party, 1789–1801" (Ph.D. diss., Columbia University), p. 7.

19. Benjamin Franklin Bache was the grandson of Benjamin Franklin and was nicknamed "Lightning Rod Jr." (Ward, "George Washington," p. 27).

20. Kobre, *Development*, p. 131; Edwin Emery and Michael Emery, *The Press and America: An Interpretive History of the Mass Media*, 5th ed. (Boston: Prentice-Hall, 1984), p. 98.

21. Stewart, *Opposition Press*, p. 520.

22. William David Sloan, "The Party Press: The Newspaper Role in National Politics, 1789–1816" (Ph.D. diss., University of Texas, 1981).

23. Kent R. Middleton, "The Partisan Press and the Rejection of a Chief Justice," *Journalism Quarterly* 53 (1976), p. 106.

24. Beyond current events and the rise of the partisan press, various other forces likely contributed to the increasing criticism of Washington. These include the rise of Democratic–Republican societies in 1793–1794 and the gradual shift in public sentiment from elitist government to more egalitarian democracy (McDonald, GW, p. 132; Sharp, *American Politics*, p. 68). Cf. Gordon S. Wood, *The Radicalism of the American Revolution* (New York: Vintage Books, 1993).

25. Writers using the classical pseudonyms Brutus, Farmer, and Sidney sharply criticized Hamilton's financial program (Ward, "George Washington," p. 24).

26. "To mollify Jefferson the word 'neutrality' was not used, but the sense was there" (McDonald, GW, p. 126).

27. Stewart, *Opposition Press*, p. 149.

28. Kobre, *Development*, p. 129; Ward, "George Washington," p. 26.

29. Ward, "George Washington," p. 26.

30. Kobre, *Development*, p. 131.

31. Sharp, *American Politics*, p. 81.

32. Ward, "George Washington" p. 26; McDonald, *American Presidency*, p. 129.

33. Humphrey, *Press*, p. 50.

34. Ibid., p. 50; McDonald, GW, p. 162.

35. McDonald, GW, pp. 162–163.

36. Humphrey, *Press*, p. 50.

37. Kobre, *Development*, p. 132.

38. Stewart, *Opposition Press*, pp. 123, 525.

39. Pollard, *Presidents*, p. 17. The press criticism of the Jay Treaty was behind another of Washington's precedents, namely, the rejection of a Supreme Court nominee. When Jay resigned as Chief Justice in early June 1795, South Carolina State Chief Justice John Rutledge wrote to Washington asking to be considered for the

vacant post. Washington appointed Rutledge as interim Chief Justice on July 1, pending confirmation when the Senate reconvened in September. However, before Rutledge heard from Washington that he had been appointed, he spoke out against the Jay Treaty on July 16. The *Aurora* printed a lengthy article on Rutledge's speech, in which he sarcastically derided the treaty as a "humble acknowledgement of our dependence upon his majesty, a surrender of our rights and privileges, for so much of his gracious favor as he should be pleased to grant." Rutledge also reportedly claimed "he had rather, the President should die, dearly as he loves him than he should sign the treaty." Having earlier approved the treaty that had since generated so much furor, the Senate was not pleased with Rutledge's criticism and thus rejected his nomination to the Court by a vote of 14 to 10. "Almost to a man, those who voted against ratification of the Jay Treaty voted to confirm Rutledge. Those who voted for the treaty voted against Rutledge" (Middleton, "Partisan Press," pp. 106–110). Had it not been for Rutledge's speech against the treaty, John Marshall would likely not have become Chief Justice, with the result that the course of American Constitutional law would likely be very different. (Charles Warren, *The Supreme Court in United States History* [Boston: Little, Brown, 1926], p. 139.)

40. Pollard, *Presidents*, p. 3.

41. McDonald, *American Presidency*, p. 218.

42. McDonald, GW, p. 25.

43. Sidney Milkis and Michael Nelson, *The American Presidency: Origins and Development, 1776–1990* (Washington, DC: Congressional Quarterly Press, 1990).

44. "Washington's caution went deeper than an appreciation of the people's fear of executive power. As the historian Gordon Wood has observed, Washington sought to live up to the 'Cincinnatus myth of Roman legend,' which celebrated the disinterested patriot who devotes his life to his country." Milkis and Nelson, *The American Presidency*, p. 72.

45. Pollard, *Presidents*, p. 6.

46. *The American Daily Advertiser*, quoted Sloan and Stovall, *The Media in America*, pp. 109–110.

47. William L. Rivers, *The Adversaries: Politics and the Press* (Boston: Beacon, 1970, p. 2).

48. Pollard, *Presidents*, p. 3.

49. McDonald, *American Presidency*, p. 211.

50. Ward, "George Washington," p. 26.

51. McDonald, *American Presidency*, p. 243.

52. Pollard, *Presidents*, p. 14; Ward, "George Washington," p. 27.

53. Sharp, *American Politics*, pp. 54–55, 122.

54. Pollard, *Presidents*, p. 14.

55. McDonald, *American Presidency*, p. 243; Kobre, *Development*, p. 132.

56. Pollard, *Presidents*, p. 17.

57. Emery and Emery, *Press*, p. 83.

58. Stephen Skowronek, *The Politics Presidents Make* (Cambridge, MA: Belknap, 1997), for example, pp. 52–54.

59. Milkis and Nelson, *The American Presidency*, pp. 80, 86.

60. Pollard, *Presidents*, p. 19.

61. Ibid., p. 23.

62. Ibid., pp. 24–26.

63. Culver H. Smith, *The Press, Politics, and Patronage: The American Government's Use of Newspapers, 1789–1875* (Athens: University Press of Georgia, 1977), p. 16.

64. Ibid., pp. 16–17.

65. Kobre, *Development*, p. 128.

66. Rivers, *Adversaries*, pp. 10–11.

67. Ibid., p. 11.

68. Rubin, *Press*, p. 13.

69. Kobre, *Development*, p. 129.

70. Cf. Nixon's use of Vice President Spiro Agnew.

71. Pollard, *Presidents*, p. 8.

72. Sharp, *American Politics*, p. 122.

73. Pollard, *Presidents*, p. 31.

74. Rivers, *Adversaries*, p. 8; Sloan and Stovall, *The Media in America*, p. 57.

75. Ward, "George Washington," p. 27.

76. Pollard, *Presidents*, pp. 8–9.

77. Ward, "George Washington," p. 25.

78. Sharp, *American Politics*, p. 55.

79. Sloan and Stovall, *The Media in America*, p. 74; Emery and Emery, *Press*, p. 99.

80. Smith, *Press*, p. 12.

Index

About the Contributors

HENRY J. ABRAHAM is James Hart professor emeritus of government at the University of Virginia and the author of 11 books and over 100 articles on Constitutional law and the judicial process.

MALCOLM L. CROSS is associate professor of political science at Tarleton State University in Texas. He is the author of several studies on political leadership and the presidency.

BYRON W. DAYNES is professor of political science at Brigham Young University and the author of numerous books and articles on the presidency.

GRAHAM G. DODDS is a Ph.D. candidate in political science at the University of Pennsylvania.

FRANK E. DUNKLE teaches history at Texas A&M University. His dissertation is a study of the development and propaganda strategies in the Boston press in the mid-1750s.

THOMAS ENGEMAN is professor of political science at Loyola University of Chicago. He is the author of numerous studies on American political thought and literature.

CAROL SUE HUMPHREY is associate professor of history at Oklahoma Baptist University and the author of numerous studies of the media in the early Republic.

JOHN W. KUEHL is associate professor of history at Old Dominion University in Virginia. He is the author of numerous articles on the early national period in U.S. history.

ELIZABETH W. MARVICK, formerly senior lecturer at the University of Bordeaux, is the author of many leading studies in political psychology.

WILLIAM D. PEDERSON is professor of political science at Louisiana State University in Shreveport. He is the editor of numerous books on the presidency.

BARBARA A. PERRY is associate professor and chair of the Department of Political Science at Sweet Briar College in Virginia. She is the author of several books on the judicial process and a former judicial fellow at the Supreme Court of the United States.

MARK J. ROZELL is associate professor of politics at The Catholic University of America in Washington, DC. He is the author of eight books on American politics.

RAYMOND TATALOVICH is professor of political science at Loyola University of Chicago. He is the author of numerous books and articles on the American presidency.

FRANK J. WILLIAMS is a judge on the Superior Court of Rhode Island and chairman of the Lincoln Forum. He is a co-editor of two earlier books on the presidency.